MW01037594

The Best Place to Be

The Story of Orange Beach, Alabama

By
Margaret Childress Long
With
Michael D. Shipler

Margaret C. Long

Michael D. Shipler

First printing Paperback Edition: March 2006

Library cataloging data:
Long, Margaret Childress.
    The best place to be: the story of
Orange Beach, Alabama / by Margaret
Childress Long with Michael D. Shipler. —
1st ed. — : , .
    x, 368 p. : ill., maps; cm.

    ISBN 0–9778049–1–7

    1. Alabama — Social life and customs —
Pictorial works.   2. Alabama – – Social life
and customs —Personal narratives.
    3. Fisheries — Alabama — Orange Beach —
History.   4. Orange Beach (Ala.) —
History.   I. Shipler, Michael D.
II. Title

976.1/21   BCL00–49379
                              AACR2 MARC

Published by
Leedon Art
Bay Minette, Alabama

Printed in the United States of America

Cover and Title page image is a pleasure sailing scene on Wolf Bay, near the
north shore of Orange Beach, Alabama. Photographer unknown – circa 1910.

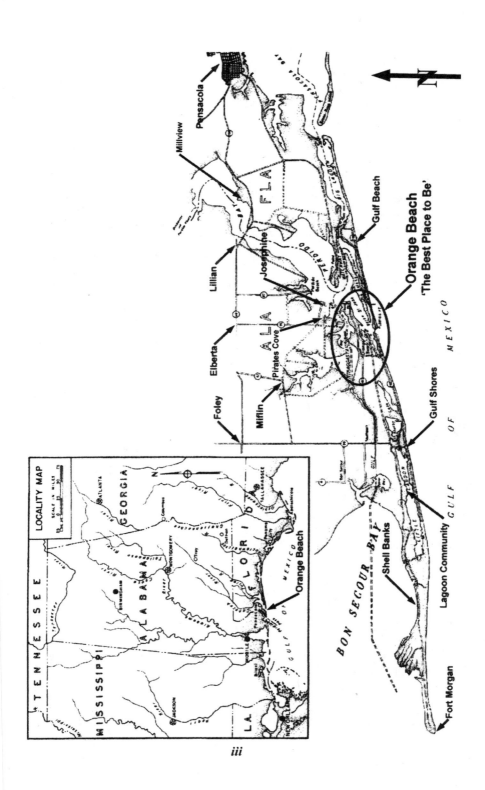

AREA MAP LEGEND

1. Alabama Point Lake
2. Artesian water well
3. Barchard Tract or Burkhart tract
4. Bay Minette District
5. Bear Point Cemetery
6. Bear Point Community Center
7. Bear Point Ferry Landing
8. Bear Point Lodge & Marina
9. Bill's Landing
10. Bird Island
11. Boat Basin
12. Boggy Point – Public Landing
13. Breakers Condo
14. Callaway/Lauder Cattle Pen
15. Callaway Marina
16. Callaway Family Property
17. Callaway Store
18. Caswell Community
19. Caswell Post Office
20. Catman Road or Rt. 2
21. Clizbe Swamp
22. Crane Pond
23. Cotton Bayou Public Landing
24. Cooks Point
25. Emmons Brown Landing
27. Farm to Market Road
28. First Deep-sea Fishing Rodeo
29. 'First' School –1910
30. Flora–Bama

31. Gilchrist Island – see Rabbit Island
32. Goat or Robinson's Island
33. Gulf Beach
34. Gulf Gate Lodge
35. Gulf Telephone Tower
36. Gulf View Park
37. Herman Callaway House
38. Hudson Marina
39. Indian Mounds
40. Indian & Sea Museum
41. James C. Callaway House
42. The Keg
43. Korner Store
44. Lauder Landing
45. Lemuel Walker, Sr. House
46. Lovick Allen Cottages
47. M & R Lodge
48. Meeks Cottages
49. Oil Well
50. Orange Beach Municipal Complex
51. Orange Beach Community Center
52. Orange Beach Elementary School
53. Orange Beach Hotel
54. Orange Beach Post Office – First
55. Orange Beach Public Library
56. Orange Beach Visitors Center
57. Paul Smith house
58. Perdido Pass Marina
59. Perdido Pass – Old

60. Peteet Shingle Mill
61. Pitcher pump water well
62. Portage Creek Bridge
63. Rabbit or Gilchrist Island
64. Roche & Martin Houses
65. Romar Beach
66. Romar Beach Road
67. Romar Beach Road Bridge
68. Safe Harbor /Sun Harbor Marina
69. Samuel Suarez Tract –see appendix
70. Sapling Point
71. Spindler place
72. 'Summer Kitchen' Post Office
73. Sun Circle Resort
74. Sunrise Service – First
75. Sun Swept Condo
76. Sweet House
77. Swim Place
78. Tanner Lodge
79. Tennis Center
80. Tillie Smith's Store
81. Tom Adam's Marina
82. Trent Marina
83. Walker Cay
84. Walker Marina
85, Walker Family Property
86. White Caps Motel
87. William Kee Tract – see appendix
88. Zeke's Marina

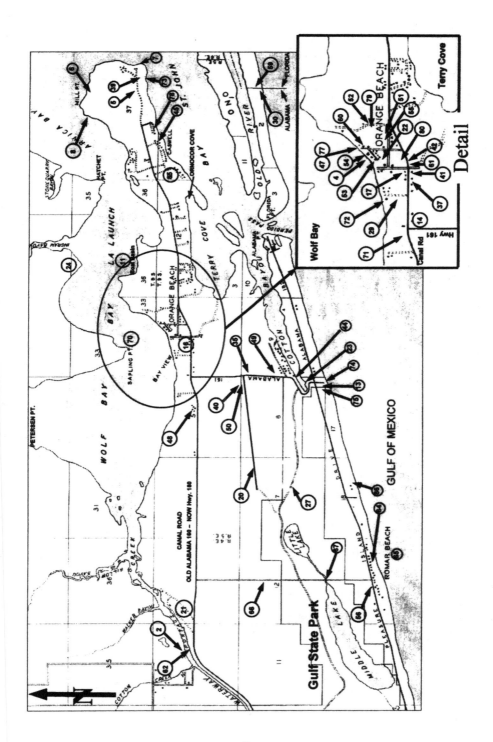

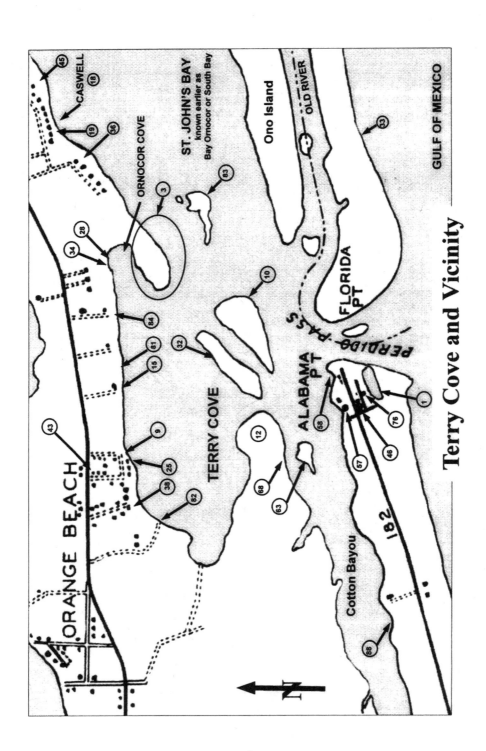

Terry Cove and Vicinity

Table of Contents

Dedication

It is with loving memory that I dedicate this book, *The Best Place to Be – The Story of Orange Beach, Alabama,* to my late father and mother, Ted and Dorothy Childress. I am proud that my father helped shape 'Pleasure Island' by dredging many of the marinas, canals, and boat slips, which we always referred to as 'ditches'. I am equally proud my mother was one of the early driving forces behind the growth of Orange Beach and, maybe more importantly, the infrastructure to handle that growth. I learned from my mother an understanding of the importance of history and genealogy. From my father I learned to fish and to appreciate the bounty of nature all around me in this wonderful place. The privilege of growing up here and learning from my parents made this book possible.

Margaret Childress Long
Orange Beach, Alabama
November 2005

Ted and Dorothy Childress

Acknowledgments

Writing a book of this nature requires the assistance of many people and organizations. First and foremost, We want to acknowledge Dorothy Brooks Childress, Margaret's beloved Mother, for her dedication to Orange Beach and the chronicling of its history. Her many talks with Margaret and her historical notes, records, and photographs have provided the basis of this work. The talks and interviews with Amel Callaway, Earl Callaway, Eleanor Callaway Lauder, Thurston Lauder, Clifford Callaway, Nolan Callaway, Eva Marie Walker Springsteen, Bertha Walker Robinson, Jerry Walker, Mary Nell Walker Hough, Gail Walker Graham, Lillian W. Ballard, James G. Bagley, Jr., Mary Lou Moore, Oscar Fell, Joe Johnson, James Huff, Ella Callaway, Beverly Callaway, Leroy Walker, Steve Walker, Roland Walker, Jr., Ronnie Resmondo, Shirley Matthews, Tom Norton, Jr., Margaret Walker, and Robin Wade were of valued assistance on the history of the 'early days'.

The notes of Brownie Callaway Lauder and Mrs. Loran D. Moore also provided much insight into the early history.

Historical articles from *The Islander*, *The Onlooker*, and *The Baldwin Times*, courtesy of Gulf Coast Newspapers, were most helpful, along with *The Pelican* newspaper of Pensacola, Florida.

A special thank you goes to Eva Marie Walker Springsteen for the hours of research in collecting the many newspaper items used throughout this book. Additionally, her work on the genealogy of both the Callaway and Walker families has been most useful.

The assistance of the South Baldwin Chamber of Commerce in Foley and the Alabama Gulf Coast Chamber of Commerce of Orange Beach and Gulf Shores in providing documents and data was and is appreciated.

We especially wish to thank the many people who provided photographs and documents which add much to a true glimpse of the past; Gail Walker Graham, Eva Marie Walker Springsteen, Jerry Walker, Leroy Walker, Steve Walker, Evonne Walker, Bertha Walker Robinson, Clifford and Myrth Callaway, Earl Callaway, Nolan Callaway, Marjorie Snook, Eleanor Callaway Lauder, Ronald Lauder, Thurston Lauder, Lillian W. Ballard, James G. Bagley, Jr., Joseph 'Joe' Johnson, Ella Callaway, Beverly Callaway, Merle Rudd Harms, Bo Lauder, Glenn Baumann, Sarah Roche Browder, Sarah DeJarnette Caldwell, Ronnie Resmondo, and the Leedon Art Gallery Oldtime Photo Collection.

Thank you for the time and energy of Myrth Callaway, of Foley, Thomas B. Norton, Jr., of Gulf Shores, George R. Smith, and Pamela Shipler of Bay Minette, who assisted in the proof reading and editing.

If we omitted acknowledgement of anyone, we sincerely apologize. We have endeavored to make this work as accurate and mistake free as possible. Errors that may occur in this book are our responsibility.

Margaret especially wishes to thank her two sons, Brooks and Wesley Moore, for encouraging her to finally complete this book. Margaret taught them to love Orange Beach and they too think it is 'the Best Place to be'.

Michael extends a special thank you to his wife, Pamela, for her involvement, endurance, and loving support during the nearly five years it has taken to write this book. He also wants to thank his longtime friends George R. Smith and Tom Norton, Jr. for their hours of discussion and proof reading and especially for still being his friends.

And last, but not least, Margaret gives a loving 'Thank You' to her husband, Horace 'Buddy' Long, Jr., who encouraged and supported her years of collecting historical information and the development of this book.

If anyone discovers errors or have additional information, information not covered in this book, or pertinent photographs, please contact us for a possible second book at: Margaret Childress Long, P.O. Box 2126, Orange Beach, Alabama 36561.

Margaret Childress Long and Michael D. Shipler
Orange Beach and Bay Minette, Alabama
November 2005

Author's Introduction
by Margaret Childress Long

This book truly began with my late mother, Dorothy Childress, who taught me many things that I have carried with me throughout my life, including a deep love for the people and the area, in which I grew up. And a delightful area it is!

My first attempt at collecting the story of Orange Beach was in 1964, when I was in high school. As part of a project, I produced a small notebook of collected information and a few early photographs.

With the astounding growth and development of the area, I was determined to expand it and update the information in that original notebook and to make it into a real book available to all the new folks who have joined us here in Orange Beach, Alabama, as visitors and residents. This book is the culmination of that desire. It is my hope that you will enjoy reading this book and come to appreciate this wonderful place as much as I do.

I have continued over the years, gathering information, maps, and photographs, and talking with descendants of the early residents.

As with any book of this nature, there are undoubtedly omissions and errors, as the subject matter is extremely complex. Any errors are the responsibility of the authors.

The object of this book is to produce as clear a history of Orange Beach, Alabama, based on recollections and facts, as possible. I remain interested in any additions, expanded historical information, other early photographs, or possible interviews that may arise as a result of publication of this book. Please send any information to me at: P.O. Box 2126, Orange Beach, Alabama 36561.

Margaret Childress Long
Orange Beach, Alabama
November 2005

Author's Introduction

by Michael D. Shipler

I was delighted to be asked by Margaret Childress Long to assist in the writing and publication of this book since I have had an avid interest in the history of south Alabama for many years and the history of Orange Beach is at the root of the growth and development of the Alabama gulf coast.

The concept for this book was born in the heart of a young girl who grew up in paradise. Margaret was raised on Cotton Bayou from age 2 through the years of change from wilderness to modern resort by parents that were actively involved in the shaping of both the land and community. She grew up with only young boys as her playmates in nature's wonderland. By age 8, she had her own Stauter Built boat, which she still owns and uses. She was treated very special. Everyone looked out for her. At an early age, she was acknowledged as the 'Queen of Cotton Bayou'.

Margaret inherited a non–stop personality and a strong sense of place from her mother. Her father taught her fishing, boating, and her love of nature.

The interviews Margaret conducted with the descendants of the early settlers of Orange Beach add depth and a touch of humanity to a history that would ordinarily be perceived as something 'dry' beyond belief. This book, with its stories and photographs, is far more than a history of a place. Hopefully this book will help you to understand what Orange Beach is all about, gaining knowledge of its people, its great charter fishing industry, and a beautiful area surrounded by water. Orange Beach is not just a resort town; it's the best place to be!

Following Margaret's introduction, we have printed the text of Margaret's original, if brief, 'History of Orange Beach'. This first history was the only known written history of Orange Beach until now. It has been used in many publications and public ceremonies, and quoted verbatim in sources too numerous to mention. Margaret's desired expansion of this history was the impetus for this book.

In this book you will follow the development of the coastal area from a remote wilderness to what is today, a dynamic family resort area. This is a big book and you will probably not want to try to read it 'cover to cover'. So, flip around, check out the photos, many of which have never been published before, pick an area of interest from the table of contents, and enjoy. Before you know it, you will have read the book and I hope will use it as a reference for years to come. You will notice as you read that there is some duplication of information. That is done on purpose to allow each section to be more complete and 'stand on its own' for quicker use as reference.

I hope you enjoy the life and times of *The Best Place to Be*!

Michael D. Shipler
Bay Minette, Alabama
November 2005

The History of Orange Beach, Alabama
By Margaret Childress
1964

Editors note: This is the first history of Orange Beach written by Margaret while she was in High School. It is printed, here without corrections, as it was originally written. Many, but not all of the photographs listed at the end of this first history are published in this book.

Introduction

I moved to Cotton Bayou in 1949 with my parents from Evergreen, Alabama. My Childress grandparents are from Chilton County, Alabama, and are no relation to the Childress mentioned in this history.

I gathered my information from facts and stories that the local citizens knew about the early settlers. Many of the early settlers were the grandparents of some of today's residents. I especially enjoyed the talks I had with people of the community.

In my report I hope to tell about the settlement of the area, the people, their interests and the accomplishments that have been made since it's settlement.

Why is this area called Orange Beach?

Early in the 1900's there were many farmers along the shores of Wolf Bay, Bay St. John, Bay La Launche and Terry's Cove. Strawberries and oranges were the most commonly grown fruits. It is told that one 12 year old tree bore 2,000 sweet oranges in one season. Many sour oranges and satsumas were also raised. Although the wind of the bays are hard on such crops and prevent growing them on a commercial scale there are still numerous orange, lemon, grapefruit, satsuma and kumquat trees to be found in the yards and gardens of the homes and there has been talk of planting the roadsides with orange trees to uphold the history of the name. It is needless to explain why the word 'Beach' is the name. A drive along highway 182 and a visit to the many homes facing the Bays and Bayou will do that.

The grandfathers of some of our citizens have told them of their lives here during the Civil War. Soldiers from Ft. Morgan came to the Orange Beach area seeking fresh fruit and vegetables to augment their army rations. Confederate troops crossed Wolf Bay on horseback enroute to and from Fort Morgan.

Dick Levin, his wife and family lived here and farmed during the Civil

War days. Some of the old timers remember Mr. Levin telling tales of the troops coming from Fort Morgan.

Capt. Percy Jones settled on the extreme end of Bear Point soon after the Civil War on property now owned by Mrs. Kemp of Selma.

James Dannelly came here soon after he lost his property on Fish River during the civil War. He settled on what is known as 'The Barchard Tract'.

In 1875, James C. Callaway married Nancy Childress and built a home on a Southern Plantation Development. He worked as a turpentine chipper and later farmed. He also had a mail route. Three of his sons are prominent citizens of the community today. In later years Mr. Callaway and his sons ran a schooner business along the Gulf.

These schooners that he built himself were the *Ellen C* and the *Morrow*. The *Ellen C* was in the lighthouse service and the *Morrow* carried freight to and from Mobile and other ports on the gulf. In 1906, Mr. Callaway and some other men dug with shovels a ditch across the Gulf. The present pass is located here even though a few changes have taken place.

The Callaway's and their boats are still important contributors to the progress of the Orange Beach Community.

In 1908, D. R. Peteet purchased 3,254 acres of land in the South end of Baldwin County. This land lies South of Portage Creek running to the gulf and the East section including about half of Bear Point. The celebrated fresh water lakes lie within its border toward the West.

In 1909, Mr. Peteet began erecting a shingle mill on Bay La Launche with Mr. Cowham as millwright. Several men came from the North to help build the mill and became residents of the area. Among them were L. H. Diehl from Holidaysburg, Pennsylvania, who bought 40 acres of land and two lots on the Bay. It was here that the first dwelling put up on Gulf Bay Tract was built. J. H. Wolbrink, from Grand Rapids, who bought a bay front lot and 5 acres of land on Bay Circle, erected the next dwelling. J. H. Hazelett bought what is known as the Swirn Place. Mr. Peteet built a small office building and later a camp house for the men who were cutting logs and hauling them to the mill. This was the beginning of Orange Beach and these were the first families to live in the area.

Others were soon attracted to South Baldwin county and in 1910 and years immediately following families moved in from various sections of the country. Among these were Harvey Spindler from Nebraska, Dr. Phil

Chappel from Grand Rapids, Michigan, the Wool's, the Pratt's, the Hendrickson's from Ohio, the McConnaughy's, from Kentucky and Richard and Carl Lockbriler from Ohio.

Mail was brought into Orange Beach via boat across Bay La Launche from Millview, Florida, through Josephine and Swift (now known as Miflin) and in 1896 a post office was established at Caswell in the home of one of the settlers. The mail was met by the Postmistress on horseback and carried to the Post Office.

In 1901, a Post Office was established at Orange Beach and Mrs. Elsie Diehl was appointed Postmistress. Later, Mr. L. H. Diehl built a two story building and moved the Post Office into this building in which he also ran a store.

In 1918, a Mr. E. R. Callaway took over the store and his wife was Postmistress until he sold out to Mr. Charles Rynd of Chicago.

In 1937, Miss Minnie Lee Callaway was appointed Postmistress. The Post Office at this time was in the Dan Callaway's 'summer kitchen'. Miss Callaway later became Mrs. Emmons Brown and is still Postmistress of the Orange Beach Post Office.

In 1952 a Rural Mail Service was established out of the Orange Beach Post Office. A new Post office was erected in 1953 and the Caswell Post Office was closed after 57 years of service. The Rural Mail carrier serves Bear Point, the Caswell area, Orange Beach, Cotton Bayou, Alabama Point and Romar Beach.

When the first school was established in the area the County paid for two months school teaching and the patrons hired a teacher for another month or two. The first school building was a log house between the Walker home and the Johnson home (now the Burkharts). In 1910 the County built the building now owned by the Baptist Church. Mrs.Tilman was the first teacher in the new building. This building was used until about 1930 when the school was consolidated with the Foley School and bus service was established. At the present time, Mrs. Ronald Lauder drives the bus and there are about sixty children from this area who ride it.

As early as 1907 the demand for tourist accommodations was felt and to meet this need the Lemuel Walkers built cottages for rent. About 1923 the Orange Beach Hotel, located on Wolf Bay was built and operated by Mrs. Hilda Dietz, who was a former Miss Callaway before her marriage.

This hotel soon became a favorite spot of many fishermen and tourists. In 1936 it was modernized and in 1953 it was owned and operated by Leo Davis and continued to serve guests comfortably and efficiently.

Sunday schools were held in the old school house as far back as 1910. Baptist church services have been held in the community since 1928. Originally it was a mission church of the First Baptist Church of Foley and was serviced by the pastors of the Foley Church. In 1953 a new church was erected and Sunday school was held every Sunday and church services were held the first and third Sunday nights. Also in 1953 the Presbyterian Church was organized. The Presbyterians held their church services the second and fourth Sunday nights in the Baptist Church building. They now have their own church building in the immediate area.

In 1951 the Orange Beach Home Demonstration Club was organized and was open to all women of Pleasure Island. One of its dreams is to eventually sponsor the erection of a community hall in Orange Beach. The annual Community Picnic is a project of the Home Demonstration Club and has become an event enjoyed by residents and visitors on Pleasure Island.

The canal as a part of the inland waterway was first discussed in 1908 and became a reality in 1932. The cutting through of this canal has created what is known as 'Pleasure Island'.

The Indian evidence indicates visits here by prehistoric Indians when they came from the interior to the Coast to fish and gather oysters. The shell mounds have frequently yielded skeletons and handiwork. In 1900 the Smithsonian Institute dug into the mounds on Bear Point.

One of the attractions of the Orange Beach Community has been the excellent fishing available in the bays and in the Gulf, which is entered through the pass at Alabama Point. The Orange Beach fishing fleet is composed of charter boats manned by capable fisherman – many of who are sons and grandsons of the early settlers.

Roads on Bear Point were trails following the beach in many places during horse and buggy days. E. G. Low, who owned the first car here, cut a road through on the ridge and later the County took it over. The road was finally surveyed and graded in 1946 and in 1947 was paved. This is State Hwy. 180, better known as the Orange Beach road. Col., E. I. Higdon was issued a permit to build a bridge and established a ferry from Bear Point to Innerarity Point in 1926. The ferry operated only about three weeks. It was during this time that Clarence Walker moved from

Pensacola to Bear Point via ferry. Highway 161 was paved to the beach around Cotton Bayou in 1945. Cotton Bayou is located West from Bay St. John and the Alabama Point Pass. It was named from blockade runners picking up cotton there during the civil War.

The Leon Comstock's built the first home on cotton Bayou in 1946. Rex Almon built the second home here shortly after. The Neil Lauder's were the next to build and are still making their home here. There are now many homes and cottages in the immediate vicinity.

Alabama Point had beautiful pine trees and large sand dunes. The storms and construction have destroyed the pine trees and the sand dunes have gone with the seasons. Route 182 was paved to Alabama Point in 1949 and the past four years 22 houses and a tourist court have been built on this road West of its intersection with 161. Both sides of the highway here offer wide views of the Gulf and Cotton Bayou. The Paul Smith's were the first family to build and live on Alabama Point.

At the extreme eastern end of Alabama Point the State has erected picnic tables and a drink concession and at the intersection of 161 and 182 maintains a beach area.

In the past few years a telephone system has been established, a bridge that connects this part of Alabama with Florida and many summer and year round homes.

The location of Orange Beach has been influential in its settlement, its growth and its livelihood. The natural beauty and its resources are continuing to attract people from all over the United States as the growing population of today proves.

Conclusion

From my research about the 'History of Orange Beach' I learned so many things that I did not know. I enjoyed writing it and I hope the information has been as interesting to you as it was to me.

The pictures loaned to me by residents helped to give me an idea about how things looked when the community was first getting started. It was interesting to compare the past with the present.

Bibliography
I.   Foley Chamber of Commerce; Articles on Pleasure Island.
II. Mrs. Loran D. Moore; Notes she has of the early settlers.
III. Mrs. Neil Lauder; Notes she has about the history.
IV. Mrs. Ronald Lauder; Pictures.
V. Mr. Amel Callaway; Talks I had with him.

Photographs

1. The 'Ellen C' Built by Mr. Amel Callaway's father. One of its main services was the lighthouse business.
2. Another of Mr. Callaway's boats.
3. Two fishermen with a large catch of King and Spanish Mackerel.
4. Boat along Perdido Bay
5. Mr. D. R. Peteet and friends
6. Record Devilfish caught in Gulf of Mexico.
7. Full view of the fish
8. Peteet's shingle mill
9. Gulf view Motel on Bear Point
10. Lauder's Landing is located at the head of Cotton Bayou. Several charter boats leave from here.
11. This is a view from the Hotel at Orange Beach.

Prehistoric land and The Early Americans

The cold mass of ice that covered much of the Northern Hemisphere was only about 500 miles to the north. The time was about 15,000 years ago. The last ice age (glacial period) was from about 25,000 to about 15,000 years ago.

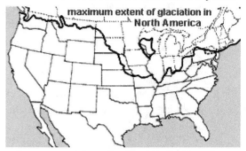

The land of Orange Beach was not empty even then. Roaming the area between that ice pack and the waters of the Gulf of Mexico were a few Mastodon and other creatures trying to survive the last epic Ice Age. Early Native Americans (Paleo–Indians) were probably in that area by then chasing the mastodon and other food sources.

Archaeological and paleontology records indicate that Paleo–Indians did not arrive until 11,500 years ago. However, some paleontologists believe that the Paleo–Indians were in the area even before the last Ice Age. It was relatively warm here and humans have always liked warm weather especially when augmented by game both large and small and a bountiful food source like the waters of the Gulf of Mexico.

The area that we know today as Orange Beach was a dramatically different place. The polar ice had sucked water out of the world's oceans into its frozen mass. When the Paleo–Indians of 11,500 years ago were here, they could not see the Gulf waters from Orange Beach. The Gulf beaches was 60 to 100 miles further south and the land here was covered with native forests.

The trickles from the glacial melt that were to become the Alabama and Tombigbee Rivers, merging together to form the Mobile and Tensaw Rivers, lay to the north and west. To the east would be born the Perdido River. Both systems were in shallow valleys that were destined to become the bays and estuaries of Mobile and Perdido. The upper Appalachian Mountains and the lands north of and around the Great Lakes had been ground down by the great scouring push of the ice as it had grown and moved south. Eventually much of that scraped off earth carried in the ice would make its way to the Gulf Coast in the ever increasing rivers of melt water as the global climate began to warm and the glaciers began to recede and eventually leaving alluvial sediment built up upon the land. The rising waters of the Gulf of Mexico from the glacial melt caused the shoreline of the Gulf to slowly creep north.

We know that the Paleo–Indians were in Orange Beach area by at least 11,500 years ago, as Clovis projectile points have been found 20 miles south of today's shoreline by modern day shrimpers dragging their nets closer to those ancient shores. Clovis hunting points, first discovered in the American Southwest and found in quantity in Kentucky and Tennessee, have been dated to that time.

Most contemporary migration maps illustrating native origin here indicate migration diagonally across the continent from the area of the northern Rocky Mountains; however, some current theory states their migration may have been by water from Mexico and Central America. The indications are that the Indian cultures in the Southwest never moved east beyond western Texas, indicating that the two areas had distinctly different contact and trade routes. Further proofs of their journey by this route may lie beneath the waters of the Gulf along the ancient shores. Wherever they originated, Native American Indians were here at least by 9500 BC (11,500 years ago), during the Pleistocene era. (Reference Appendix chart on cultural chronology)

Typical Clovis Point

The first apparent native civilization (as we think of civilization) began forming in this area during what is known as the Late Archaic period (3500 BC to 1000 BC). Those Indians created the earliest known 'shell mounds'. They further developed in the Woodland period between 1,000 BC through about 1000 AD. During this period is when the first 'burial mounds' were built.

During the Mississippian period (1000 AD to about 1500 AD) the native Indians developed a much more sophisticated civilization. These Indians were the 'temple mound' builders. Their civilization was quite advanced with a central government housed atop their huge mounds located in the Tensaw Delta swamps at Bottle Creek in north Baldwin County and at Moundville, Alabama. The governmental city at Bottle Creek with its individual family dwellings was the 'Capitol City' of a large part of the Southeast. Their trade area may well have included all of the Gulf Coast, Mexico and Central America as well as inland areas of North America.

After a brutal encounter with the army of the early Spanish explorer DeSoto, the Mississippians began to fade away, breaking up into smaller tribes or disappearing. We do know that they were replaced with the Muskogee civilization or 'modern' Indian tribes of the Cherokee, Chickasaw, Choctaw, and Creek during what is called the Historic period between 1500 and 1850 AD. The Muskogee settled around the rivers of Mississippi, Alabama, and Western Georgia.

The French befriended the Indians wherever they encountered them and utilized their friendship to their benefit during their years of occupation in North America. The French moved the Tensaw Indians from Louisiana, after the Tensaw dispute with the Chickasaw, to the Eastern Shore of Mobile Bay for a short time during the French control of the area.

The Appalachee Indians of northwest Florida had been nearly destroyed by the British and moved themselves under the protection of the French about 1704. They were settled on the present site of Blakeley in Baldwin County, Alabama, and remained there until the French lost control of the area, at which time they moved westward with the French in 1763.

The Native American Indians, although not living permanently in the Orange Beach area,

came from their inland villages to fish, gather oysters, and other seafood from the bountiful harvest found here. Archeologists believe that their visits were seasonal, but of long enough duration, that villages were actually built. The 'mounds' on Bear Point and surrounding areas are remaining evidence of their frequent trips.

Based upon an interview in the early 1960's, it was believed that in 1900, the Smithsonian Institute had dug in these mounds. However, on further research, it was discovered that the Smithsonian did not dig in these mounds. Clarence Bloomfield Moore was the first 'archaeologist' to dig here. He investigated two of the mounds on Bear Point in 1901. Moore was a wealthy, educated, amateur archeologist and his early work was important. The reports of his digs during the time span of 1901 to 1918 are still referenced by modern archeologists.

The exploration of these mounds yielded skeletons and many early Indian artifacts that are now in the Smithsonian's collection. Those recovered artifacts took a circuitous route to the Smithsonian. It seems that Moore widely distributed many of his artifacts with a large number going to the Academy of Natural Sciences in Philadelphia. Later, George Heye, of the Museum of the American Indian in New York bought them. Ultimately, the Smithsonian Museum of the American Indian, purchased the artifacts, where they now reside.

David L. DeJarnette, a geologist with the University of Alabama and the Alabama Museum of Natural History, conducted digs and research at these mounds during the

David L. DeJarnette

1930's. David DeJarnette is considered the early guiding force behind archaeology in Alabama. DeJarnette is the father of Sarah DeJarnette Caldwell, current owner of the Dan Callaway house.

The University of South Alabama Archaeology Department was called

in during April 2004, to research the site of the new 'Caswell Place' development. This type of research 'dig' is required of coastal development sites in Alabama. Under the direction of Archeologist Bonnie L. Gums, it was soon discovered that the site had been an early Indian seasonal village. Artifacts have been

Pottery shards from the Caswell dig by Bonnie L. Gums of the University of South Alabama, May 2004.

recovered that date to at least 1,700 years ago. This was the site of the old 'Gulf View Park', which was Walker family property at Caswell (recently sold by Bertha Walker Robinson). A full report will require more than a year to produce. It is anticipated that some of the trailer loads of artifacts will eventually end up in the Orange Beach Indian and Sea Museum.

Although local residents and visitors have dug in these sites and other mounds in the area over the time of 'modern' occupation causing damage and loss of artifacts, the artifacts and research information they still contain are now protected under Alabama law.

There is some historical research that indicates the Creek Indians may have done extensive coastal trading from this area with the Indians of Mexico and Central America. Artifacts dug in this area tend to support trade routes with these Indians. In a conversation with Herman Smith, the archeologist for the Central American country of Belize, he accepted these trade routes as fact, supported by his research of Indian cultures in Belize and Guatemala.

The American Indians have lived on the lands of North America for countless generations and have had a profound impact upon the successful development of the European colonization of America. For the most part the Indians lived with and on the land without the concept of individual land ownership, a much different concept than that of the colonial Europeans who coveted land ownership. Yet the Native Americans not only allowed the colonist's to settle on the land they used, but actually fed them through their first winters and even taught them what to grow and how to grow it to be able to feed themselves.

The involvement of the Native American Indians in trade and war with the various European countries had major effect on the actual political configuration of the 'New World', the timing of European expansion, and which European peoples would ultimately colonize the land.

Without the Indians, European colonization would probably not have succeeded when it did and who knows which country would have been the ultimate winner of America.

European exploration begins

The topography of the area has basically remained the same since the time that European explorers first trod the lands of Orange Beach over 500 years ago. Those explorers and the countries they represented make a list that reads like a 'Who's Who' of early North American history. At varying times each of these nations and peoples have claimed ownership of this jewel on the Alabama Coast.

There is a persistent story of very early exploration by the Welshman Prince Madoc ab Owain Gwnedd who may have been the first European to set foot in the area around 1170 AD. There is no known written evidence to confirm Madoc's explorations in the New World. There are however, some unexplained oddities of fair skinned and red–haired Indians, words spoken by them from the Welsh language, and indications that the Mandan Indians near the Great Lakes may have hosted these visiting Welshmen during their inland travels from here. The story has grown to legendary status.

Some historians believe that the Portuguese explorer Prince Henry the Navigator may have landed here before the Spanish. Portuguese explorers were quite adventuresome. However, no record of these possible explorations seems to exist. One explanation for this lack of written record may be that the Roman Catholic Pope in 1493 had declared this part of the New World to be the domain for Spanish exploration and the Portuguese would not have chanced excommunication from their church by documenting any such exploration. Bear in mind that this was the time of the infamous Spanish Inquisition by the Catholic Church.

Spanish Soldier

In 1497, shortly after Christopher Columbus' 'discovery' of the 'New World' for Spain, Italian explorer, Amerigo Vespucci (the man for whom the America's are named) also made voyages to the New World for Spain. It is believed by some that he may have charted Mobile Bay as the bay shows up on a European map in 1507 and there is no record of any other European explorers here before that time.

During the early period of Spanish explorations, Diego Miruelo mapped Bay Ochuse, believed by many to be Pensacola Bay, Florida, in 1516. In

29

this same time frame Juan Ponce de Leon (searcher for the 'Fountain of Youth') landed in Florida and charted the gulf coast as far north as Sarasota, opening the gulf coast to further exploration.

Alonso Alvarez de Pineda, another Spanish explorer and mapmaker, was sent by his government in 1519 to explore and chart the Gulf Coast from Florida to Mexico. During this expedition, he explored the Mobile Bay area for nearly 2 months.

Veteran Spanish soldier Panfilo de Narvaez with about 250 to 300 men led an expedition from 1527 to 1536. Alvar Nunez Cabeza de Vacca, a member of the expedition, wrote journals of the trip. The expedition was a disaster. They battled hurricanes during their voyage from the Caribbean and fought hostile Indians on their arrival in Florida. Add to all that, the ships that brought his expedition to this new land set sail for Mexico, leaving the expedition stranded near Tampa Bay. Narvaez and his men then walked north to the area of Panama City where they built rafts and headed west along the coast. They landed at Pensacola in 1528, but were attacked by Indians who drove them on west to Mobile Bay. From there they again coasted on west ultimately reaching Mexico with only 4 survivors.

Spanish explorer Hernando DeSoto in 1539 was among the first of the

major explorers to investigate this area, well after the 'discovery' of the 'New World' by Columbus. His multi–year odyssey covered much of the Southeast and parts of the Midwest. By August of 1540 he was in the Mobile area, where he met Chief Tuskaloosa, of the Maubila Indians. DeSoto was here in search of gold and riches any way he could get them. Therefore, it did not take long for a major battle to ensue which decimated the tribe, left their city of Maubila in ashes, and many of DeSoto's men dead or wounded.

Hernando DeSoto

Following the battle with the Maubila, DeSoto and the remainder of his men continued northwest on their quest for gold. Soon after crossing the Mississippi River, DeSoto died. The few survivors of the expedition eventually made their way to Spanish held Mexico.

While DeSoto was wandering the countryside, as part of a prearranged plan, his fleet commander Francisco Maldonado, sailed with the fleet from Tampa to Bay Ochuse (believed to be Pensacola Bay, but may have been confused at the time with Mobile Bay) where he was to wait for DeSoto and his expedition.

An interesting discovery was reported to have been made about 50 years ago when an arquebus (a Spanish matchlock musket of the period) was found grown into the crotch of a tree in what is now the eastern part of Gulf State Park. If this report is true, it could lead to speculation of a number of possible actions by Maldonado. Maldonado may have had a camp there where he could have watched both Pensacola and Mobile Bays possibly being unsure which bay was Ochuse. One may even consider that Maldonado might have anchored his fleet in Perdido Bay to be between each of the possible bays making it easier to monitor both bays. Perdido Bay is more protected from major storms, shallow enough to enable the scraping of his ships' hulls, and being near his possible camp while he awaited DeSoto's return.

Wherever Maldonado waited, it would be hard to imagine that he and his crew did not explore the area while he waited in vain for two years.

The year 1558 brought another Spanish explorer, Guido de las Bazares, to the Pensacola Bay area scouting for a possible site for a permanent Spanish settlement.

In 1559 Tristan de Luna y Arellano sailed with a dozen or so ships and nearly 2000 soldiers and colonists for the Central Gulf Coast. Landing in Mobile Bay, known to him as Bahia Filipina, he endeavored to establish a colony on the Eastern Shore and did considerable exploration of the area. For unknown reasons, he moved to Pensacola Bay. Within two months of

the move, all but three of his ships, most of his food, and supplies were destroyed by a hurricane. It would be four years before the expedition was rescued.

Through all of this exploration by the Spanish, only a small outpost was established at Pensacola, Florida.

Then came the French

The French began their interest in the Central Gulf Coast in 1682 when Rene'– Robert Cavelier, Sieur de La Salle, came down the Mississippi River from Canada and claimed all lands affected by the river for France. This was the establishment of the French Louisiana Territory later to become lands included in the Louisiana Purchase.

In 1698, Pierre LeMoyne Sieur d'Iberville set out

French Soldier

31

from the Caribbean to the Gulf Coast with his younger brother Jean Baptiste LeMoyne, Sieur d'Bienville, along with all the people and supplies required

Bienville

to establish a colony. After stopping briefly at Pensacola and Mobile Bay, they proceeded on to establish a colony at present day Biloxi, Mississippi.

Iberville left d'Sauvole, his second in command, in charge of the Biloxi settlement when he returned to France.

Iberville

Sauvole died in 1701, leaving the 21 year old Bienville in charge. Bienville moved the colony to Mobile Bay in 1702, an area he thought held more promise for permanent settlement, thus bringing the first French control to the area.

By 1702 war broke out with France and Spain allied against England. Called Queen Anne's War or War of Spanish Secession, the war continued until 1713. The war was about, among other things, France's control of Canadian trade and the English control of the eastern North American coast. Spain was caught in the middle with their settlements in Pensacola and St. Augustine, Florida. A force of English troops supported by American Colonials captured a French fort in Nova Scotia. With additional English victories in Europe, France and Spain were forced to seek an armistice. The subsequent Treaty of Utrecht gave possession of Newfoundland and Nova Scotia to England. Through this time, Bienville twice captured the small Spanish held, Pensacola outpost.

Additional wars followed with other countries added to the mix:

War of the Quadruple Alliance (1718–1720). A conflict broke out between France and Spain. By 1718 Spain found itself opposed by not only at war with France, but also England, Austria, and the Netherlands. One of the results of this war was that the French, then in control of Pensacola, gave Pensacola back to Spain.

King George's War or War of Jenkin's Ear (1739–1742). A war between England and Spain. Spanish privateers were harassing English merchant shipping. A Spanish privateer stopped an English ship for smuggling. The English Captain Jenkins' ear was cut off by one of the privateers. The result of the incident was a declaration of war by England against Spain. Although there were frequent attacks back and forth the result was basically a draw.

French and Indian War or Seven Years War (1754–1763). Another war over European domination of North America with the French and Indians allied against England (again with Spanish held territory caught in the middle of some of the action). Major results of the war were that France lost their control of their Louisiana Territory to Spain and Spain gave up control of Pensacola and East Florida to England for recognition of Spain's control of Cuba. In 1762, France ceded Louisiana to Spain in the secret treaty of Fontainbleau. In 1763, the Fontainbleau Treaty was confirmed and Spain ceded its Florida Territory to England. This war left England with serious debts that ultimately led to over taxation of the American colonies. One of the new taxes, the infamous Stamp Act, was part of the prelude to the American Revolution.

American Revolutionary War (1776–1781). The war of American Independence with the American colonies allied (later) with France against England. The colonies won the war beginning the end of European domination of America.

American Revolutionary War battles were fought at Old Spanish Fort  (to the north of Orange Beach on the Eastern Shore of Mobile Bay) and at Pensacola (to the East of Orange Beach), not by Americans, but by the Spaniard Bernardó de Galvez against the British!

Seeing a possibly weakened England, involved in a major war with the American colonists, Spain began its own war against England in 1779. Galvez was the Governor of Louisiana at the time and Mobile and Pensacola were then under British rule. Galvez, along with his army of Spanish

Colonial Soldier

regulars, Creoles, Indians, and free Blacks, gave great support to the American colonies just when they needed it by attacking the British at Baton Rouge and Natchez. The following year he attacked and captured Mobile and Pensacola, helping to eliminate the British forces along the Gulf and preventing a possible British attack on the American colonies from the south.

With the surrender of British General Cornwallis

Galvez

33

and the signing of the Treaty of Paris in 1782, the United States of America began to take charge of the area. England ceded control of West Florida to the new United States of America.

There were still border disputes between the U.S., England, Spain, and the Native Americans, to whom most of the land in the central Gulf coast actually belonged.

In the Treaty of San Ildefonso in 1800, Spain was required to give its Louisiana Territory back to France. Within 3 short years the United States purchased the Louisiana Territory from France for fifteen million dollars. This was one of the last removals of European colonial rule from North America.

War of 1812 (1812–1814). The final conflict between the newly independent United States of America and England.

American Andrew Jackson and his army whipped the British in nearby Pensacola. From Pensacola, Jackson moved his troops and equipment by raft across Perdido Bay to Bear Point as he passed through Orange Beach on his way west for his battles with the British at New Orleans.

The War of 1812 at last removed England as a British Soldier

colonial power in America, but unfortunately brought on the disputes with the Native American Indians in the Southeast due to the colonists desire for additional land for the burgeoning American population. These disputes culminated in the First Creek Indian War of 1814, fought in Alabama, and the 1831 to 1837, 'Trail of Tears' expulsion of most of the Native Americans to the newly established Indian Territory (now the State of Oklahoma). The Second Creek War of 1837 fought mostly in neighboring Northwest Florida along with the Seminole War further south in Florida was their last gasp. For the most part, all these wars and their associated skirmishes were fought over the lands of the Gulf Coast.

A Few Pirates Sprinkled In

During the early colonial days, pirates roamed the area and at least one chest of pirate treasure is known to have been dug up from the sands along the bay shore. Pirates Cove just east of Wolf Bay is named for these visitors.

It is believed that the famed pirate Jean LaFitte hulled his ships in Perdido Bay. 'Hulling' was a process whereby the ship would be driven into a shallow area. When the tide subsided, the ship would be forced onto one side to enable the sailors to scrape barnacles, replace

Spanish Galleon

planking, or re–caulk the hull. At the next tide the process would be repeated for the other side.

The coves and inlets in the area would have made for good hideouts and launching places for raids on British merchant ships and Spanish gold bearing galleons that sailed along the coast on their way home to England or Spain.

We think of these galleons sailing straight across the Caribbean from Mexico and South America on their way to Spain. However, they actually sailed north along the coast of Central America, Mexico, along the Gulf coast, and south down the west coast of Florida with a stop in Cuba before heading on to their destination. Losing so many ships in hurricanes, it only made sense to stay close to land.

From the beginning of European exploration of the New World, control of Florida and the lands of the Gulf coast was hotly contested. Each nation that had control left their mark and the resulting cultural diversity of this area is legendary. The Gulf Coast is indeed the land of 'Five Flags' and more!

The United States stakes its claim

There was an important, but often historically overlooked, treaty signed in 1795 between the newly formed United States of America and Spain. This treaty, called the Treaty of San Lorenzo or Pinckney's Treaty, defined the first international boundaries for the United States. Maybe its most important features were the agreements to allow U. S. citizens the 'right to deposit' their exports in Spanish held New Orleans and to engage in commercial business there. The treaty for the first time recognized the southern and western boundaries of the U. S. The western boundary being the Mississippi River, thereby allowing access to the river for commerce for the rapidly expanding frontier population. The southern boundary allowed U. S. access to what would become the northern areas of the States of Alabama and Mississippi.

Noted surveyor Andrew Ellicott was appointed Commissioner of the survey of the border between the United States of America and the Spanish held lands of West Florida by President George Washington, his former business partner. Ellicott and Esteban Minor of Spain jointly surveyed the line in 1799 to define the 31 degrees North Latitude line agreed to as the separation line of the two countries in the Treaty of San Lorenzo. The line is often referred to as the 'Ellicott Line' or 'Mound Line' due to the three feet high, fifteen feet diameter mounds used to mark survey points every mile on the line. This line runs through the community of Stockton in the northern end of Baldwin County.

Toward the end of the American Revolutionary War, the migration into the area which would become Baldwin County began. Many 'Tories' (people loyal to the English Crown) left, or were run out of, the Carolinas and moved to the area of North Baldwin on the new southern frontier.

Baldwin County, as an entity, actually predates the State of Alabama. It was formed in 1809, while this area of the county was part of the Mississippi Territory. At that time the southern half of the county was still part of Spanish/British West Florida.

Upon the admission of the State of Mississippi into the Union,

December 10, 1817, Baldwin County became part of the newly established Alabama Territory. The county came to its present north–south shape with the admission of the State of Alabama as the 22nd State, on December 14, 1819.

Subtle changes on the north end of the county occurred during the time of Reconstruction (a time of military occupation in the South, 1865 to 1877) after the War of Southern Independence 1861–1865 (The Civil War). In 1865 the north end of Baldwin County actually extended east over the northwest corner of the State of Florida. But in 1866, Escambia County, Alabama, was carved out of Baldwin and Covington Counties aligning Baldwin County to its current configuration.

Baldwin County was named for Abraham Baldwin who was born in Connecticut, but was a resident of Georgia during the last 20 years of his life. He was a delegate from Georgia at the Constitutional Convention and a signer of the Constitution.

The Civil War

Orange Beach was basically undeveloped during the time of the War of Southern Independence. There was only a few farmers in the area and due to its remoteness and numerous bays and coves, it was an ideal area for the 'blockade runners' (private merchant ships and boats) to pickup and land their cargoes.

Cotton Bayou got its name from the 'blockade runners' hauling 'King Cotton' from the bayou to assist the Confederacy. These ships would attempt to sneak past the blockades of southern harbors by the Union fleets to supply the armaments and life necessities to the Confederacy.

The story of a young soldier named Lemuel Walker Jr., illustrates the importance of fishing in

Confederate Soldier

the area. 'Lem' as he was called, enlisted in Company 'F' of the 21st Regiment of the Alabama Volunteers on October 13, 1861. The 21st Alabama manned the area fortifications and many of the regiment were involved in the major Battle of Shiloh, Tennessee. Private Lem however, was assigned to the

A blockade running schooner

batteries at Choctaw Bluff on the Tombigbee River for protection of the important salt works near there in Clarke County, Alabama. Until, that is, it was discovered that he was only 16 years old. Being under age for service, he was discharged August 30, 1862. That did not stop him from serving his homeland however, and he re–enlisted in September of 1863. Lem rejoined his old unit for '3 years or the war.' According to his muster roll, he was immediately detached from the unit 'to fish' by Department of the Gulf Commander, Major General Dabney H. Maury. Feeding the Confederacy was an important function as the war dragged on and supplies dwindled and Lem had the needed skills.

Once while fishing in Mobile Bay, Lem and his party were captured by Yankees. The Yankees then sent them out, with guards, to continue fishing, only this time for the Union. One night, while fishing the lower bay, they pushed their guards overboard and returned to their own units.

Lem married Fanny Strong of the Shell Banks community after the war and they moved to Caswell in 1884, to be near his aging father who lived on Bear Point. The land deed to his new home was recorded in 1890 and Lem spent the balance of his life on that land in Caswell.

His life long career of fishing in the bays and the open Gulf might be considered the beginning of the fishing industry in Orange Beach area.

Some of the 'old timers' remember tales told by early resident   Richard 'Dick' Leavins of the Confederate troops that came here during the war from Fort Morgan at the entrance to Mobile Bay. There has been a fort there from the early days of exploration and it was named Fort Bowyer during the War of 1812. The current brick fortification was completed in 1836 and named for Revolutionary War hero Daniel Morgan. The soldiers came to the Orange Beach area   seeking fresh fruit and vegetables from the local farmers to augment their military rations. The troops came overland by horse on their route from and to the fort.

The tough times of the four years of the war did not stop with the end of the war in April 1865. Following the end of the war, the entire South was under rigid Federal Military occupation and was 'disenfranchised' until 1877, a period known as 'Reconstruction'. No other group of States has ever endured such action. Most areas of the South were destitute with crops and machinery destroyed from war actions, but such was not the case in Orange Beach. With the fertile land and the resources of the Gulf of Mexico at their doorstep, Orange Beach not only survived, but grew. Many of the men who had served in the area returned here after the war.

The Land and Gulf

Orange Beach, 'The Gem of the Gulf Coast', is located on the eastern

end of 'Pleasure Island', along the southwest coast of the State of Alabama. It is nestled next to the azure blue waters of the Gulf of Mexico and nearly surrounded by bays, coves and bayous.

'Where the land meets the sea' is what Orange Beach is all about. From its early days, the Gulf of Mexico has been the lure that has brought many visitors. The ultra fine 'sugar white' sand dunes and beaches, the abundance of stately pines, live oaks often festooned with Spanish moss, flowering oleander trees and azaleas, and year around access to the great outdoors make visiting or living here like being in paradise. The combination of the mild winters and balmy summer breezes of a semi–tropical climate zone and the casual resort life style contribute to the growth of the area.

Although fishing has always been a major attraction, most of the early settlers farmed and raised cattle, goats, and truck gardens, primarily for sustenance and meager export for cash flow. Timber   logging for lumber and pine tar collection for the production of turpentine and naval stores were early industries. Wooden ships of the day used pine tars to coat ropes and riggings and for sealing their hulls and decks. The uses of turpentine, another product of pine tar, seemed to be limited only by their imagination.

Although the occasional hurricane cause some problems, they give us plenty of warning to get out of their way. The generally long periods of delightful living between 'storms' more than make up for their problems. Hurricanes do have some effect however, sometimes changing the configuration of beaches, low lands, and islands, and on occasion causing damage to structures and roadways when they come ashore. (See appendix for further information about tropical storms and hurricanes.)

The normal coastal currents of the central Gulf Coast run from east to west. Along with these currents, normal tidal action, which is generally only about one foot, causes continual changes along the Gulf front beaches as the sands shift with the currents. South Alabama is the only place in the world where the famous and warm ocean current, the Gulf Stream, actually touches land during the summer months. This is one of the reasons for the terrific fishing in the area.

The effects caused by the heating and cooling of the land and the generally stable temperatures of the Gulf waters create delightful breezes. The breeze from the Gulf to the land during the day and the reverse at night makes for comfortable living conditions.

The Islands

There are many small islands in the area which add to the 'feel' of a tropical resort. The largest of these, Ono Island, located on Old River just north of Gulf Beach, is now a very upscale place, but it was not always that way. Before the 1960's, George Kee and his brother Harville raised about 5,000 goats there. The brothers were bridge tenders in the area. They lived in a small shack and sold goats for milk, meat, and pasture at 50 cents each if you caught your own goat or 1–dollar if they caught it. Surprisingly, the locals never called the island Goat Island. That moniker was given to the island now known as Robinson Island near the mouth of Terry Cove. Ono Island purportedly got its name during negotiations between the State of Alabama and the State of Florida over ownership of the island with each saying 'Oh, No!' when the other stated that the island was theirs'.

The island just off Caswell near Burkart Point is called Walker Cay. That island got its name from the Walker family that lived in nearby Caswell. An interesting incident turned Walker Cay into a port in need as reported in the Foley Onlooker newspaper, March 11, 1920:

'Mr. Bill of Orange Beach, started out one afternoon last week with Claude Peteet and another gentleman to Walker's Inn (Gulf View Park), where Mr. Peteet and his friend intended spending the night. Mr. Bill had trouble with the engine and went adrift, the three men spent the night on the little island which was not more than two hundred yards from the main land if they had only known where they were.'

Being adrift, lost in the fog, and making land fall on the island, they spent a wet and uncomfortable night. Upon awakening the next morning with the lifting fog, they could see their destination port only 200 yards away!

According to James Huff who had talked to a Terry family member while working in Mobile in the 1970's, Terry Cove was named for an

41

early sea Captain, probably George Terry, who came frequently to Orange Beach and anchored in the Cove that now carries his name. In 1879, George Terry purchased land in the area.

The small Island at the entrance to Cotton Bayou is Rabbit Island. No story seems to accompany that name, but one may make a reasonable assumption. The Orange Beach City Council renamed Rabbit Island in 1980 to Gilchrist Island, named for Dr. Gilchrist of Mobile, who bought land in the area. The Island however, is still called Rabbit Island by most locals.

Another island made from dredge spoilage from dredging of Perdido Pass, is located just south of Robinson Island near the pass. It is frequently used for picnics by day boaters and seems generally to be known as Bird Island.

Lakes

There are 3 fresh water lakes in the Gulf State Park to the west of Orange Beach: from west to east, Lake Shelby, the largest, Middle Lake, and Little Lake. These lakes are spring fed and Lake Shelby is known to be the closest naturally occurring fresh water lake to salt water (the Gulf of Mexico). These lakes are great for fishing, swimming, and canoeing.

There was another fresh water lake as well. This unnamed lake of about 7 acres in size was located on Alabama Point and existed for many years, but was swept away with the sand during Hurricane Flossy on September 24, 1956.

What's in the name?

The name 'Orange Beach' came about slowly as the area grew from the war period of the 1860's to the early 1900's. During that time there were several farmers along the shores of Wolf Bay, Bay La Launche, Arnica Bay, Bay St. John, and Terry Cove.

Citrus was brought to the 'New World' by the Spanish by 1565 and spread the plantings along the Gulf Coast. Small plantings of sour and Satsuma Oranges (Mandarin type oranges) developed in the area by the 1890's. Oranges and strawberries were the most commonly grown produce. It is told that one 12 year old tree bore 2,000 sweet oranges in one season. The wind off the bays and the occasional freezes during the winter months are hard on such crops and prevent growing them on a commercial scale today. One such hard–freeze occurred in the winter of 1916–1917 that destroyed most citrus trees throughout the Deep South. Another devastating hard–freeze occurred in 1926. After replanting

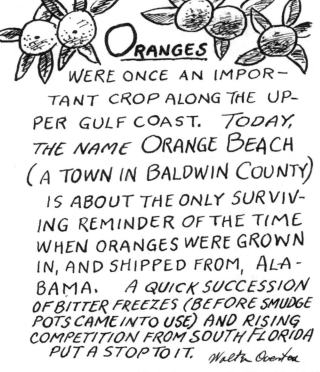

ORANGES WERE ONCE AN IMPOR-
TANT CROP ALONG THE UP-
PER GULF COAST. TODAY,
THE NAME ORANGE BEACH
(A TOWN IN BALDWIN COUNTY)
IS ABOUT THE ONLY SURVIV-
ING REMINDER OF THE TIME
WHEN ORANGES WERE GROWN
IN, AND SHIPPED FROM, ALA-
BAMA. A QUICK SUCCESSION
OF BITTER FREEZES (BEFORE SMUDGE
POTS CAME INTO USE) AND RISING
COMPETITION FROM SOUTH FLORIDA
PUT A STOP TO IT. Walter Overton

Above is an illustration that was published as part of a 'Southland Sketches' panel by noted artist Walter Overton. These panels were published weekly in the *Mobile Register* newspapers from 1937 to 1976.

however; there are to this day many orange, lemon, grapefruit, Satsuma, and kumquat trees to be found in the yards and gardens of area homes. There has been continuing talk of planting the roadsides with orange trees to uphold the history of the name. It is needless to explain why the word 'Beach' is part of the name

The Environment

Through the years of Orange Beach's history, its environment has been one of its primary attractions. The environment all around us is what has brought the people, residents and visitors alike. As more people have come to Orange Beach, the protection of the resources and environment has become more and more important.

In 1931, a daughter, named Joy Morrill, was born to Charter Captain Willard Smith 'Bill' Morrill and Frances 'Frank' Walker Morrill in a hospital at Pensacola. Her father brought her home to Caswell in his charter boat, *Perdido Maid*, Joy's sister Betty Morrill Dubuisson, accompanied them.

Joy grew up learning about her environment under her father's tutelage. As a child, Joy began planning the study of the sea life of Perdido Bay. Her desire carried her to the University of Alabama where she graduated in 1953, then to a master's degree in marine biology, and on to a doctorate in marine botany from the University of North Carolina.

After working and teaching all over the country, she returned to Caswell in 1986. Joy Morrill was astounded by  the marine destruction of Perdido Bay and became concerned over the rapid building and development in what became 'her' environment. In 1993 she founded the Alabama Coastal Heritage Trust, an organization devoted to preservation of critical habitat. Joy Morrill became a major voice for her fragile environment. She filed lawsuits against developers, spoke at City Council meetings and other public forums.

Joy Morrill

Joy's last crusade was to save 588 acres of what she called 'one of the last pristine maritime forests' that had been acquired by the city in 1990. Joy Morrill's long fight to save those 588 acres of maritime forest may have indeed succeeded, only time will tell. Her use of scientific and legal knowledge and her public speaking and leadership has provided a legacy of knowledge and concern to the citizens of Orange Beach. Joy Morrill passed away July 27, 1997, but will not soon be forgotten as a protector of the fragile coastal environment of Orange Beach.

Other chapters will discuss the artificial reef program and maritime fishing restrictions that help ensure the continued productivity of Gulf charter fishing industry and the zoning, building restrictions, and other infrastructures and programs begun by the city that help keep Orange Beach a clean family oriented resort community.

A Little Genealogy

From the 1870's through to today the community of Orange Beach has had two prominent families, the Callaways and the Walkers. Of course, other families were involved with the development of the community, but even many of them quickly became connected with these families. To understand the development of Orange Beach, one needs to understand these family connections.

The Callaway Family

James Spruell Callaway lived in the Lagoon community west of Gulf Shores and never lived in Orange Beach. He was killed during the War of Southern Independence at the end of the Battle of Jonesboro, Georgia, and is buried there. His son, James Clifford Callaway, born in Montrose on the Eastern Shore of Mobile Bay, moved to Orange Beach in 1875 and was the founder of the Orange Beach Callaway's. James C. was a farmer and seaman with his schooners becoming the primary lifeblood to the early growth of Orange Beach. James C. reared his sons as seafarers.

Other families of note with Callaway connections are Brown, Childress, Dietz, Ewing, Lauder, Nelson, Shelby, Walker, Wallace, and Williams. These names are seen throughout this book.

Portraits of Captain James Clifford Callaway and his wife Nancy Ellen Childress Callaway. James was born in Montrose, Alabama, in 1854. Ellen was born in Gasque, Alabama, in 1857. They moved to Orange Beach at the time of their marriage, November 1875. They had eleven children – eight boys and three girls.

The above 1895 photo is of James C. Callaway and three of his sons. From left to right are Elver, James C., Herman, and Childress Callaway.

This photo was taken at a Callaway Family Reunion during the 1950's. Left to right – kneeling: Marion Lauder holding Susan Lauder, Earl Callaway, Ronnie Callaway, Marie Lauder, Ella Callaway, David Callaway, Debbie Callaway, Kathleen Callaway, and Richard Callaway held by Billy Callaway.
Standing: Brownie Callaway, Thurston Lauder, Neil Lauder, Ronald Lauder, James Callaway, Elinor Callaway, Mildred Callaway, Amel Callaway, Ray Callaway, Macklin Callaway, Ellen Callaway, Eleanor Callaway, Jimmy Lauder, Bobby Lauder, and Jimmy Harrell.

The Walker Family

Lemuel Walker, Sr., like his Callaway counter part, was not born in Orange Beach, but he did come here early...about 1865. We know very little about Lemuel, Sr., other than he had two children by his first wife, Rosine Patterson Gabel, and seven children by his second wife, Lovey Styron. He died in 1896. Lemuel, Sr.'s home is still standing in Caswell, although over the years it has been extensively renovated.

His son Lemuel, Jr., was a soldier during the War of Southern Independence. Lem, as he was called, was born in Point Clear, Alabama, and moved to Orange Beach by 1890 to be near his aging father. Lemuel, Jr., took a very active part in the growth of the fishing industry in Orange Beach. His descendants are active in the charter fishing industry today.

Families with Walker family connections are Bill, Caswell, Callaway, Dietz, Low, Morrill, Robinson, Strong, Styron, and White. The inter–relationship of the Walkers with these community names further illustrates the domination of the Walkers and Callaways in the community.

A portrait of Lemuel 'Lem' Walker, Jr. and his wife Mary Frances 'Fanny' Strong Walker. Lem was born in Point Clear, Alabama in 1846. Fanny was born in Shell Banks, Alabama, in 1849. They were married following the Civil War in 1866. They had twelve children ...seven boys and five girls. They moved to Orange Beach about 1890 to be near his aging father.

Above are some of the sons of Rufus Walker Sr.: Shown left to right: Gladwin, Ruben, Raymond, Roland Sr., 'Bob', Rabun, Roy, and Rufus, Jr.

This is a photograph of the Walker Family Reunion in July 1930. Back row, left to right: Bob Walker, Edwin Bill, Rex Walker, Harry Bill, Edna Bill, and Roland Walker. Front row: Abbie (Bill) Walker, Ray Walker, Rufus Walker Sr., Gladwin Walker, Ruben Walker, Crockett 'CS' White, Jr., Edna Walker White, and Elbert White on Edna's lap.

The Callaway and Walker families have collaborated in many ways over the years to the benefit of the community. They have each carved out their own niches from time to time, as with the early freight and lighthouse service of the Callaway schooners and the early prominence in the area of U.S. Mail boat service by the Walkers.

Their work together in their participation in the Orange Beach Community Center and the establishment of the charter fishing industry has given purpose to the community. The beginnings of the Orange Beach Fishing Association, the push for a safer pass to the Gulf, and their early work in the artificial reef programs are but a few of their joint accomplishments.

Yet, through it all, there has always been that unspoken family competition that has provided the impetus for constant gain and growth. Even in passing from this world, the families seem to be with their family groups. Many of the Callaway family are buried with their ancestors on the west–end of the island at Miller Memorial Cemetery in Shellbanks and the Lagoon Community, while many of the Walker family are buried in Bear Point Cemetery near their early established community of Caswell.

For an outline descendents list of the Callaway and Walker families, see the Appendix.

Early Settlement

During the time of Spanish occupation of West Florida, which included Orange Beach, Spain granted 559.56 acres of land to Samuel Suarez, which was most of the eastern end of Bear Point. Adjacent to the west was a similar grant of 567.17 acres to William Kee, who is believed to be Samuel Suarez' brother–in–law. These two land grants covered most of what we know today as Orange Beach. These grants were not issued United States land patents until May 1925 and September 1923 respectively. Joseph Suarez, who is believed to be a brother of Samuel, was granted land in the area of Perdido Beach and another brother, Francis Suarez, was granted 698.77 acres on the west end of 'Pleasure Island' in the area of Fort Morgan. We know little about these men or the reason they were given Spanish grants. Several descendants of the Suarez family served in the Confederate Army during the War of Southern Independence and many descendents still live in the area. (See the Appendix for the Land Patents and map of the Suarez and Kee grants)

At the time of Alabama Statehood in 1819, this area was a pristine coastal wilderness. It was a peninsula back then, not an island. The area was sparsely populated with stalwart settlers, along with alligator, deer, bear, wild hog, raccoon, myriad bird life, and other wild creatures. Other than the occasional boater or fisherman and the few folks who lived on the north shore of Arnica Bay, Bay La Launche, Pirates Cove, and Wolf Bay, little happened here until the War of Southern Independence.

- Foley Onlooker – Orange Beach community news November 27, 1924:
  'Intensive and successful trapping is being conducted here by Edward Ewing and Amel Callaway and as a result our chickens will be safer.'

Richard 'Dick' Leavins, was an early settler to Orange Beach along with his wife and family, who farmed in Orange Beach during the war days.

Captain Percy Jones settled on the extreme eastern end of Bear Point soon after the war.

James Dannelly also moved here after he lost his property on Fish River during the war. Dannelly settled on what is now known as 'The Barchard Tract'. It was on his place at Fish River, then known as Dannelly's Mills, that the Union Army troops gathered for their march and subsequent attacks on Spanish Fort and Fort Blakeley in March and April of 1865 (the last major battles of the war).

By 1874, the Lemuel Walker, Sr., family made their home here. The James C. Callaway family arrived about 1875.

Josephine Community

The area of Josephine, on the mainland shore of Arnica Bay, was an important connection to the relatively isolated settlers in Orange Beach and Caswell. Josephine was established many years before settlement in Orange Beach, providing a nearby source of farm goodsand merchandise stores.

In 1881, Josephine got its first Post Office which was named for the daughter of Amos Ross who had been a resident since 1858. After a century of service, mail delivery by the Josephine Post Office was consolidated into the Elberta Post Office in 1959.

The home of Admiral Raphael Semmes of Confederate cruiser *CSS Alabama* fame, was on Semmes Bayou (now Roberts Bayou). Semmes' moved his family to Josephine from Maryland in 1846. Semmes and his wife Elizabeth raised four children there. He was a Naval Midshipman stationed in Pensacola assigned to the Lighthouse Service at the time. Semmes' large two story home became the Mexiwana Hotel, owned by Leon O. McPherson, after Semmes had moved to Mobile. The home/hotel burned in 1935. McPherson, who had moved to Josephine from Chicago, Illinois, additionally operated a small local freight and mail boat also called the *Mexiwana.*

Adm. Raphael Semmes

The area of Josephine was used by the Spanish American War troops stationed in Pensacola for R & R (Rest and Relaxation) during 1898.

John McKee Climmie moved to Josephine from Ontario, Canada, via Selma, Alabama, in 1904. Climmie owned several shops in the area including a plumbing shop, tin smithing shop, a boat yard, and a sawmill. He is also credited with building the first ferry that provided important transportation across Perdido Bay at Lillian, the only route from the area to Pensacola without circling around Perdido Bay. Leon Climmie was the grandfather of life long resident, Austin Ballard, husband of Lillian Walker Ballard who is a Josephine Community historian with no known connection to the local Walker family.

Other important residents to the Josephine area were Joe and Elizabeth Pasaura who operated an open–air bakery and an enclosed pavilion restaurant that supplied fresh baked goods to the entire area via the U.S. Mail boat. The bakery was located beside the Post Office on Semmes Bayou. Remains of the baking oven still stand.

During the 1920's, the Luey Brannon family operated a turpentine still near Pirates Cove. Many Orange Beach residents worked in the turpentine industry.

Area entertainment was provided at Pirates Cove after the Coves' development by Max Lawrenz, Sr., who had moved to the area in 1916. The area's first jukebox was located here along with other entertainment.

Change comes to the area

In 1875, James C. Callaway married Nancy Childress and moved to Orange Beach from the community of Lagoon. They built a home on land that was located on what is now Highway 180, just east of Highway 161. He operated a schooner freight service, worked as a turpentine chipper in the pine forests of the area, and also farmed.

Capt. James C. Callaway

Have you ever heard the term 'cat faced' pines? They are the 'V' shaped cuts on pine tree trunks that were made by 'chippers', a special tool made for the job. The pine sap seeped from these cuts and was collected in pans attached to the tree. This collecting of pine sap was referred to as 'turpentining' and was one of the first major industries in Baldwin County. In those days, turpentine was used for just about everything. As the turpentine industry began to grow in the area, the workers were housed at the old Harvey Spindler place on the west side of Orange Beach.

By the 1890's, James C. and his sons ran the schooner freight business and with the addition of a second schooner also worked in the lighthouse service along the Gulf Coast. His schooners were the *J. S. Murrow* and the *Ellen C.*

James C. Callaway was a man of many talents. He was a superior boat builder, noted seafarer, lighthouse keeper, self taught doctor for both humans and animals, turpentine chipper, carpenter, farmer, stockman, mail carrier, shell collector, and what ever else was required to live in what was a remote area. He was the epitome of the phrase 'jack of all trades'. 'Captain Jim', as he was called, taught these traits and skills to his sons.

One of his grandsons, Clifford Callaway, tells a story that illustrates the talents of James C. It seems that an uncle by marriage shot himself with a 38 caliber pistol in the yard of his family home. His family put him in a wheelbarrow and pushed him to the *Ellen C*, where James C. sailed him to Mobile. The Mobile doctor was unable to remove the bullet and he was sent home to recover. Later while serving on the *Ellen C*, he complained of headaches, where upon James C. Callaway using his pocketknife, successfully removed the bullet!

Captain Callaway bought the schooner, *J. S. Murrow*, when he first

A view of the harbor at the Boat Basin. The schooner at left is the *Ellen C*, at the right is James C. Callaway's other schooner *J. S. Murrow*.

arrived in Orange Beach in 1875 and it was used in the lighthouse service routinely checking and maintaining coastal beacons and lighthouses.

James C. Callaway, with the help of Mr. Cook, a ship builder from Pensacola, and James' sons built the *Ellen C* from the keel up, even felling and cutting their own lumber. Contrary to what many people believe, the schooner was not built in Orange Beach. Clifford Callaway, states that the schooner was built in a shipyard on Sapling Point at the east foot of Wolf Bay, because that location was protected from the cold north wind that blows during the deep winter months. Captain Jim's schooner *Ellen C* was used primarily to carry freight to and from Mobile and other ports of call on the Gulf of Mexico.

These schooners were the lifeblood of the early Orange Beach settlers. The descendants of James C. Callaway and their boats were important contributors to the progress of the Orange Beach Community.

- Foley Onlooker – Orange Beach community news November 27, 1924 – 'Between lumber and naval supplies Capt. Callaway and the Murrow are kept pretty busy these days.'

The *J. S. Murrow* later met her end during a storm when she was blown aground on the shore of Wolf Bay. She was abandoned and later burned where she sat after salvage of her engine and usable parts. The other Callaway schooner, *Ellen C,* was sold into Mexico in 1920 after the passing of James C. Callaway and was lost to history.

Other notables to early development

A group of men, primarily from Iowa, purchased the Southern Plantation Company, a company that had been selling land in central Baldwin County for about 2 years. They renamed the company, Southern Plantation Development Company and the new company purchased 80,000 additional acres from the Southern States Lumber Company. The Southern States Lumber Company was a large lumber company that owned huge tracts of forest land. Southern States had been formed by the merger of the Muscogee Lumber Company, Seminole Lumber Company, and the George W. Robinson Company. By 1904, Southern Plantation Development realized that better transportation was needed if they were going to develop their land. With that in mind they set about the donation of cash, rights–of–way through their land, built depots, and furnished rail ties, thereby enticing the L&N Railroad to extend a branch line from Bay Minette into south Baldwin. By 1906, they had brought 250 settlers to the rich farmlands of central Baldwin County.

As the area began to grow, others were also attracted to south Baldwin County and the Orange Beach area. John Foley, a patent medicine manufacturer from Chicago, founded the City of Foley in 1905. Foley had purchased 55,000 acres of land, in and around the current site of the City of Foley, that he offered for sale by lots and acreage. John Foley and his Magnolia Land Company (still operated by his descendants) also helped with materials and rights–of–way in the extension of the railroad from Robertsdale to his new town.

John Foley organized many 'Real Estate' trains in the Chicago area that brought prospective new settlers to his new city, putting them up in his 'modern' new hotel, the 'Magnolia', that still stands in downtown Foley and is now open as a 'bed and breakfast'. These 'Real Estate' trains were greeted in the cities of central and south Baldwin by the sounds of community bands

A 'Real Estate' train from up north arriving in Summerdale – July 21, 1910.

55

and folks in all their Sunday best. John Foley's new town and the actions of the SouthernPlantation Development Company were an important part of the development of central and south Baldwin.

In 1908, D. R. Peteet moved to Orange Beach from Birmingham, Alabama, and purchased 3,254 acres of land in the area. His land extended from Portage Creek on the north (now part of the Intracoastal Canal), just west of the three fresh water lakes, to about half way to Bear Point on the east. Although stories of D. R. Peteet picture

D. R. Peteet shown standing on the porch of his office on the Boat Basin.

him as an unfriendly, hard driving businessman, his brother Claude, who brokered real estate in the area and was a Notary Public, was extremely well liked in the community.

D. R. Peteet erected a shingle mill on the south shore of Bay La Launche in 1909, with Mr. Cowan as millwright. Peteet built a small office building and later a camp house for the men who were cutting logs and hauling them to the mill. He hired several men from the North to help build the mill, and enchanted, with the area, they soon became residents. Among them was L. H. Diehl from Holidaysburg, Pennsylvania, who bought 40 acres of land from Peteet along with two lots on the Bay near the mill. It was here that the first dwelling was built on what is known as Gulf Bay Tract. J. H. Wolbrink, from Grand Rapids, Michigan, purchased 5 acres of land on Bay Circle and a bay front lot, erected the next dwelling. J. H. Hazelett bought what is known as the Swirn Place (named after Andrew Swirn who had a farm there). This small settlement around Peteet's mill was the true beginning of what was to become the City of Orange Beach.

Frank Barchard, Sr. came from Illinois, bought land around Foley, and was further intrigued by the Caswell area on Bear Point. Barchard purchased land there establishing the Barchard Tract in 1923. He moved to the area and eventually bought the Foley Onlooker newspaper as a birthday gift to his son Frank, Jr. This purchase and gift made Frank, Jr. the youngest newspaper editor in the State of Alabama at the age of 13 or 14. Eventually, Frank, Jr. inherited the rest of the property. Kitty Barchard, Frank's daughter, joined the Callaway family by her marriage to Nolan Callaway, a grandson of James C. Callaway.

Are you beginning to see that Yankees developed and populated much of south Baldwin County and Orange Beach in particular from the late 1890s? For the most part, south Baldwin County was 'colonized' by northern land developers. Our winter 'snow bird' visitors are just continuing the migration and like most of the rest of us, they liked it here and many of them have stayed.

Orange Beach developed it's own independent culture. A culture developed by its history, land, and location to the Gulf, not a culture imported by the people who moved here. Many other communities in south Baldwin were literally colonized by ethnic or locational populations, such as Elberta (German), Silverhill (Scandinavian and Bohemian), Malbis Plantation (Greek), Foley (Chicago), or Perdido Beach (Montgomery).

Until the early 20th century, the only means of transportation into the areas south of Wolf Bay on the east and Bon Secour Bay on the west was by water, horseback, or wagon. As a result, prior to the dredging of the Intercoastal Canal, both ends of the 'island' were the only areas developed, as these were the only areas with water access to protected bays and bayous. The only developed areas on the east end were south of Wolf Bay, Bay La Launche, and Arnica Bay with the settlements of Bear Point, Caswell, Orange Beach, and Romar Beach. The communities of Shell Banks, Gasque, Pilot Town at Navy Cove, and Ft. Morgan were on the west end with only the community of Lagoon in between.

By 1910 and the years immediately following, families moved into the Orange Beach area from various sections of the country. Among these were the Harvey Spindler's from Nebraska, Dr. Philo Chappel from Grand Rapids, Michigan, the Hendrickson's from Ohio, the McConnaughy's from Kentucky, and Richard and Carl Lockbriler from Ohio, along with the Wool's, and the Pratt's. Most of these folks were hired to come here by D. R. Peteet for his shingle mill. Many of them stayed.

- Foley Onlooker – Orange Beach community news
  November 27, 1924: 'Carter and Nichols are getting logs
  ready for a number of log houses for Frank Barchard to be

erected by B.T. Hudson on his Orange Beach subdivision.'

'Mr. and Mrs. Jacob Wolbrink were here for a couple of days working on their property here.'

- Foley Onlooker – Orange Beach community news June 3, 1925: 'There were a couple of men from Bay Minette here Saturday looking over some land.'

- Foley Onlooker – Orange Beach community news 1929–1933: 'Two prospectors from Iowa were here last week looking for a hotel site and were very profuse in praise for our bathing beach.'

Story of Romar Beach

Romar Beach is important because it is the location of some of the first houses on the beach. Good friends Spurgeon Roche and Carl Taylor 'Zeke' Martin, both businessmen of Mobile, homesteaded the land with 3 miles of beachfront covering the area from Gulf State Park on the west to today's public beach area at Cotton Bayou on the east...now only 480 feet. Although you see the Roche name spelled many ways, descendant Sarah Roche Browder confirms the spelling of both first and last names of her ancestor as you see them here. They named their location Romar Beach, the 'Ro' for the Roche family and 'Mar' for the Martin family.

They built their small neighboring houses about 1924 as the ultimate isolated 'get away' for their families. And isolated it was!

Romar Beach about 1925. The original Martin house on the left...the Roche house on the right.

Getting there in those early days was a challenge. The first challenge was to cut a road from the sand road, which later became 'Highway 180', south to their beach property. The roadway was 'corduroyed' across the sand and swampy land and required a wooden bridge over one of the three fresh water lakes. 'Corduroying' a road means stabilizing the roadbed with logs or lumber across the roadway, then covering them with packed dirt or sand. Getting stuck in the sand was common here as it was elsewhere in the Orange Beach area. The road is still there, but is now impassible. A few remaining pilings of the old bridge can be seen sticking out of the water today. Power lines now follow the old roadway from Highway 180 south to Highway 182.

A view from Mack Shelby's driveway as a car heads for Romar Beach on the old road in 1949.

59

Mack Shelby lived on the road and was caretaker for the Romar property. Lake Shelby, the largest of the fresh water lakes in Gulf State Park is named for him.

As true homestead property under the Government Homestead Act, Roche and Martin were required to 'till the soil'. To qualify for homestead status, they planted gardens and even with great effort still had little success, only the original oleander trees survive.

Their small cottages survived the hurricane of 1926 with little damage and continued in family use through the Great Depression.

Zeke's Landing Restaurant and Marina on Cotton Bayou was named for Carl Taylor 'Zeke' Martin. Zeke's Landing where many charter fishing boats once docked was sold for private condominiums in 2005.

In 1947, after World War II, a major remodel was done to the Roche house. The cottage was raised to a second floor level on 14 foot pilings. The now expanded and open bottom area was screened–in to enjoy bug free breezes. The upper floor was enclosed with jalousie windows and provided extra sleeping space for all their extended families and visitors. As many as 25 folks would be there for the night, with the boys sleeping in hammocks and chairs on one side and the girls and families on the other.

By 1980, Romar House as the Roche place became known had a new owner, Jerry Gilbreath of Laurel, Mississippi. The house suffered roof damage from Hurricane Frederic, but little structural damage. Gilbreath began another restoration, eventually opening the home in 1991 as the 'Original Romar House Bed and Breakfast', Alabama's first seaside bed and breakfast inn.

U. S. Mail Service

Most of us are aware of United States Postal Service Post Offices handling local pickup and delivery of letters and packages and extending that service to surrounding rural areas. Rural mail service in the early days of our nation was handled by private individuals or companies through contracts with the United States Postal Service and such was the case in the Perdido Bay area. Mail service into the Perdido Bay area was operated through the Pensacola, Florida, Post Office and was handled by contract mail service.

The first contract mail service to the area in the late 1890s was provided to Peterson Point on the western foot of Wolf Bay. Mail was brought from Pensacola by land routes to Peterson Point. Mail contractor, Brown 'B.T.' Hudson, father of Orange Beach boat builder Jim Hudson, picked up the mail and delivered it into the area by boat.

There were many 'water routes' across the nation in those days. Today, there are only 2 water mail routes remaining, one of which operates in Magnolia Springs, only a few miles from Orange Beach.

Due to the difficulty and time delays of land travel in the area, it was not long before the mail began to be picked up at the lumber boom town of Millview, on the Florida side of Perdido Bay. The contract U. S. mail boat then distributed the mail to the communities of Caswell, Josephine, Miflin, Perdido Beach, and Lillian. After the sawmills at Millview shut down, the mail was picked up at Innerarity Point.

Rufus Walker Sr. sold his property on Bear Point to his brother Clarence and moved to Miflin about 1910, to take over the U. S. Mail contract. The Walker family operated the mail boat *Hollybird* and later the *Edna* out of there for many years. Walker family members Rufus, Sr., Lemuel, Jr., Leroy, and Clarence were

Rufus Walker Sr.'s, mail boat *Edna* at the head of Miflin Bay near where his home was located.

the captains with Wilmer Miller as the mate on one of their boats. The mail was delivered every day to post offices in the area, rain or shine.

The Walker's moved back to Orange Beach in the early 1930's when B. T. Hudson again had the mail contract.

- Foley Onlooker – advertisement – 1920:
  'US Mail boat 'Hollybird' – Miflin, Alabama – Millview, Florida and way points – six days a week – $1.75 round trip – open for charters on Sunday each week $10.00 – R. E. Walker owner – Miflin, Alabama'

- Foley Onlooker – Orange Beach community news 1929–1933: 'B.T. Hudson, who was quite sick from blood poison, has fully recovered and put in the entire week working on an engine for his mail boat, Jim has been running the mail.'

The post office at the small community of Caswell on the south side of

Edna Bill and Alice Caswell (the first Postmaster at Caswell). Photo taken November 1896 at Caswell.

Bear Point was established in 1896, in the home of the Caswell's, one of the early families to settle the area. The mail boat was met by the first Postmaster Alice L. Caswell who picked up the mail and carried it to the Post Office.

The mail boat also carried passengers and freight and often delivered fresh bread and pastries along its route from the open–air bakery in Josephine.

- Baldwin Times newspaper – Bear Point community news – June 27, 1895: 'R. H. Caswell and family have just returned from a trip to Mobile. A daily mail is to be established between Bear Point and Millview next month. It will be carried by a steamboat.'

- Baldwin Times newspaper – Bear Point community news article – January 7, 1897: 'It will be good for the people of Baldwin to know through the columns of your worthy paper that this morning starts the first mail from our new Post Office on Bear Point. It is named Caswell. The good book says 'That the first shall be last and the last shall be First'. I am glad the colony are well pleased and are doing well. Understand we

Orange Beach Post Office Circa 1921.

are in the tropical region of Baldwin Co., where we have plenty of green and ripe tomatoes, young pears and blooms, all kinds of fish, oysters, and plenty of hog and hominy.'

A post office was established in Orange Beach at Bay La Launche in 1901, and Mrs. Elsie E. Diehl was appointed the first Postmaster. Later, her husband, L. H. Diehl, built a two story building nearby and moved the post office to this building in which he also ran a mercantile store. Elver R. Callaway took over the store in 1918, with his wife, Mina, appointed as postmaster. He sold out to Charles H. Rynd, from Chicago, who became postmaster in 1920.

- Foley Onlooker newspaper – Orange Beach Community news – January 18, 1923: 'The mail boat 'Holly Bird' had a mighty close escape from disaster last Wednesday night when about two miles from Perdido Beach on its return trip of the day it struck a piece of submerged planking that is being thrown from the decking of the Lillian Bridge into the water. It caught into the wheel and tore into the bottom of the boat. Prompt action by Capt. Walker kept her afloat and then a long tedious wait for him and his passengers while they slowly drifted to shallow water. They then waded to shore and walked in their wet cloths to Perdido Beach and got a small boat to carry them to Bear Point, where they stayed the rest of the night. It seems a rather dangerous way of getting rid of the old planking by dumping it into the bay, as that is constantly a menace to every boat on the bay.'

Philo S. Chappell was postmaster from 1926 to 1937. Minnie Lee Callaway became Postmaster in February 1937. The post office was located in her father's (Dan Callaway), 'summer kitchen'; a small building behind their home which still stands today.

The 'summer kitchen' also contained a small store operated by Emmons Brown. The store had a porch on the front and a gasoline pump to service the small boats and the few cars in the area.

Working in close proximity every day, Minnie Lee Callaway and Emmons Brown fell in love and were married December 8, 1937. Mrs. Emmons Brown remained the Postmaster of the Orange Beach Post Office until 1967.

Dan Callaway's 'Summer Kitchen' – one of the early Post Offices in Orange Beach, currently under restoration.

The Dan Callaway property was bought by Alabama geologist David L. DeJarnette in 1971, from the Rudd family. The property was inherited by his daughter, Sarah DeJarnette Caldwell. Dan Callaway's, 'summer kitchen' and home are currently being restored by James and Sarah Caldwell and they hope to get the 'summer kitchen' placed on the National Register of Historic Places.

There is an old lifeboat that sits in the yard of the house…this is the lifeboat that saved the captain, crew, and passengers from the *Lady Lake* after sinking in the Gulf.

Rural Mail Service was operated by the Caswell Post Office until 1952 when it was moved to the Orange Beach Post Office. The Rural Mail carrier served Bear Point, the Caswell area, Orange Beach, Cotton Bayou, Alabama Point, and Romar Beach.

A new U. S. Post Office was erected in Orange Beach in 1953 which became the main area Post Office. It was located on the south side of Highway 180 in front of where The Keg is now located.

The Caswell Post Office was closed on October 1, 1954, after 57 years of faithful service.

The post office on Highway 180 operated until 1987. A new post office was built in the Municipal Complex on Highway 161. The old Highway 180 post office was purchased in April 1987 and operated as Orange Beach Seafood until 1990. After the Orange Beach Seafood moved, the building became in order, a florist shop, then a string of other shops and offices...video store, Water Board office, wicker shop, and a junk shop before being torn down 1998.

Early Stores

The Korner Store, an early food store and gathering place for the community, was built in 1938 by Emma Brown, mother of Emmons Brown. The Korner Store, near Hudson's Marina, was located in the building where the Snapper Lounge is now on the corner of Highway 180 and Wilson Blvd.

Clarence and Alta Lehr (Alta was Orland Huff's sister) moved to  Orange Beach about 1944 and purchased the Korner Store. Emmons and Minnie Lee Callaway Brown owned the Korner Store at the time, having inherited it from Emmons mother. Alta Lehr loved cats and there were always a bunch of them around the store as well as her home.

The Korner Store on Highway 180 circa 1940.

Orland and Modene Huff moved to Orange Beach in late 1945, settling on Cook's Point with their family. Modene quickly became a 'fixture' at the Korner Store.

Modene Huff did everything at the store from cutting meat and cheese, checking out customers, to clean up, but she always had a smile for everyone. She was a cornerstone of the community. Modene continued working there even after the Lehr's sold the store to Arthur Robinson of Bay Minette in 1968.

The Korner Store was a rather unique place. Not only was the store a place to purchase food items, Lehr had a special license for the drinking of alcoholic beverages on premises. As a result, a little table was located in the back of the store where the locals gathered. As a boy, Modene Huff's son, James, worked with his mother at the store and remembers some of the visitors to the table in the back. One was an old boatman and boat repairman from Norway named John Carlson who had come here during WWII. Another was the Russian, Andrew Swirn, who owned a boatyard on the north bay just down the road opposite the Presbyterian Church. The stories of boat building, fishing, and life on the high seas flowed continuously. Most locals were frequent customers.

A trip to the Korner Store was a highlight for the children in Orange

Beach. They were sent to the store for needed foodstuffs or pick up mail at the post office.

The Korner Store 'closed' in the early 1970's, when it was sold to Bill and Paulette Stevenson who operated it as a deli and sandwich shop. They in turn sold it to the current owner, Sonny Brice, who renamed the building Snapper's Lounge.

Modene Huff passed away in November 2002.

Another store was the Smith Store owned and operated by Tillie Smith. Tillie Smith and her husband lived with and cared for Philo S.Chappell who had been the Orange Beach Postmaster during the 1920's and 30's. When he passed away, the store and property were willed to the Smith's. Mr. Smith had been Principal of Foley Elementary School where Tillie was a teacher.

The Smith Store, referred to as Tillie's Store by locals, was originally on the old Orange Beach Road (Highway 180). At the time, the highway turned north for a block in the area near the Keg, then east for the some distance (where Tillie's Store sat), then returned to its current location. After the straightening of Highway 180, the Smith Store was moved by the State to the south side of the Smith property to be back on the main highway. Tillie's store operated Texaco gasoline pumps that were the only gas pumps for many years on the main road. The Texaco distributor in Foley was Arthur Boller, who provided service to the Orange Beach area and moved the pumps and gasoline storage tanks to Tillie's new location. The building that housed Tillie's Store still stands today.

To the west and across the street from Tillie's Store was a hand pitcher pump from which most of the area residents came to get the best tasting drinking water available in the area. The old pitcher pump where most folks got their drinking and washing water was removed and the well closed after the opening of the water system.

There were a few other small stores in the area. Oscar and Edna Callaway had a small store located on Highway 180. Emmons Brown operated the store in Dan Callaway's 'summer kitchen' that also housed the Orange Beach Post Office around 1938.

Callaway Store July 1941. The baby in foreground is Beverly Callaway.

Emmons Brown later operated Brown's Landing on Terry Cove, where he rented his 14 skiffs for 50 cents a day. A small store at Gulf View Park was operated by the Clarence Walker's.

How could all these stores survive during those years when the population was small? It seems as though each of those stores had their own specialty that drew customers. The Korner Store appears to be the only one that offered meat and an 'on premises' drinking license. The Tillie Smith Store was on the only main road (Highway 180), that sold gasoline, and was a Post Office for a while. The Callaway Store had an icehouse. Emmons Brown's Store was located in the post office for a fairly long time, had gasoline, and was located on the south shore of Wolf Bay, the main early business area. The store at Gulf View Park in Caswell catered to the marine trade and was the first store seen by boats returning through the pass from the Gulf.

Each of these stores had varying incomes, but you must remember that those times were not filled with tourists...subsistence was the name of the game.

The Childress family comes to Baldwin County
The progenitor of the spark for the growth of Orange Beach came to Baldwin County by covered wagon. Hermie Thompson 'H.T.' Childress was beckoned south by the fertile farmland. In 1924, he packed his wife, Dovie, eight children (four more would be born in Baldwin County), and personal affects in a covered wagon, loaded the heavier equipment, supplies and animals in rail cars, left Chilton County and headed south. The journey took seven days. Even before they arrived in Loxley, the word began to spread throughout the citizenry that this rag tag assemblage was a circus coming to town. On their arrival, children and adults alike lined the main street to welcome the would be excitement. Although some disappointment passed through the gathered crowd, the new family was welcomed. H.T. would become Justice of the Peace in Loxley and little did they realize the effect that their son Ted would eventually bring to Orange Beach.

Ted Childress grew up in Loxley then left home to attend college at Alabama Polytechnic Institute (Auburn University). Upon graduation he became an Assistant County Agent in Conecuh County, the only County Agent slot open at the time, although he wanted to return to Baldwin County. As county agent, it was only natural for him to meet the families of the prominent citizens of the area including Doctor Brooks, a two term Mayor of Evergreen...they met and became friends. Ted was especially taken with his delightful daughter, Dorothy. A romance ensued and Ted and Dorothy were married in 1938.

Ted loved the area of south Baldwin and frequently brought his 4–H boys, as well as other county agents, to the Orange Beach Hotel for fishing and boating. Shortly after his marriage, he began buying farmland between Robertsdale and Summerdale. In 1945, Ted resigned his position in Conecuh County and became a farmer in Summerdale. During his time away from his wife and family in Evergreen, Ted would wander the few roads in Orange Beach and fish in Cotton Bayou.

Dorothy Brooks was the daughter of John R. Brooks, a prominent dentist and leading citizen in Evergreen. She was raised in affluence and high social standing in this old Alabama town. Servants and cooks were part of her every day life. Dorothy was well educated in the ways of society and her role within the community. She was a strong willed young lady with an abundance of self–confidence. Those traits she would pass on to her daughter.

Dr. Amos Garrett, Dorothy Brooks Childress' first cousin, was a dentist in Robertsdale for many years. Dr. Garrett was the Mayor of Robertsdale and is credited with saving the city from financial ruin during the Depression. He was known as a compassionate man with a love of his community, county, state and fellow man. During the 1930's Garrett began buying land in the Orange Beach area, getting most of it for taxes owed. Remember that the Great Depression was in full bloom and most folks were struggling to survive. Dr. Garrett and business associate Mack McFall, bought large tracts of land on Alabama Point, around Cotton Bayou, the Catman Road area and Ono Island. By 1944, Dr. Garrett began development of the Garrett Sub–Division Number One on Cotton Bayou. This was the first sub–division in Orange Beach.

To help develop his sub–division, Dr. Garrett offered to give Ted and  Dorothy a lot there, but they turned it down. Dr. Garrett had built a house in the sub–division for his wife Sarah, in 1946, but she didn't like it and stayed in Robertsdale. The U.S. War Department gave permission July 15, 1947 to construct a boathouse and wharf for the property. This was in the aftermath of World War

View of the north shore of Cotton Bayou in 1950.

II and the War Department still had control of the Army Corps of Engineers. The Corps still controls construction on coastal and inland waterways. Ted and Dorothy Childress eventually purchased the house and property in September 1948 for $12,500. Not used to small 50 foot wide lots, Ted had immediately purchased the adjoining five lots to expand their property. This was the fourth house built on Cotton Bayou. Other houses then on the Bayou were those of the Leon Comstock's (1946), Neil Lauder's (1945), Rex Almon, and the Esternel's.

As the area began to develop in 1949, the Ted and Dorothy Childress family moved here from Evergreen. When Ted and Dorothy Childress arrived on Cotton Bayou in Orange Beach, they were only the second year–round residents on the bayou, the Neil Lauder Family being the first. Dorothy at first did not like living in a wilderness. There were few roads, no restaurants, no department

Neil and Brownie Callaway Lauder at their Orange Beach home 1937.

stores, no telephones, no churches, no schools and not much else in the area. No servants came with her. She had to learn how to cook, haul drinking water, clean house, take care of her children, and keep the wild hogs out of their garbage cans. As Dorothy had always said, 'We were the first outsiders to move to Cotton Bayou.'

Ted Childress with son Foster and daughter Margaret. Photo taken at the end of Hwy. 161 in April 1951.

Daughter Margaret was only two when they moved here and quickly adapted to the laid–back life style. Margaret and her older brother Foster were raised on these delightful shores. As she grew up, she became known as the 'Queen of Cotton Bayou', being the only little girl on the Bayou. Everyone in the area looked out for her.

'When we moved here,' stated Dorothy exuberantly, 'we didn't even have a voting box. We had to drive to the Lagoon Community on Ft. Morgan Road or to Foley to cast our ballots.' That didn't last long, for she successfully lobbied for and got a local precinct and ballot box. 'There wasn't any town to speak of,' Dorothy recalled. 'There was one small store, operated by Mrs. Tillie Smith, on Alabama 160 (now Highway 180) near where the Community Center is now. There was also the Korner Store on Highway 160. This was the main store, because it had meat and vegetables. Besides the stores, there were a few cottages for rent, plus the old Orange Beach Hotel on Highway 160. Ray and Ella Callaway operated the Orange Beach Cottages at the time,' Dorothy related. 'Those were the only businesses besides the charter and commercial fishing boats, and there weren't too many of them,' Dorothy stated.

Although most everyone had his or her own water well, most of the well water tasted terrible. To get good drinking water Dorothy or her children would go weekly to the pitcher pump well across the street from the old post office on Highway 180, pump it by hand, then haul the water back home. You had to be careful about storing the water in glass containers as sunlight passing through the glass could and did occasionally cause fires...you had to keep them covered.

A nine–mile drive took the Childress' to Gus Kennedy's Store north of the Old Canal Bridge, where Highway 180 now makes a right angle in Gulf Shores...beyond that 'we had to go to Foley for practically everything.' There was no Perdido Pass Bridge to Pensacola at the time.

Dorothy Childress organized and was the first President of the Home Demonstration Club of Orange Beach, a civic group that raised funds to help purchase land for the Orange Beach Community Center. They organized fish fry's and made jams and jellies, with the proceeds going to their project. One of their biggest projects was the Annual Orange Beach Picnic. Her efforts with the club also helped her learn how to cook. Her best friend, Brownie Lauder, showed her the fine points of cooking and living in the wilderness. There wasn't much about the community of Orange Beach in which Dorothy was not involved, including the incorporation of the City and founding the Orange Beach Water, Sewer and Fire

Dorothy Childress when she was President of the Home Demonstration Club...1951.

70

Protection Authority. Dorothy Childress remained active in community affairs until her passing in 2000.

If there is a canal, boat slip or marina that was dredged out in Orange Beach or Gulf Shores prior to the passing of Ted Childress, it was probably dug by Ted's company, 'Ted E. Childress and Son'. In some cases the payment for his work was traded in lots along the 'ditches', as he called the canals, dug for new developments. His dragline operator was William Giles and William's brother Oliver, the bulldozer operator, they were well known to residents and developers alike.

Later, the Paul Smith's were the first family to build and live on Alabama Point. Paul was the first world famous 'Marlboro Man' advertising for Marlboro cigarettes.

For a short time during the 1950's, a 'Tea Room' operated just west of the Crane Pond in the area referred to as the 'Bay Minette District'. The building still stands, but no more tearoom. The old Swirn place was also in this area along with D. R. Peteet's office building.

Discussion of the Crane Pond brought memories from Clifford Callaway. He states, how he and some of his friends made 'pocket' money by catching baby cranes at the Crane Pond for the 'Crane Lady' who banded the small birds for the government. He also commented about land prices in that area saying that 'land could be bought here for 50 cents an acre when he was a boy (late 1920's).'

Travel in the Wilderness

During horse and buggy days, roads on Bear Point were sand trails following the beach line in many places. Travel was by foot or horse. E. G. Low, who was a farm implement dealer in Robertsdale and owned the first car in Orange Beach, cut a road through on the Ridge. The Ridge is an area of high ground that traverses Pleasure Island from east to west. This road was named Highway 160 when the County assumed maintenance. After eventual straightening of

1919 Model T Ford truck driven by E.G. Low. Believed to be the first truck in Orange Beach.

the road by the State, the Highway was re–numbered Highway 180, as we know it today, but still referred to as the Canal Road by the locals.

In those early days, most everyone had a horse and no story of those times is complete without a tale or two. Dan Callaway's horse was named 'Charlie' and Charlie could at times be quite cantankerous. It seems that on a particular day Charlie did not want to pull the family filled wagon back home. To get his attention, Dan touched Charlie's rear end with a Model 'T' battery. Well, that did it. Charlie took off, bouncing Dan, his kids, and nephews out of the wagon. Charlie eventually wrapped the wagon around a large Magnolia tree at the end of his rampage. After checking for bumps and bruises, everyone laughed, picked up the wagon pieces, calmed Charlie down, and walked on home.

Clifford Callaway was a young boy on that trip and many years later, he

Ray and David Callaway pictured with their horse 'Fanny'.

saw that old Magnolia and low and behold, the old wagon axle was still wrapped around the base!

Amel Callaway's horse was named 'Cargan'. The area kids were there whenever he was walking around and around as he powered the grinder that crushed the latest sugar cane crop. Crushing sugar cane for juice is like having a neighborhood candy store...its sweet juice all around. According to Godbee Smith, when Amel Callaway was crushing sugar cane, the returning school bus would stop, the kids would all pile out, and enjoy the sweet treat.

Because of the sand trails and roads on the 'Island', horses could get around a lot better than cars. Horses were used for practical transportation in the Orange Beach area for many years and were even used by the military for beach patrols during WWII. After the paving of the main roads, cars finally came into their own, but travel in the early days required time and patience.

- Foley Onlooker – Orange Beach community news January 31, 1924 – 'Mrs. Hilda Dietz and son returned Saturday evening from a two weeks trip to Mobile. Her mother, Mrs. Callaway, who also has been away for two months on a visit, came home with her.'

   'Capt. Dan Callaway and entire family returned home from a weeks trip to Mobile. He brought along for his own consumption a fine lot of select oysters. Think of it, it only took 25 to make a solid quart.'

- Foley Onlooker – news item February 21, 1929 – (This was a little more than a year after the building of the Mobile Causeway):
   'Traffic Across Mobile Bridge Gains Heavily'
   'Traffic across the Mobile bay bridge showed an increase of 11% in January over the corresponding month of last year, according to figures announced by the Mobile Bay Bridge Company. The report showed a total of 15,735 vehicles crossed the bridge last month, from which the revenues from tolls amounted to $17,985.95.
      The increased traffic in January over the same month of a year ago is in line with the general gain recorded in the use of the structure during the last several months. The December gain showed a still higher percentage then January, reaching 28%.'

The following excerpt from the '1938 Tour Guide to South Baldwin' published by The Golden Rod Studio gives a good idea of what travel in the area was like in the early days:

'Orange Beach and Caswell Highway'

'The highway to Orange Beach and Caswell leads eastward from a point on the Sibley Holmes Trail (now Highway 59). It leads to the deep–sea fishing camps that lie opposite the Gulf of Mexico inlet to Perdido Bay. Between Orange Beach and Caswell on this highway is located the scene of the Baldwin County Annual Deep–Sea Rodeo. Under varying weather conditions the highway surface is sometimes a little rough. Reasonable caution is advised in the case of those driving the trail for the first time. If this suggestion is complied with the ride will be as safe and enjoyable as any other, as the highway is the regular approach to these villages and is under constant use by everyone. At about three–and–a–half miles the highway makes a right turn to cross the Intracoastal Canal. A left turn and Orange Beach and Caswell is straight ahead. The map (not show here) shows their splendid anchorage for small craft, which may approach by way of the inland canal from either direction and lie here in safe harbor with all supplies available, and yet be only a moment's motoring from the outlet to gulf waters which abound with Tarpon, Ling (Cobia), Sailfish, King and Spanish Mackerel, Bluefish, Bonita, Cavallo (sic) and all the other hard–fighting beauties of the Gulf Stream waters...A fleet of charter boats is available at most reasonable rates, with experienced fishing guides and navigators in charge. Living accommodations can be secured in either Orange Beach or Caswell.'

Considering the difficulty of travel during the early 20th century in general and specifically in the Orange Beach area it is truly amazing how many people were lured to Orange Beach. The following items from the Foley Onlooker newspaper – Orange Beach community news for the years 1929–1933 demonstrate how strong the lure of Orange Beach really was:

'A big party of 4 cars headed by A. F. Wesley and wife of Robertsdale drove down and spent Sunday enjoying themselves with a picnic dinner on the beautiful Barchard–Herbert property just east of the village. The party embraced Mr. and Mrs. John Mikulecky, Mr. and Mrs. Joseph Dvorak, Mr. and Mrs. George Mach, Mr. and Mrs. Alois Ryznar, Frank Novak, Sr., and Frank Novak Jr., and Mr. and Mrs. John Kavarik, of Chicago. They are all coming back next Sunday and make a trip to the Gulf if the weather is favorable.'

'Our old neighbors, Mr. and Mrs. George Hayes and Mr. and Mrs. Perry Hughes, who have only recently arrived from their home in Clinton, Ill., being detained till now by sickness, spent Sunday with old friends here and certainly looked good. We miss these old Orange Beach people for they were always fore most in everything for the good of entertainment of the place.'

'Mr. and Mrs. Charles Rynd and Mrs. Rynd's sister, Mrs. Pennock of Michigan and Arthur spent three days in Loxley at their brother's home, D. S. Comstock. One of the most interesting trips while there was a trip over the Old Spanish Trail as far as the Sage bridge.'

'The three Mr. Lotts of Robertsdale drove down Sunday but had the misfortune to break a radius rod on their "Henry" necessitating an extra trip to the city for repairs and then some expert work by Mr. Hudson.'

'R. (sic) T. Hudson and sons Jim and Willie made a business trip to Miflin Sunday in search for some parts to a touring car.'

State Highway 180, better known as Canal Road or Orange Beach Road, was finally surveyed and graded in 1946 and within a year it was paved.

Travel to Foley from Orange Beach before Highway 180 was completed was not easy. One had to cross the corduroy section (wood planks or logs covered with sand or dirt) that crossed through Clizbe Swamp in the area just east of the Foley Express Bridge.

The Clizbe Swamp was named for Rosco J. Clizbe who purchased the 160.12–acre area in 1906. The area was a Cypress tree swamp at the time. During the late 1920's Clifford Callaway remembers that Clizbe logged off all the cypress leaving the swampy area that had to be 'corduroyed' to be able to cross it.

Then the road turned north and crossed over a one–lane pontoon bridge over Portage Creek near the southwest corner of Wolf Bay. The bridge was of the swing type to allow boats to pass through, as boats were sometimes kept further up in the fresh water of Portage Creek and Walker Creek to remove sea worms from their hulls and for protection from major storms. Later a hand–cranked, draw–type bridge was built just to the east that replaced the original pontoon bridge, from that point, travel was on

dirt roads to Foley.

Most of that difficult travel changed with the dredging of the Intracoastal Canal in 1932 and the building of the first Intracoastal Canal bridge at Gulf Shores on Highway 59. At that point, the Portage Creek Bridge was removed.

This is actually the second Canal Bridge. The first bridge was a floating concrete barge that swung to open the canal to traffic. Photo 1959.

The first canal bridge, built after the completion of the Intracoastal Canal, was a concrete swing barge winched open and closed by a V–8 Ford engine. Brothers Weldon and Dwight Steele operated the 'bridge'. There were however, many long waits to cross the old Canal Bridge, as the canal became a primary route for commercial barges, tugs and sailboats. When a 'real' bridge replaced this one, fishermen in Orange Beach bought that first 'bridge' for use as an artificial fishing reef in the Gulf of Mexico. The 'real' bridge that replaced the barge was located where Highway 180 (Canal Road) makes the right angle turn south into Gulf Shores. In 1972, the new 4–lane high–rise W. C. Holmes Bridge was constructed to the west of the old one with all new approaches and realignment of State Highway 59 (the old Sibley Holmes Trail). Dr. W. C. Holmes had been in medical practice in Foley from 1927 until his death in 1961.

In the days before the Canal Bridge, a trip to Pensacola, the nearest large city, only 27 miles away, was a major event. Travel through the area of Clizbe Swamp and over the one–lane pontoon bridge at Portage Creek was slow enough. Then you had the ride to Lillian to catch the ferry where you probably had a long wait, assuming the ferry was even running that day. John Climmie of Josephine built and operated a 20 by 40 foot ferry that crossed Perdido Bay. The ferry was powered by a 35 horse power motor…not exactly speed, but eventually it did cross the bay. On the Florida side the roads into Pensacola were sand. You generally planned to spend the night before the return trip.

The ferry operated until the storm of 1916 when it was severely damaged. A wooden bridge then replaced the ferry.

Travel to Fort Morgan and other places

Visits to Fort Morgan on the west end at Mobile Point has always been an attraction to both locals and visitors, but getting there was not always easy.

Clifford Callaway's Grandfather Chester Williams was the lighthouse keeper at Fort Morgan where he and his wife lived. The light was kerosene fired then. When Clifford and his father Herman would go to visit them during the late 1920's they would drive to the end of Highway 59 (a sand road at the time) and if the tide was out, they would drive on the hard packed sand of the beach all the way to Fort Morgan. According to Clifford, as strange as is sounds, that way was faster than taking the Fort Morgan Road which was mostly soft sand and bogs.

Beverly Callaway and Merle Rudd Harms related a story of visiting relatives in the Lagoon and Shell Banks communities when they were young girls by 'walking to the Fresh Water Lakes, then taking a skiff to Lagoon and walking from there to Shellbanks.'

In 1926, Col. E. I. Higdon was issued a permit to build a bridge or establish a ferry from Bear Point to Innerarity Point, Florida, across the lower reaches of Perdido Bay. He never built the bridge, but he did build a ferry. Dan Callaway operated the ferry and used one of the *J. S. Murrow's* salvaged engines to power it. The ferry only operated for about three weeks since there were not many cars and the sound of the engine and all the water scared the horses. It was a great idea whose time had not yet come. It was during this time, however, that Clarence Walker moved his family from Pensacola to Bear Point utilizing the ferry service. Clarence Walker moved to his family's place at Caswell and developed 'Gulf View Park'.

By 1939, land was given to the State of Alabama for the development of the Gulf State Park that now separates Orange Beach from the Town of Gulf Shores. The central part of Pleasure Island was basically undeveloped, except for the Lagoon community, prior to the offering of land to the State of Alabama by property owner George Meyer. The offer was made in exchange for state help in building roads into the area. Except for the foresight of Meyer and the dredging of the Intracoastal Canal, development of the area would have been much later. Much of the land at that time was bayous and marsh with very little access. The first 'real' road into this area was through Gulf State Park. That road traveled from the canal through the park to the beach Casino where the park convention center now stands. This roadway is still the primary route through the park. During the 40's Meyer began construction of primitive roads into the area that is now Gulf Shores. However, even with the paving of the extension of State Highway 59 from the canal to the beach, there was still little convenient passage east and west until State Highway 182, 'The Beach Road', was completed.

Cotton Bayou Road

Amos Garrett traded his land south of the west–end of Cotton Bayou to Robin Swift, Sr. in exchange for Swift to complete Highway 161 from Cotton Bayou on to the beach. Highway 161 (Cotton Bayou Road) was completed and paved in 1945 finally connecting Canal Road (Highway 180) to the Beach Road (Highway 182). The twists and turns of Highway 161 were straightened out and the roadway widened in 1990.

There was another important road into Cotton Bayou, which was built during the first administration of Governor Jim Folsom (1947 – 1951) as a 'farm to market' road. This road followed what would later be part of 'Catman Road' from the State Park entry road. The 'Farm to Market' road veered southeast just past Lake Shelby to the head of Cotton Bayou. This road became the primary route of travel for the growing development around the Bayou until it was closed when Route 2 or the 'Catman Road' as it is more popularly known, was completed connecting further north on Highway 161. Although later blocked to auto traffic after severe fires in that part of the State Park, 'Catman Road' was still used by cyclists and hikers for several years and was ultimately repaved and designated as the current 'biking trail' in 2001.

The legendary 'Catman Road' now a biking trail off of Highway 161. The stories about this road seemed to start in the early 1940's.

According to James Huff, the 'Catman Road' name came from teenagers during the 1940's hiding in the brush and making strange noises and cat sounds to scare people on the lonely road at night. It is quite possible that this activity of the local children grew out of a strange murder mystery that occurred on the other end of the island on Ft. Morgan Road. The stories of creatures and noises on this road have grown over the years to near legendary proportions!

The Leon Comstock family built the first home on Cotton Bayou in

1946. Shortly thereafter, Rex Almon built the second home and the Neil Lauders' were the next to build. Neil Lauder owned and operated Lauder's Landing on the Bayou and was a Baldwin County Commissioner for many years.

1949 brought the paving of Highway 182 (Beach Road) from the State Park to Alabama Point. After paving, the State erected picnic tables and a drink concession at the eastern end of Alabama Point and also at the intersection of Highways 161 and 182 where the State continues to maintain a public beach area.

Travel was still not easy, even after the bridge was established at Lillian, as storms and bridge fires caused the bridge to be frequently out of commission. The first public owned concrete Lillian Bridge was not completed until 1932 and was replaced with a new wider and more substantial bridge dedicated on August 10, 1980.

The first bridge connecting Orange Beach to Florida Point (Gulf Beach as it was known then by the locals – later became Perdido Key) was dedicated on May 12, 1962. Governors John Patterson of Alabama and Farris Bryant of Florida were in attendance along with hundreds of other area people. Orange Beach residents Mary Nell Walker and Margaret Childress cut

The first Perdido Pass Bridge under construction March 1959.

the ribbon. Orange Beach now had direct access to Pensacola, Florida, Perdido Key, and Ono Island. Hurricane Frederic in September 1979 severely damaged supports of the bridge.

The current Perdido Pass Bridge was constructed and dedicated August 28, 1989. Mary Nell Walker and Margaret Childress also cut the dedication ribbon for this new bridge.

The turn of the millennium brought the new Foley Express Bridge and toll road from Highway 59 just north of Foley connecting to the Canal Road (Highway 180) near Clizbe Swamp.

Another new bridge was proposed in 1996 referred to as the Highway 161 Bridge. Due to a change in Governors, the bridge was moved out 10 years and the 'Foley Express' toll bridge was accepted. The Foley Express Bridge was initially privately funded. The City of Orange Beach bought into the bridge in 2003. The Highway 161 Bridge is currently on schedule for 2006 and is already funded by the State fuel tax that was established for maintenance and building of roads and bridges.

These bridges, along with the W. C. Holmes Bridge on Highway 59 crossing the Intracoastal Canal into Gulf Shores, now provide easy access to Pleasure Island as well as quick evacuation routes in the event of hurricanes or other natural disasters.

General Photo Section

This scene shows the collection of pine tar (sap) from the large forests in early Baldwin County. The term 'cat facing' refers to the 'chipping' of the tree trunk in a 'V' shape to allow the sap to flow into collection trays.

The collection of pine tar (naval stores) was the first major industry in Baldwin County, other than farming and fishing. Many of the early settlers in Orange Beach were involved in this industry. The schooners of J.C. Callaway shipped many barrels of pine tar to ports throughout the Gulf of Mexico for processing.

Above is a photo from the early 1900s of the home of Lemuel Walker, Jr. that was located in Caswell. Lemuel, Jr. had previously lived in a large home in Miflin. He cut that house in half and moved it to Caswell to be closer to his aging father.

This is the home of Captain James C. Callaway that was located on the south side of Canal Road just east of what would later become Nancy Lane. Photo from late 1890s.

This photograph of Civil War veteran, Lemuel Walker Jr, and wife Mary Frances Strong Walker, was believed taken in the early 1900s at their home in Caswell. Lem, as he was known, spent his life fishing and raised twelve children, many of whom became prominent charter fishing captains.

This is Captain James Clifford Callaway shown with part of his immense shell collection. His schooners *J. S. Murrow* and *Ellen C* plied the waters and ports of the Caribbean and the Gulf of Mexico giving him ample opportunity to add to his shell collection. The photo is believed from the 1890's and shows him in the yard of his home on Canal Road.

Above is the Lemuel Walker, Sr. house originally built between 1874–1878 on Bear Point on Bay St. John. This photo shows the home in 2001, after many years of extensive remodeling.

Below is a view of the Lemuel Walker, Sr., home from the waters of Bay St. John. This photo taken in 2004.

This photograph from the 1890s is of Edith Caswell Bill and her husband, Gillman C. 'G. C.' Bill, at their home in Caswell. G. C. owned a large tract of land on Bear Point in the Caswell area. His youngest daughter, Abbie M. Bill married Rufus Walker, Sr. in 1899, and on the death of her father, she inherited her share of the land, where she and her husband settled after leaving Miflin.

The photo above shows a herd of goats on the old Swirn place on Wolf Bay, where the M & R Lodge is now located. The folks in the background are believed to be a Mr. Stanley, Andrew Swirn, and his wife Elizabeth. Andrew Swirn operated a boat yard at his place as well as a sustenance farm. Mrs. Elisabeth Swirn celebrated her 103rd birthday in 2004!

Captain James C. Callaway and Captain Ronald Lauder branding cattle in their pen near the junction of Highway 161 and Highway 180 (Canal Road) circa 1910.

Above is pictured Elizabeth Swirn, widow of Andrew Swirn, and friend Harry Crawford. Harry had been manager of Safe Harbor Marina during the mid 1960's, and had rented a cottage from the Swirn's. He became a life long friend and still takes Elizabeth dancing at the Community Center. Elizabeth celebrated her 103rd birthday in 2004. Photo from 2004.

Above are Clifford Callaway (on left) and his cousin Ray Callaway. Clifford and Ray served together in the Merchant Marine during WWII. Photo taken in 2002 at Clifford's home in Foley.

D. R. Peteet's shingle mill was constructed in 1909 on the south shore of Wolf Bay on the Gulf Bay Tract. Other than farming and 'turpentining', this was the first industry in Orange Beach. The area around the mill grew as Peteet added office buildings and the workers he had brought in from up north began to buy land and build homes which provided the nucleus for the growth of the city.

You can't have a shingle mill without the trees to make the shingles. The photo above, thought to be taken in the Miflin area shows a 'Big Wheel' with oxen, which was typically used to haul logs to the mill.

The view above, of the bay front on Bay La Launche is a different perspective of the same area as the photo below. Note the white sand beach at the waterline. Beach play and swimming were routine summertime activities for the children.

This is a view of the area (same as above photo) where the first stores in Orange Beach were established. Note the rails on the wharf; these were used for a hand car to assist in loading and unloading cargo from boats such as the Callaway schooners. The young lad standing on the wharf is believed to be Clifford Callaway. The photo was made about 1928.

Although this was not truly the first school building in Orange Beach, it is often referred to as such. It was however, the first school built by the county school system. This was a very modern structure when it was built The tall girl on the left is Vallie Callaway, daughter of Captain Dan Callaway. The school was located on the south shore of Bay La Launche near the Baptist Church.

The 1910 school shown in the top photograph, after considerable remodeling, is now the Indian and Sea Museum relocated to Marjorie Snook Park near the Municipal Complex on Highway 161. The museum is owned by the City of Orange Beach and is operated by Gail Walker Graham, the daughter of Captain Rabun Walker. The museum receives visitors from around the world and displays relics of Native American cultures and Orange Beach's maritime and charter fishing industry. Ms. Graham also provides historical information about the area.

On the left is a photo taken in the early 1900s of the home of Captain Dan Callaway, third son of Captain James C. Callaway. The house still stands and is located on the south shore of Wolf Bay. The house is currently being restored by James and Sarah DeJarnette Caldwell.

On the right is a photo taken in the late 1920s of Vallie Callaway Williams, the second daughter of Captain Dan Callaway.

At left is a photo taken circa 1910 of Captain Dan Callaway while in Key West picking up and delivering supplies while captaining the schooner *J. S. Murrow*.

At right is Captain Amel Callaway with his daughter Brownie Callaway Lauder Photo taken on Garrett Lane in Orange Beach, circa 1940. Captain Amel was the younger brother of Captain Dan Callaway.

Above: This photograph shows Wolf Creek Landing where the Walker family landed for Sunday School when living in Miflin. The photo was taken in the early 1900's.

At left: 'Bob' Walker, Sr. and Roland Walker, Sr. are shown on the front gate of their Miflin Home. Both of these young lads grew up to become charter boat captains and an integral part of the Orange Beach charter fishing industry. The Walker family lived in Miflin for a number of years when their father, Captain Rufus Walker, Sr., held the U.S. mail contract and delivered the mail by boat out of Miflin into the area, before moving back to Orange Beach.

At left is Rufus Walker Sr., with his wife Abbie, daughter Edna is standing left), daughter Lida at right, and Rufus Jr. is on his lap. Lida died in February 1909, just a few weeks after this photo was taken, from blood poisoning after stepping on a nail.

The photo below taken in the yard of their Miflin home, circa 1920, shows the sons of Rufus, Sr., from left, Roland, Bob, Rabun, and Rex with a calf. Their Miflin home was located close to the ferry. Captain Rufus held the U.S. Mail contract during the time he lived in Miflin.

Rufus Walker Sr., holding son Rex, with the his family, Roland, Ruben, Rabun, Roy, Rufus Jr., and Edna. The photo was taken in Miflin where Rufus based his U.S. Mail boat.

The photo above shows several of the sons of Captain Rufus Walker, Sr. at the Roy Walker Marina on Terry Cove believed during the 1950s. From left are, Roy, Roland Sr., Ray, Ruben, and Gladwin.

The photo above shows Dan Callaway's 'Summer Kitchen' which by 1937, was the third Post Office in Orange Beach. Captain Dan's daughter, Minnie Lee Callaway, was the Postmaster. The building also housed a small store and had gas pumps out front. The store was operated by Emmons Brown. Minnie Lee and Emmons fell in love while working there and married. The building still stands and is currently being restored.

Below is the second Post Office in Orange Beach. The building was built by L. H. Diehl (husband of the first Postmaster Elsie E. Diehl) and was located on Wolf Bay south shore. Photo taken in 1921.

Pictured at left is Edna Bill and her Aunt Alice L. Caswell. Alice was the first Postmaster of the Caswell community, appointed November 11, 1896. The Caswell Post Office closed October 1, 1954, after mail handling was transferred to the Orange Beach Post Office.

The photo at the right is of Mina Laura Callaway, wife of Elver Callaway, Sr. Mina Laura was appointed the second Postmaster of the Post Office in Orange Beach on April 4, 1918.

The Orange Beach Post Office was established in 1910 with Elsie E. Diehl as the first Postmaster, appointed March 5, 1910. Mina Laura Callaway was a sister of Elsie Diehl.

The area known as Romar Beach was land homesteaded by good friends Spurgeon Roche and Carl Taylor 'Zeke' Martin, both businessmen of Mobile, as a family 'get–away' place. This photo from circa 1924 shows the Martin house on the left and the Roche house on the right. The land originally included about three miles of beach property from Gulf State Park to Cotton Bayou, now only about 480 feet.

The photo below from 1949 shows the Roche house after extensive remodeling. The house was raised on pilings and 'sleeping' porches were added for the growing family and friends that came for the week ends. Romar House as it became known was sold about 1980 to Jerry Gilbreath of Laurel, Mississippi, who eventually opened the home in 1991 as the 'Original Romar House Bed and Breakfast'. The 'B&B' was Alabama's first seaside bed and breakfast inn.

This is a photograph of Gulf View Park operated by Clarence 'Ted' and Hazel Walker for many years. Gulf View was kind of an early 'resort' supplying not only charter fishing, but a place to stay with meals and a small store. Their little girl, Bertha, is on the car (later became Bertha Walker Robinson), and was the last owner of Gulf View. The property has been sold and plans are now underway for the 'Caswell Place' development.

This photo is the gas station and store in Gulf View Park at Caswell. The store catered primarily to fishermen with day snacks (crackers and sardines), drinks, and fuel and oil for skiffs and small boats.

The Orange Beach Hotel was built about 1923 by Mrs. Hilda Callaway Dietz, who operated it for many years. The hotel, located on the south shore of Wolf Bay, was a community gathering place and 'home' to many visitors and fishermen, as well as local folks who needed a place to stay while building their own homes in the area. The boy on the left is Lloyd Callaway (son of Captain Herman Callaway) and the boy with the fishing pole is Al Dietz (Hilda's son). It is one of the few remaining buildings of Orange Beach's early days. The hotel is currently used as the home and gallery of the Pleasure Island Art Association.

This was the view to the northwest across the lower portion of Wolf Bay from the Orange Beach Hotel. This photo was taken about 1924. Notice the white sand beaches. The location is now Orange Beach Waterfront Park. The Orange Beach hotel has been restored and should be on the list of Alabama Historic Places by the time this book is published.

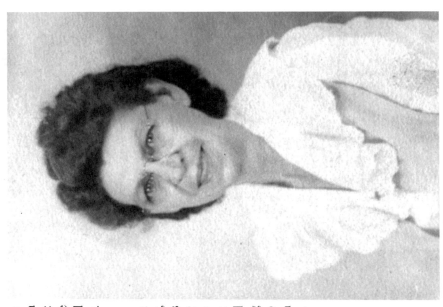

At left is a photo of the children of Edward and Hilda Callaway Dietz. Left to right: Eva, Al, and Alma Dietz. The two daughters were adopted sisters. Photo from circa 1920.

At right is a photo taken in 1938 of Hilda Callaway Dietz, a daughter of Captain James C. Callaway. Hilda and her husband Edward built the Orange Beach Hotel about 1923. Edward was a medical doctor from Ohio and during the depression went back to Ohio to work. Edward died in 1931 while in Ohio. Hilda continued to operate the hotel for many years.

Above is a photo of children playing in the summer waters of Wolf Bay at the Orange Beach Hotel, circa 1923. Pictured from left are Eleanor Callaway, Lois Callaway, Eva Dietz, Al Dietz (in foreground), Brownie Callaway, and Alma Dietz.

At right are some of Captain Herman Callaway's boys having fun by pretending to 'fill up' their horse at a gasoline pump in front of their uncle Amel's house. Amel Callaway had the gas pump for use by the school bus that he bought and maintained. From left are Marion, Billy, and Clifford Callaway circa 1931.

On the left is a view of Bear Point Marina taken from the beach on the south shore of Arnica Bay. (circa 1940)

On the right is an image of Burkart Cottages on Terry Cove (near the location of Gulf Gate Lodge). The little boy in the foreground is believed to be LeeRoy Walker, eldest son of Captain Roy Walker. (circa 1934)

The photo above shows one of the cottages that was part of Gulf View Park. The lady in the swing is Bertha Walker Robinson. The land where her home and this cottage once stood was founded as Gulf View by her grandfather Hart Low and expanded into Gulf View Park by her father.

The photo at left shows Bertha Walker Robinson, daughter of Clarence 'Ted' Walker, standing by the palm tree planted by her grandfather, Lemuel Walker, Jr., when he first settled in Orange Beach in the late 1800s. Bertha sold the property in 2004 for development and the house and the tree are now gone. The area where her house once stood was excavated by the University of South Alabama Archeological Department in 2004 and they discovered the remains of a transient Indian fishing village that may be three thousand years old.

Above is Eleanor Callaway Lauder who was the primary school bus driver after the Orange Beach school was consolidated with Foley about 1930. She drove bus #13 which was so familiar with many current area residents.

At left is Emily Davis Cowan, known as 'Bom', an early school teacher in Orange Beach. Emily was born in 1869 and came to Orange Beach from Wisconsin with her husband who was the millwright for D. R. Peteet's shingle mill. Emily passed away in 1965.

This photo of students was the last group of Orange Beach school students before consolidation of the Orange Beach school into the Foley school in 1930. Only five of these students have been identified; front row, third from right, holding a child is Eva Brasher Dietz (later to become Mrs. Roy Walker); standing at left is Oscar Callaway, son of Captain Dan Callaway; Vallie Callaway (5th from left), daughter of Captain Dan Callaway; Brownie Callaway (2nd from right – later to become Mrs. Neil Lauder, daughter of Captain Amel Callaway; Alma Brasher Dietz (at right – sister to Eva), later to become Mrs. Rabun Walker. Photo taken on the grounds of the 1910 school on Bay Circle.

This photo is a view north at the cantilever–swing bridge across the Intracoastal Canal. This was actually the second bridge operated at this location. It was located at the western end of Highway 180 (Canal Road). The first bridge was also a 'swing' type, but was a floating barge that swung open for canal traffic. Long waits were normal here when trying to get to Foley, as the Canal has been busy since it opened in 1932. The building in left center was Royce Chancey's Bait Shop. Gus Kennedy's store was just up the road.

This 1940 photograph of the Korner Store is one of the few early photos known to exist of the store. The Korner Store was built in 1938 by Emma Brown, mother of Emmons Brown. The store was a meeting place and primary grocery store for many years, with Modene Huff greeting the customers every day from 1945 until it closed in the early 1970s. The store still sits on the corner of Highway 180 and Wilson Blvd. as the Snapper Lounge.

The above photo from 2002 shows the Tillie Smith Store that operated on Highway 180 near Bay Circle. The store is shown in the background and was for a time, the Orange Beach Post Office and had Texaco gas pumps out front. Captain Herman Callaway stopped at this store nearly every day to purchase gas for his charter boat.

The company of 'Ted E. Childress and Son' played an important part in the development of Orange Beach with their drag line and bulldozer. The company dug most of the boat slips, canals, and marinas in the area. The photo shows their drag line in action at Walker Marina.

The above photo demonstrates the laid back life style at Walker Marina in 1946. The unidentified lad in foreground is enjoying the great life. Countless children have spent their summer days on the waters of Orange Beach.

On the left is a photo of the Gulf Gate Lodge on Terry Cove, taken in 1966. At right is a photo of Eva Marie Walker, daughter of Captain Rabun Walker, with her dog at the site of the Gulf Gate Lodge about 1949, while the lodge was under construction. Gulf Gate Lodge construction was started by Crockett White, Sr., Eva Marie's uncle, but he ran out of money and the lodge was purchased and completed by 'Chunky' Baldwin. The Gulf Gate Lodge was torn down in the mid 1980's.

The paving of Highway 182 (Beach Road) from Gulf State Park to Alabama Point was done in 1949. The photo above shows Governor 'Big Jim' Folsom cutting the ribbon.

At left: Captain Roland Walker, Sr., is shown talking with Foley Mayor, Arthur Holk at the Perdido Pass Bridge dedication, August 28, 1989. The relationship between Foley and Orange Beach has been long and supportive, including being a major supplier of goods and services to the citizens of Orange Beach and sixty years of consolidated school in Foley.

Ft. Morgan, seen here in the 1950's, was one of the primary destinations of the Alabama Beach Bus Service. Ft. Morgan has always been a busy tourist site, since even the locals took visitors there, and still do. During the 1950's, it was not uncommon for visitors to stay a week at a time at the Ft. Morgan Inn located in these old officers quarters from the Spanish American War of 1898. The Ft. Morgan Inn and most of the other out buildings no longer exist, but the fort itself is still a major tourist attraction.

The Alabama Beach Bus Service, owned and operated by James Bagley, Jr., ran from Orange Beach to Ft. Morgan and Foley. It operated for about a year during 1949–50.

Invocation
    Rev. Marvin Bryant
Welcome
    Mrs. Clate Low
Group Singing
    "Down Yonder"
    "By the Light of the
    Silvery Moon"
Honorary Citizenship Award
"School Days"
    Margaret Childress
    Ronnie and Mike Low
Monologue - - "Junior"
    Marian Lauder
Song - "In the Evening by the
    Moonlight"
    Frances Osborne
    Marie and Marian Lauder
    "The Orange Pickers"
Song - "Cruising Down the River"
    "The Orange Pickers"

Guitar Solo
    Marion Williams
Reading
    Mrs. Rebecca Davis
"The Indelible Inkspots"
    Marion Williams
    "Mac" Callaway
Pantomine - "This Ole House"
    Roland Walker
    James Huff
    Leslie Hammond
    Marion Williams
Song - "Waiting on the Robert
    E. Lee"
    Mary Jean Walker
    Marian Lauder
Group Singing
    "Dixie"
Song - "I'll See You in My Dreams"
    "The Orange Pickers"
Benediction
    Rev. Marvin Edge

Above is the program for the 'Orange Beach Community Picnic' that was held August 17, 1954 and sponsored by the Home Demonstration Club of Orange Beach. The Picnic was started by the Home Demonstration Club and has gone on to become an annual community event

At left: A scene from the Home Demonstration Club (1954). The two Club members are Rebecca Davis and Mary Hayes, both of Montgomery, Alabama, and summer residents with houses on Cotton Bayou.

At right: Dorothy Childress when President and founder of the Orange Beach Home Demonstration Club in 1951. The club was organized to provide activities for lady residents and to raise funds for the purchase of land for a community center; a goal which they achieved. The Orange Beach Community Center is still a vibrant part of the community.

Above is a photo of Thurston Lauder , son of Captain Neil Lauder, on the dock at Lauder Landing on Cotton Bayou. Thurston was the author's closest playmate while growing up on Cotton Bayou.

Below is a photo from a day of frolic on the waters of Cotton Bayou.Growing up on Cotton Bayou meant that you had access to a boat and good times. Shown here is Thurston Lauder with the paddle and Margaret Childress in the bow of the boat. Margaret's brother, Foster, can be seen swimming near the stern. This photo was taken at Lauder Landing with Captain Neil Lauder's charter boat *Duchess* in the background at left.

The photographs on this page are the only ones known to survive of an oil well drilled in Orange Beach. This photo was taken of the oil well derrick in March, 1952. The stock of South Baldwin Oil Company, Inc., was held mostly by local men. The well was located to the south of the current Gulftel telephone exchange on Highway 161 (Cotton Bayou Road). No oil or gas was hit and the well rig was removed.

For a short while the area became a local dump. (See the Appendix for a copy of

This photo shows James Bagley, Jr., holding his daughter Lynn while Nancy stands on the 'corduroy' road leading across the sand from the Cotton Bayou Road (Hwy. 161) to the oil well. Circa 1952.

Above is a photo taken at the old Herman Callaway home on Canal Road (Hwy. 180). Pictured is Clifford Callaway, son of Captain Herman Callaway, and his wife Myrth. Clifford and his brother Nolan were born in the house in 1923 & 1927 respectively. The family property was sold in the summer of 2004.

Above is the front yard of the Captain Herman Callaway house on Canal Road (looking west). The area on the far side of the large trees is where Captain Herman built the charter boat *Dixie Maid*.

The 113 foot tower at left was the transmitting tower that brought telephone service to Orange Beach in 1956. The Gulf Telephone tower provided a wireless transmission to a receiver on the water tower in Foley and was the first system of its kind in the U. S. The tower was located on Hwy. 161 just across from where the City Municipal Complex is now located.

At right is a portrait of John McClure Snook of Gulf Telephone. John and his wife Marjorie donated land for the City Complex and Marjorie Snook Park.

The low angle aerial photo above shows the White Caps which was the first 'real' motel on the beach. Located west of Romar Beach, the White Caps was built by Dr. Gray from Tennessee, about 1959. The motel had the distinction of having the first swimming pool in the area.

Below is the White Caps during the early 1980s with its swimming pool in the foreground. From the time the White Caps was built until the 1990s, the motel had a series of owners and managers. The last owner of the White Caps was Glenn Baumann. The 'Summer House' now stands where the White Caps once stood.

A large crowd is shown above at the dedication of the first Perdido Pass bridge at Alabama Point on May 12, 1962. This bridge dedication was well attended by dignitaries and people from both Alabama and Florida, since it connected the two islands of Perdido Key and Pleasure Island for the first time.

After the first bridge at Perdido Pass was severely damaged during Hurricane Frederic in September 1979, a new wider and taller bridge was built and dedicated. Ribbon cutting at the new Perdido Pass Bridge was held August 28, 1989. Author, Margaret Childress Long is on the right and her friend Mary Nell Walker Hough is second from left, they helped cut the ribbon on both bridges.

The photograph above shows the existing Perdido Pass Bridge...a four–lane structure that crosses Perdido Pass from Alabama Point to Florida Point. After the first bridge was severely damaged in Hurricane Frederic in September 1979, this new bridge was built and dedicated August 28, 1989.

Below is the first Perdido Pass Bridge, a two lane concrete bridge. Construction began on this bridge in 1958 with the dedication May 12, 1962. The strong and ever changing currents in Perdido Pass made construction difficult. After damage Hurricane Frederic and construction of the new bridge, the old bridge was torn down.

The house seen in the background of the above photo was the Henry Sweet house. Henry Sweet was the head of the Army Corps of Engineers – Mobile District during the 1950s, when he was given land by Amos Garrett for this house on Alabama Point . During Hurricane Flossy on September 24, 1956, the pass was hit hard, removing the lake on Alabama Point and eroding sand severely in front of Sweet's house. A steel piling sea wall was installed to stop future erosion.

Hurricane Betsy hit the area on Labor Day, September 8, 1965. The photo above shows the resulting damage with sand washed out behind the steel piling sea wall. The photo below shows a close up of the house hanging out over the water of the pass. Sweet sued the State of Alabama for the damage to his home and won. The result of the damage, the law suit, and the constant push by the Orange Beach Fishing Association for more permanent improvements to Perdido Pass was what we see today in the concrete sea wall, the rock jetties, and other navigational improvements.

left: At U.S. Capitol in Washington, D.C., Roland Walker represented the Orange Beach Fishing Association along with Alabama Representative Bill Dickinson in their quest for dredging and navigational aids for Perdido Pass. Pictured from left: Roland Walker, Harry Crawford, Walter Mims, Alabama Senator John Sparkman, Bill Dickinson, and Gulf Shores Mayor Johnny Sims. Dickinson also assisted the Orange Beach Fishing Association with development of the Artificial Reef program. Dickinson became involved with the program after fishing with Roland Walker over one of his 'home–built' reefs with great success.

Right: Roland Walker with one of the early artificial reefs. Later reefs were made of piles of concrete pipe, car bodies, and WWII Liberty ships. The Orange Beach Fishing Association still promotes their 'Adopt–a–Reef' program to enhance bottom fishing in the Gulf.

The photo above, from the 'Foley Onlooker', shows Dorothy Childress drawing her last bottle of water from the only public well with good tasting water. On this day, January 15, 1974, the Orange Beach water system began operation. Prior to that time, Dorothy hauled water for drinking and washing purposes from that well tap near 'The Keg' to her home on Cotton Bayou

The photo below shows the Water Board members gathered for the ceremony of turning on the new city water system. Board members from left: Ted Ray, Betty Ray, E. M. Karcher, Dorothy Childress, Mrs. Karcher, J. B. Hill, and A. W. Robinson.

Above is the Clarence 'Ted' and Ellen Tampary house after Hurrican Frederic. The Home was close to the Flora–Bama and right on the beach. The Tampary's built the now famous Flora–Bama Package Store and Lounge.

Above is the Ted and Dorothy Childress house on Cotton Bayou showing the damage after Hurricane Frederic in September 1979. The hurricane came in straight up Mobile Bay as a category 3 storm and dealt heavy effects along the Gulf coast and inland areas of Alabama and Mississippi.

A Walker family reunion held at Douglas Walker's summer place, November 1, 1981. Kneeling from left: Ann and Sidney Walker Sr., Kevin Walker, Sidney Walker Jr., Loretta and Ken Walker, Gail and Rickey Graham. Standing: Nora and Gladwin Walker, Ray and Mary Gene Walker, Margaret and Roland Walker Sr., Roy and Eva Walker, Rabun and Alma Walker.

This is a photo of the first Sunday services in the new addition to the Orange Beach Presbyterian Church, October 17, 1982. The Presbyterians organized and broke ground for their first church in 1953. For many years, the Presbyterians shared the First Baptist Church for their services.

Above is a photo of the swearing–in of the first City Council of Orange Beach, October 15, 1985, at the Orange Beach Community Center. The group was sworn–in by Baldwin County Probate Judge Harry D'Olive (seen at far left). From left to right are City Officers: Council Place 2, J. F. 'Jack' Govan; Council Place 3, William S. 'Steven' Garner; Mayor Ronnie Callaway; Council Place 5, J. D. 'Jim' Snell; Council Place 1, Rose Williams; Council Place 4 and Mayor Pro Tem, John F. 'Frank' Ellis.

Below is the Orange Beach City Council in August 2004. Shown left to right: seated, Pete Blalock and Mayor Steve Russo. Standing: Ed Carroll, Joni Blalock, Jeff Silvers, and Tony Kennon.

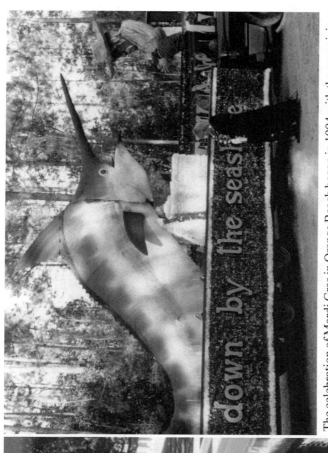

The celebration of Mardi Gras in Orange Beach began in 1994 with the organizing of the 'Crewe of Mystic Isle' by Sylvia and Dean Howland and Captain Earl Callaway (Sylvia is shown at left) . Above is one of the many floats that parade on Fat Tuesday each year. The celebration has expanded with the addition of several other Mystic Societies.

129

In March 1994, the Orange Beach Garden Club began planting 62 trees in the city recreational park on the north side of Highway 180 between Walker Lane and Wilson Boulevard. The trees were purchased with a Shell Oil Company 'Petals' program grant. The club remains very active in the community. From left are club members Elinor Callaway Haynes, Lois Brown, Myrth Callaway (President at the time of the grant), Margaret McFarland, Tina Bakker, Jan Borum, Jaunita Eubanks, Jeannine Newsome, Becky Gregory, and Joyce Morris.

The dedication of the Marjorie Snook Park in October 1999. The land for the municipal complex and the park was donated to the City of Orange Beach by John and Marjorie Snook. Mayor Steve Russo is shown at the podium.

Above is a photo from 1980 taken at the Orange Beach Community Center. Shown left to right are: Captain Leroy Walker, Captain Carl McDuffie, and Captain Raymond Walker. The Orange Beach Community Center had been a project of the Home Demonstration Club and became a reality in 1972.

This photo from February 2003 is of the new Orange Beach Senior Activity Center. This facility is located in Waterfront Park on the south shore of Wolf Bay.

The Orange Beach Municipal Complex located on Highway 161, south of Highway 180. Photo from 2002.

The Orange Beach Elementary School on Wilson Boulevard was taken in 2002. The school was opened in 1997 for kindergarten through fifth grade. This was the first school built in Orange Beach since 1910.

Orange Beach Public Library on the south shore of Wolf Bay is shown above in this 2002 photo. The Orange Beach library was begun by the city in 1991 and due to public demand has expanded and moved several times, until the present library was built and opened its doors on May 7, 2001.

Orange Beach began fire service in 1961 with the organization of the Orange Beach Volunteer Fire Service. This volunteer fire service grew and continued service to the community until 1994 when it merged into the city as the Orange Beach Fire and Rescue service and has grown steadily to keep pace with the growth of the city. The current Orange Beach Fire and Rescue building is shown below.

The Orange Beach Police Department in 1995. Seated left to right: Scott Beaman, Kimberly Wasdin, Vera Doty, Sgt. Lyle Dodd, Sgt. T. J. McVickers, Maj. Gerald Poe, Chief Robert Vinson, Sgt. Greg Duck, Sgt. Mike Talley, Anthony Grigsby, Gina Long, and Sec. Eunice Stewart. Standing: Paula Knight, Tim Brown, Mike Hamilton, David Groover, Earlie Roberts, Robert Wiser, and Richard Duggan. Not pictured: Rick Rouse, Jim Harris, and Frank Hobbs.

The above rare aerial photograph was taken in the early 1950's. What makes this aerial rare is that it shows the large lake that existed for many years on Alabama Point which was eroded away by Hurricane Flossy, September 24, 1956. The view is to the north–northeast with Perdido Pass (in the right center) prior to the construction of the first Perdido Pass Bridge. The island above Alabama Point is Robinson or Goat Island with Terry Cove just above it.

The 1950 photograph below of Alabama Point, shows the Sweet house below the lake and the Lovick Allen Cottages just below the Sweet house. The Paul Smith house is in the foreground on Cotton Bayou. Paul Smith was the world famous 'Marlboro Man' of cigarette advertising.

Above is an aerial photo of Perdido Pass viewed to the east–northeast. Date is unknown, but probably in the early 1970s.

Below is an aerial photo looking northwest showing Perdido Pass, the entrance to Cotton Bayou at the left and Terry Cove at the top. This photo was taken in February 2002.

Above is an aerial photo from January 1978 looking northeast across Alabama Point and Perdido Pass. Cotton Bayou is in the center foreground with Terry Cove and Bear Point above it . Ono Island is to the left of the beach above Perdido Pass.

This aerial photo of Terry Cove was also taken in January 1978. The view is to the north from above Perdido Pass. On the right is Burkart Point with Robinson Island on the left.

Above is a low level aerial photograph of the first Perdido Pass Bridge viewed to the southeast from over Cotton Bayou. The bridge underpinning was severely damaged during Hurricane Frederic in September 1979. The new bridge opened in 1989.

Below is an aerial photograph of Perdido Pass looking to the northeast. This photo was taken about 1963 before the installation of the concrete sea wall and rock jetties in 1969.

Above is an aerial view to the east–northeast along Highway 182 (Beach Road) showing Alabama Point, Perdido Pass, and bridge. Cotton Bayou is in the lower left with Terry Cove above it. Bay St. John is at the top center with Ono Island, Old River, and Perdido Key (once known as Gulf Beach) to the upper right. Photo taken in February 2002.

This is an aerial view to the southeast from Bay La Launche across Bear Point to Bay St. John, Ono Island, Perdido Key, and the Gulf of Mexico. Photo taken February 2002.

Above is an aerial view to the southeast showing the Foley Express Toll Bridge that opened in 2000, across the Intracoastal Canal. This bridge connects the Foley Expressway from the Canal road (Highway 180) to Highway 59 just north of Foley. 'The Wharf' development is currently planned for the area on the south side of the canal, just to the left of the bridge. The 'River Walk – swim with the Dolphins' and 'Portage Creek Condos' developments are set for the area to the left of the bridge toll booths on the north side of the canal. Photo taken in February 2002.

This aerial view to the south from lower Wolf Bay, shows Highway 161 (Cotton Bayou Road) on the right that connects to Highway 182 (Beach Road) with Cotton Bayou, Alabama Point, and at the top, the Gulf of Mexico. Perdido Pass is shown in the upper left. Photo taken February 2002.

Let Tourism Begin

Hart M. Low, Grandfather of Bertha Walker Robinson, moved from Ohio to Robertsdale, then to Orange Beach, about 1912. Low bought 210 acres that had been part of the 'Samuel Suarez Tract' on Bear Point. Seven and a half acres of this land had a small one–room house on it.

Low expanded the house and named it 'Gulf View'.

In the early 1930's Clarence and Hazel Walker further developed the property that was located on Bay Ornocor (called South Bay before 1920, but now Bay St. John) into the first

Gulf View Park as seen from the water. Operated by Clarence & Hazel Walker , this was one of the first fishing 'resorts' in the area.

full–scale resort in the area renaming it 'Gulf View Park'. Coming in through the Pass from the Gulf, 'Gulf View Park' was one of the first places you saw. The park not only had lodge–sleeping accommodations for visitors and fishermen, it had five individual cabins, a small Texaco gas station and store offering day snacks and ice, and had skiffs for rent. The small store closed in 1943 and the buildings of 'Gulf View Park' were torn down in 1975.

Clarence, the first born of Lemuel Walker, Sr., was called 'Uncle Ted' by friends and family and grew up in a fishing family. Clarence worked for the L&N Railroad in Pensacola and commuted back and forth until he and Hazel married in 1915. They then lived in Pensacola until 1926 when they moved back to Caswell where they stayed until the WWII years. Moving to Mobile during WWII, they ultimately moved to Huntsville, Alabama, to be near their only daughter.

The original home of Lemuel Walker, Sr. still stands on Bay St. John not far to the east of 'Gulf View Park', but has been extensively remodeled over the years.

The charter boat *Jimmy* was one of the first 'factory built' charter boats in the area. The *Jimmy* was actually owned by J. U. Blacksher, a businessman from Mobile who loved to fish the waters of Orange Beach. The boat was reserved for Blacksher's use every Thursday. Through a unique arrangement with Blacksher, Captain Clarence Walker had use of the *Jimmy*, maintained it, and kept the revenue.

The following excerpts from the Foley Onlooker newspaper community news section gives evidence of the growing tourism of the early 1900's.

The Lemuel Walker, Jr. house at Caswell

- Early 1920
  'Frank Stewart, "The Picture Man", of Fairhope and his friend, Mr. Powers, of Iowa, are here for a few days recreation will probably fish some, boat some with his old friend, George Samson, and on the side take some more of these lovely views that are popular with all tourists.'

- April 23, 1925 – 'Mr. and Mrs. George Mach of Robertsdale spent a week here in their cottage having rented the Wolbrink cottage for the year and expect to spend many more happy days here this summer. They will as soon as they can get to it, build a home on the land acquired by them just east of the village.'

  'Word was received from Mrs. Reid who spent four weeks recently in the Rynd cottage that she will return in August with her husband and most probably with her father who was utterly carried away with her description of the oystering, crabbing and fishing they enjoyed and also the good time enjoyed while here.'

- June 13, 1933 or 1935 – 'Mr. and Mrs. W.M. Moore and children of Bay Minette, and Miss Beulah White and T.H. Moore and family of Montgomery are spending a month here enjoying the good bathing and fishing to be found.'

- 'Mr. Talmadge E. Ross, son–in–law of Mr. Kent came in last week from Clinton, Ill. and joined his wife and little boy who preceded him. They are installed in the Shamrock cottage. Mr. Minor T. Bishop, a friend, accompanied him.'

M and R Lodge, located on Bay La Launche near the Crane Pond, (also know as the Old Swirn Place) was another of the early cottages for rent to fishermen. Mr. Stanley was the manager before the Swirn's arrived in the late 1930's. Stanley later married the Swirn's daughter.

In 1923 the Orange Beach Hotel, located on the south shore of Wolf

Bay, was built and operated by Hilda Callaway Dietz. The youngest daughter of James C. Callaway, Hilda had married Edward George Dietz, a medical Doctor from Cleveland, Ohio, in December 1913 in the home of her father. The hotel was built on land Hilda had inherited from her father. After his death,

Orange Beach Hotel circa 1947

her mother, Nancy Ellen Childress Callaway, donated 30 feet of land on the west side of the hotel to the county for a road from Highway 180 to Wolf Bay and the hotel, so that her family would always have a way to the water. This right of way still bears her name as 'Nancy Lane'. This hotel soon became a favorite spot of many fishermen, tourists, and locals. Hilda's husband went back to Cleveland during the depression to support his family. While there, he became ill and died in June 1931.

- Foley Onlooker – Orange Beach Community news – January 18, 1923:
  'Mrs. Hilda Dietz having purchased the unused building at Perdido Beach owned by her brother–in–law Henry Harms took a crew of men from here and wrecked it and will bring the lumber here to use in the construction of her new hotel. Work will soon start on said building and Orange Beach will then have a first class stopping place for guests that will fill a lot felt want.'

By 1936 the hotel was modernized with the addition of electric lights using a 32–volt Delco generator electric system with a bank of Edison glass batteries rated at one–half volt each. After her father's death, Hilda cared for her mother who lived with her at the hotel. The hotel had four small cottages around it; each painted a different bright color. At the time there was a 30 feet wide beach of white sand in front of the hotel. It was a great place for bathers and just relaxing.

The importance of the Orange Beach Hotel is illustrated by the following community news items in the Foley Onlooker newspaper:

- April 23, 1925 – 'Mr. Ed Dietz of Cleveland, Ohio, proprietor of the Bay View hotel at this place is here for the first time in a number of years. The hotel was built entirely during his absence under the able supervision of his wife Mrs. Hilda Dietz and is a gem of a building and is already favored with a considerable patronage.'

- May 21, 1925 – 'Mrs. Edwin Dietz proprietor of the Orange Beach Hotel, was a business visitor here last week. This is a new hotel, beautifully located when completed it will be convenient and modern in every respect, a fact to be appreciated by the large number who annually visit Orange Beach, which is one of the finest resorts in this section, the bathing being considered the best in the bay district. Two large boats are nearing completion by the owners, living at Orange Beach. They will be for hire, adding to the opportunities for real sport in hunting for cavalia, ling and tarpon, each of which inhabit nearby waters.'

- October 17, 1929 – 'Alasarian Dietz (Hilda's son) with the help of his Uncle Leon 'Len' Callaway is erecting a nice pier with chute and spring board for benefit of the bathers at Hotel Orange Beach.'

Orange Beach Hotel pier and platform was a very busy place. Photo about 1930.

Hilda Dietz was held in high esteem by both her hotel patrons and local residents as demonstrated by this article in the Foley Onlooker Orange Beach community section of the December 5, 1929:

'Surprise Party Given Honors Mrs. Hilda Dietz'
'Miss Evelyn Dietz gave a lovely surprise party Saturday evening in honor of her mother's birthday, Mrs. Hilda Dietz. There were about 40 guests and all enjoyed themselves playing bridge and

dancing. Some guests from Miflin furnished pretty string   music.
A beautifully decorated birthday cake, made by the Malbis
Bakery, was presented to the honoree.
Refreshments consisted of cake and cocoa.
Many beautiful and useful gifts were presented with best wishes
for many more happy birthdays.
Messrs. Raymond Ard, Roy Walker, Willard and Leonard Leigh
attended a surprise party for Mrs. Hilda Dietz at Orange Beach
Saturday.'

At the beginning of World War II, Hilda sold the hotel and moved with
her mother to Mobile.

By 1953 the hotel was owned and operated by Leo Davis. Ray
Callaway was talking to Davis one afternoon in 1955, when Davis made
the comment that he wanted to sell the hotel. Following the   conversation,
Ray went home to talk to his wife Ella about purchasing it. They had
$5,000 on hand and gave that to Davis to consummate the deal. Total
price for the hotel, $10,000. Ray and Ella operated the hotel for the next 8
years. They sold the hotel in 1963 for $30,000. Bill and Sandy Campbell
purchased the hotel operating it until the City of Orange Beach purchased
it and the surrounding property in 2001 for $1.2 million to use as the new
Waterfront Park. Through the efforts of Margaret Childress Long, the old
hotel was saved from the wrecking ball and has now been renovated
again. The building has since served briefly as the Orange Beach Senior
Citizens Center and now as the Pleasure Island Art Association gallery.
The Orange Beach Hotel has now been placed on the register of Alabama's
historic places.

The 1940 'Highlights and Highway of Baldwin' tourist guide lists 'Camp,
Hotel and tourist Home' rates for Caswell and Orange Beach:

Caswell:

Bear Point Fishing Lodge	$3.00 per day	$21.00 per week
Cabins	3.00	21.00
Gulf View Park	2.50	15.00
Cottages	2.50 up	14.00 up

Orange Beach:

Orange Beach Hotel	2.50	15.00
Cabins	2.50	14.00

A vacationer by the name of James G. Bagley, Jr. came to Orange
Beach in 1948;. Like others before him, he moved here as a resident in
September 1949.

In those days, things to entertain visitors were limited to three: 1) go fishing 2) dig arrowheads at the Indian Mound on Bear Point or 3) visit Fort Morgan on the other end of the island. Bagley saw the need for a local bus service. He purchased a bus and began the Alabama Beach Bus Service. Originally his bus ran from Foley to Fort Morgan and back. On this run, he states that he would pass five Greyhound buses a day, which gives the indication of the popularity of a visit to Fort Morgan. After the first year, Bagley expanded his service to include runs between Orange Beach and Gulf Shores. He ran the service continuously until one day in October of 1950 when he had one passenger in the morning with the same person returning in the afternoon. He told that person that he would have to hitch–hike the next day since he was closing the service that night. James Bagley went into the insurance business, not leaving Orange Beach.

About 1950, Lovick Allen built a group of small cottages on Alabama Point near where the Outrigger once stood. Lovick died in 1963, but his family continued to live there for many years, supported by the income from the cottages operated by his daughter Suella.

Bill and Mildred Meeks owned and operated Meeks Cottages on Canal Road west of Highway 161 beginning in the 1950s. The cottages are gone now, and the property is now being developed.

The White Caps on the Gulf front west of Romar Beach, was the first 'real' motel in Orange Beach. Dr. Gray from Tennessee built the White Caps during 1959–60. The White Caps had the distinction of having the first swimming pool in the area. His wife had no interest in the area, so he sold it to Mr. and Mrs. Crawford who also owned the Sea Horse in Gulf Shores. Glenn Baumann and Gordon Miller took over payments from Crawford in September 1962. During 1967 – 1970, Ted Verdonschet of the Netherlands was the manager of the property. In 1973, the motel had a serious fire, but it was soon built back bigger and better than ever. Bob and Janet Hastings operated the motel from 1980 to 1984. Glenn Baumann was the last owner of the White Caps. The condominium Summer House is now located where the White Caps once stood.

'The Breakers' and the 'Sun Swept', both located on Highway 182, west of Highway 161, were the first two condominiums built in Orange Beach.

Prior to the 1950's, restaurants were few and far between. Most 'sit down' foodservice was provided by the camps and hotels or in the homes of the charter captains.

Crockett White Sr., started construction on Gulf Gate Lodge in 1949, but ran out of money and turned the unfinished lodge back to Farmers and Merchants Bank of Foley. 'Chunky' Baldwin, an advertising businessman of St. Louis, Missouri, purchased the building and completed construction. When the lodge finally opened with Pat Patrick and his wife as managers, it was a smash hit! The lodge rapidly gained a reputation with locals and visitors alike for good food and hospitality.

Gulf Gate Lodge circa 1966.

Margaret Childress sold crabs to the lodge, live for 60 cents per dozen and dressed for 85 cents each. Later in the summer of 1966, she became a waitress and cleaned cottages. That was her first job.

Joe and Sally McCarran purchased the lodge from 'Chunky' Baldwin about 1970. The McCarran's had been coming to Orange Beach as tourists since 1953 and saw the lodge as an opportunity to become permanent residents. To survive through the slow winter months, they established the 'Turnip Green Festival' to bring in more business. McCarran's first cousin, Katherine Floyd, was the first 'Turnip Green Festival Queen'. The first 'Deep Sea Rodeo' was held at this location in 1938 and it was 'hosted' by the lodge about 1979. The lodge was eventually sold and torn down in the mid 1980's.

Bear Point Lodge circa 1940.

One can not forget that another popular place through the years was the Bear Point Lodge and Marina. The lodge located on Arnica Bay near Mill Point was operated in its early years by Calla Mae Lanner and her four children; Ed (killed in Europe in 1945), Walter, Ella Hill Lanner Hamburg and Mary Ann Lanner Callaway.

The Keg, on Highway 180, has been a favorite place for many years, serving up their famous 'Keg Burger'. The Keg began its life when five volunteer firemen got together to start the lounge. It was then located west of Sam's Stop and Shop on Canal Road, where the restaurant 'Mexico Rock' was located, now 'Fish Camp' restaurant. The original owners were Roger Faulk, Glen Jerkins, Homer McNiel, Weldon Oulliber, and Kyle Carter. This group sold the business to Glenn and Dora Scott.

In 1985, Don Miller bought The Keg and the old Orange Beach Post Office building further west on Highway 180. He built the current Keg building behind the Post Office in 1986. Dean and Sylvia Howland purchased the property in 1987 and in turn sold to the current owners Howard and Jeannie Gann in 1997. The old Post Office was torn down in 1998 to expand parking and visibility. An interesting note is that The Keg, located in what could be called 'downtown Orange Beach', was the last property to be annexed into the city.

However, the 'grand daddy' of local clubs has to be 'Flora–Bama, Package, Lounge & Oyster Bar'. The 'Flora–Bama' straddles the State line between Florida

Flora–Bama, Package, Lounge & Oyster Bar

and Alabama and sits right on the beach on Perdido Key. Ted and Ellen Tampary built this   unusual place in 1964. However, the day   before it was set to open, the building burned to the ground with arson the suspected cause. This fire did not stop the Tamparys however, as they quickly rebuilt the lounge. With the varying drinking laws between the States of Florida and Alabama, the place soon became a hit and its reputation has since grown to some international notoriety.

The 'Flora–Bama' has been immortalized in a book by popular novelist John Grisham and in a song by noted singer/song writer Jimmy Buffet, who occasionally shows up there. The Interstate Mullet Toss and other events gather very large crowds and of course having super star, National Football League Quarterback, Kenny Stabler, throw out the first mullet for the first few years at the 'Mullet Toss' didn't hurt. Maybe the biggest event established by the 'Flora–Bama' has been the ever expanding 'Frank Brown Song Writers Festival'

On a sadder note, the 'Flora–Bama' was destroyed by Hurricane Ivan September 16, 2004, however its many events are still going and they have plans to rebuild.

The Speed of Change Picks Up

Following the major Hurricane Frederic on September 12, 1979, the speed of development increased dramatically. While Orange Beach did not have the damage that neighboring Gulf Shores experienced from Frederic... it was enough. The damage along the beach in both cities was considerable. The houses behind the dune line faired reasonably well, but structures like the Tampary house and the 'Flora–Bama' on Gulf Beach were all but demolished. The Gulf storm surge broke through the dunes about one hundred feet wide into Lake Shelby just west of the State Beach Pavilion in Gulf State Park.

One of the results of the damage was that many part–time and some full–time residents of Pleasure Island packed up and left. This brought a lot of property on the market, especially beachfront property. Those that stayed did well for their futures, as this was a time of incredible investment opportunities.

Hurricane Frederic brought concern and subsequent planning for the future to the folks in the Orange Beach area and to the City of Gulf Shores. Mayor Thomas B. Norton, Sr., of Gulf Shores, went into action. He established new disaster programs, instituted improved   utility systems, improved building regulations, developed rebuilding programs, purchased beach property for future public use, and established a fund for his city for future disasters. All this brought money, lots of money, to the area. Developers began purchasing   property and not just beachfront, but all of 'Pleasure Island'. In the ten years after Hurricane Frederic, literally billions of dollars were invested on the island. The condominium building boom was on! The developers had seen the growth potential in the area and now saw an opportunity to participate.

The remaining residents of Orange Beach had been through this before, but not on this scale since the storm of 1926. They in turn saw the future and were determined to be ready for the coming population explosion. One of these people was Dorothy Childress who had already been involved with the establishment of many community services. She joined forces with Joe Johnson, A. E. Cooper, Bob Milsap, and others to begin talking about incorporating the city.

The area population, both resident and non–resident, began to increase rapidly. The influx of visitors changed the area from a normal summer season destination to a year–round resort with places for our visiting winter 'Snow Birds' to stay. When the super market chains of 'Winn–Dixie' and 'Delchamps' (now Bruno's) arrived in Orange Beach, it was a sure sign that the city had come of age.

The increase in services and places to stay brought even more people, which in turn brought more building. That is until the 'Savings and Loan Bust' of the 1980's. With the failure of some of the big national S & L's, property foreclosures became common place for several years until the nation's financial systems began to recover. By the early 1990's things were back on course. Even through all that, the area continued to grow and develop.

1993 brought organization of the Alabama Gulf Coast Convention and Visitors Bureau, allowing Orange Beach and Gulf Shores to work together in the promotion and development of 'Pleasure Island'. Prior to that time the South Baldwin Chamber of Commerce in Foley, was THE source for visitor and development information for Orange Beach.

The tourism industry has grown substantially over the years. According to the Alabama Gulf Coast Convention and Visitors Bureau, lodging and retail tax revenue collected by Gulf Shores and Orange Beach during 1994 was $7,222,740. By 2002, that revenue had increased to $17,742,953!

Reminiscing the Merchant Marine
and World Wars

The sea was a tradition from the start with the Callaways. The operation of James C. Callaway's schooner's *Ellen C* and *J. S. Murrow* in the Gulf and Caribbean was in their blood. Several in the family turned to the merchant marine for a living.

The following comments are from the Orange Beach community news items in the Foley Onlooker:

- January 31, 1924 – 'Commander Elver R. Callaway of U.S. shipping board vessel came home from Mobile the first time in about three years to make a visit to this, his old home.'

- November 14, 1929 – 'Capt. Callaway Named Master of "Seatrain"' 'Captain Elver R. Callaway, of Mobile and whose home as a boy was at Orange Beach, has been appointed master of the "Seatrain" which operates between New Orleans and Havana, according to word received from Mobile. Captain Callaway was formerly Captain of the Waterman steamer "Lake Benton", which recently was sold to Europeana.
   During his seafaring career of 30 years he has sailed regularly out of Mobile. He was chief officer of the old Windward Island line and chief officer of the Page and Jones steamship "Hancock". For the past six years he has been in the employ of the Waterman Steamship Corporation. When the "Lake Benton" was sold he was appointed master of the "Lake Treba".'

- 1929–1933 – 'Captain Elver Callaway who was here on a visit as well as business trip returned to Mobile last Saturday. While here he had his residence repaired and his acreage plowed and planted to trees.'

- June 13, 1933 or 1935 – 'Leon and Captain Elver Callaway were welcome visitors to their mother Mrs. J. C. Callaway this week. Capt. Callaway's boat is on the way for repairs making it possible for his visit at this time before making another trip across the big pond.'

During World War I, Childress Callaway was in the secret OSS where his maritime experience was put to good use. Childress' nephews, Clifford Callaway and his first cousin Raymond, both went into the Merchant Marine to join the action of World War II. Service in the Merchant Marine was not easy. According to Clifford, on one return trip to Mobile, both cousins were sick and placed in the hospital for recovery. The ship left without them and was sunk by a German submarine about 30 miles south of Ft. Morgan; only three survived of the forty–five onboard.

Another harrowing trip was as a single unescorted ship passing through the Panama Canal and on to the island of New Guinea in the South Pacific carrying radio equipment to U. S. forces on the island. Being an unescorted ship was vulnerable and open to enemy submarine attack. Fortunately this trip had no major incidents.

Ray and Clifford Callaway on leave in Mobile from the Merchant Marine during WWII.

During the war, 77 merchant ships were sunk in the Gulf of Mexico and the Merchant Marine lost 5,682 lives during the war. Clifford Callaway spent 14 ½ years in the Merchant Marine.

Roland Walker, Sr., was also in the Merchant Marine aboard the Liberty ship 'John W. McKay', a ship similar to the ones he would later arrange to sink in the Gulf of Mexico for artificial fishing reefs in support of the Orange Beach Charter fishing industry.

The *Miss Kay*, Roy Walker's charter boat, was used by the U.S. Coast Guard during the war and still proudly carries a service plaque in honor of that duty.

Cotton Bayou was an exciting place during World War II. Naval aircraft from Pensacola Naval Air Station used the bayou for machine gun practice on water borne targets. Old River on the south side of Ono Island was used for bomb practice using dummy bombs. Military bomber and fighter aircraft flew over the houses along the Bayou nearly every day. Nothing quite like war in your backyard!

Walter Tanner was the first person from Orange Beach to be killed in action in WW II. He died in Europe, September 1945. His body was returned to Orange Beach a year later and was laid to rest at Pine Rest Cemetery in Foley. Tanner owned the small Tanner Lodge on St. Johns Bay, just east of Caswell. His wife Ella continued operating the lodge.

The charter fishing business was basically brought to a halt by the war with the danger of German submarines and a shortage of fuel. Many Orange Beach residents moved to Pensacola or Mobile during the war years working in the ship building industry or civilian naval employment in support of the war effort.

Soldiers from Fort Morgan (the Fort was reactivated during WW II) patrolled the beaches on horseback watching for enemy submarines or agents slipping ashore. Even with 'blacked out' windows to keep submarines from defining the land, as the guards would come by the few homes of beach residents, they would open their doors and offer them coffee or cold drinks depending on the time of year.

One of the benefits of WWII was the availability of fathometers. For the first time, charter boats could read water depth without using a lead line and could locate large schools of fish. These delightful new pieces of electronics were a major help to safety from grounding and for locating fish!

Charter boat fishing begins

Fishing was an every day part of life for the Native American Indians, the early Spanish, French, and English settlements and by the early 1800's, the stalwart early settlers along the bays and bayous.

Through those early years almost everyone did at least some fishing. As the population grew, commercial fishing began to develop to supply a food source for those that primarily lived in the larger local settlements and for the farmers that spent all their time on the land. The turpentine industry developed producing naval stores for the related commercial fishing and water transport industries. In the days of sail, turpentine was a necessary worldwide commodity.

The early commercial or net fishermen kept their catches in 'live wells' and transported them to Pensacola where they were sold 'live'. Ice was not a common commodity on fishing boats in those days.

During the early 1900's a new concept arrived in Orange Beach, one called 'fishing for hire'. Clifford and Nolan Callaway's family records show that the first license to operate a boat 'for hire' was issued at the custom house in Mobile, Alabama, to Herman Callaway. Herman was one of the sons of James C. and Nancy Ellen Callaway. He started with an un–named 24 foot boat, then the *Resolute*, a 26 footer that he built himself. Herman's original license is kept in the Callaway family archives. He held operators license dated from February 1, 1913 through February 16, 1966. Herman also held an engineers license from September 12, 1913 through May 7, 1952.

According to Thurston Lauder, his Grandfather, Amel Callaway, remember his first experience of 'fishing for hire" was with Robin Swift, Sr. of Atmore, Alabama. Swift was visiting the area and wanted to go fishing, but did not have a boat. He approached Amel to take him out in the Gulf in his small boat *Red Wing*. Amel thought it was a little strange for someone to pay money to fish for fun, but 75 cents was 75 cents in those days.

It wasn't long before the concept caught on. You have to admit that it was a good concept. Who else knows better

Captain Amel Callaway on the *Red Wing*. Man in background unidentified.

where the fish are than someone that fishes for a living? The idea quickly grew. By the late 1920's, several fishermen were augmenting their living by 'charter fishing', the new name for 'fishing for hire'. During the 30's there were enough fishermen coming to Orange Beach to warrant starting a fishing association and Perdido Pass Fishing Association, one of the forerunners of today's Orange Beach Fishing Association was born.

The association was not just some boat captains getting together to decide how much to charge for their services. This group discussed safety of the pass channel, shared ideas for comfort of their fares, boat maintenance, and discussed standards for members of their association. By 1939, the dozen or so members of the organization were advertising their services in area publications and the industry began to grow.

Fishermen began to wire requests for date and time to their favorite captains via Western Union in Foley. From Foley, the messages were hand delivered to the appropriate Captain in Orange Beach. When telephone communication arrived in 1956 arranging a charter became a lot easier.

Today, there are over 125 charter boats operating out of Orange Beach with most of them members of the Orange Beach Fishing Association.

Commercial fishing is still big business along with the shrimping, crabbing, and oyster gathering, but the charter boats are way too busy for that.

Deep Sea Trolling
(6 PERSON PARTY)
ALL TACKLE FURNISHED
N. A. LAUDER
AT LAUDER'S LANDING
Orange Beach, Ala. - Contact Western Union

Above is a typical charter fishing ad in a 1949 publication.

The following news items from the Foley Onlooker Orange Beach community news talks about charter boat fishing:

- May 6, 1920 – 'Amel Callaway and Hudie Ewing of Orange Beach are in Caswell this week running one of Lee Walker's fishing boats while the Pompano are plentiful. They loaded up about 500 lbs. Monday A.M. There is only about six weeks in a season for Pompano and both the Callaway's and Walker's are after them.'
- June 3, 1925 – 'Mr. and Mrs. George Hayes and Mr. Hughes,

157

of Foley, were at the Beach the other day and were accompanied by Mr. and Mrs. Huff to Bill Landing and in 2 hours caught 75 large white trout.'

- October 17, 1929 – 'There was 30 King mackerel, 6 Spanish mackerel, 2 large ling, 1 nice blue fish and 2 bonitas, all in large sizes caught by J.N. Webb, Jerry Aristialle, W. Meder and T.T. Shepperd all of Mobile, they were put with Amel Callaway the well known fisherman of Orange Beach.'

- October 17, 1929 – 'Mrs. N.G. Lock and Johnson Dortuck of Mobile were guest of Hotel Orange Beach for three days catching a real large catch both days. They were fishing with Amel Callaway the first day, but the second day with Herman Callaway making a large catch the last day. They said we are taking our six pound fish home and show our friends what we can catch at Orange Beach.'

Taxing the fleet

About the time that the Orange Beach charter fleet was really beginning to grow, the Federal Government decided that they wanted a piece of the action and put a tax on charter boats and yachts. All charter captains paid it, except Herman Callaway, according to his son Clifford. Herman refused to pay as he considered it an unfair tax. At varying times several agents of the Federal Bureau of Investigation visited Herman at his home. Herman basically asked them to leave. One day another man in a suit rode up to the house, Herman had to be thinking 'here we go again', but this time it turned out to be the President of Waterman Steam Ship Corporation and he agreed with Herman about the tax. More importantly, Waterman Steam Ship had the money to fight the government. And fight they did...and they won! The tax was repealed. It is said that Herman Callaway beat the government!

Roy Walker earned his Captain's license in 1932, a license he held for over 60 years with most of those years spent on his favorite boat *Miss Kay*. At one time he was the oldest person in the United States with a Captain's license. By 1939, Roy had built a house in Orange Beach and his marina on Terry Cove. At the time, there were only one other full service marinas in the area, Hudson Marina operated by Jim Hudson.

Jim Hudson was a unique character. He was a charter fisherman, boat builder, boat repairman, and marina owner/operator. He was easy to recognize, since he always wore overalls and went barefoot regardless of the season.

Walker Marina had a serious fire in the early 1960's, but it was quickly rebuilt. A Model 'A' Ford engine was used to pull boats out of the water at Walker Marina, at least until Hurricane Frederic when the motor was stolen during the aftermath of the storm. Hurricane Frederic in September 1979 brought serious damage to all area marinas.

Iris Ethridge was the first female charter captain in Orange Beach. She owned and operated her boat, *On the Crosstie,* with her husband Bill serving as her first mate. They shared their business venture for a decade. Iris has served on the Orange Beach City Council and in 2002 was the first 'Ms. Senior Baldwin County'.

The Orange Beach Fishing Association established a fishing rodeo in 1938. This is a contest of who can catch the largest fish in several different categories. The first Orange Beach Deep–Sea Fishing Rodeo was headquartered on Terry Cove near where Gulf Gate Lodge would be built. Beside all the great fishing

The first Orange Beach Deep Sea Fishing Rodeo at Terry Cove – July 1938.

and the visitors waiting at the dock for the boats to arrive with their catches, there was great food available for all. A grand weekend was had and an annual event was begun. In later years, Gulf Gate Lodge would host the event.

During one of the early rodeos, Herman Callaway was in the Gulf with a small charter party when he was notified of a hurricane headed their way. The U. S. Coast Guard dropped a buoy from their airplane with a note attached telling him to 'get to safe harbor – that a hurricane was coming'. He ignored the note since the people were making good catches. He knew he had a few hours before the hurricane would be upon them. Besides they had time before the closing hour of the days contest.

It wasn't long before, the Coast Guard plane flew over again and dropped another buoy. This time the message 'demanded' that he head for safe harbor, so lines were reeled in and to the dock they went. His party did well in the rodeo and remained safe from the hurricane.

The 1940 'Highlights and Highway of Baldwin' tourist guide lists 'boats for hire' rates for Caswell and Orange Beach:

'For bay fishing, powerboats (with gas, pilot, etc.) can be had for $1.00 to 2.50 per hour. For Gulf fishing, $1.50 to 2.50 per hour. Skiffs can be rented for 50 cents per hour, but most camps supply them free with cottages. Outboard motors can be had for $1.50 to 2.50 per day.'

By 1966 charter fishing was in such demand that rates had increased to $60.00 for a half day trip on the Gulf.

Development of area Marinas and Landings

Important to any large fishing fleets are the marinas where they tie up and replenish supplies while in port. Among the first of these was Bill's Landing. Lauder Landing was later built on Cotton Bayou at the west-end of the bayou. Neil Lauder owned the landing and the following early

captains kept their charter boats there: Neil Lauder, Ronald Lauder, Ray Callaway, Amel Callaway, and Pop Messerill, although Pop owned a motel on Fort Morgan Road, way to the west. The Callaway's later built a dock on Terry Cove near Trent Marina.

This is a photograph of Lauder Landing with Captain Neil Lauder's charter boat *Duchess* tied up. This was at the head of Cotton Bayou.

Ray and Ella Callaway purchased a site on Terry Cove for the Callaway Marina in 1963 from a Mr. Dryer of Daphne with the capital from their sale of the Orange Beach Hotel. They paid $90 a front foot for the marina site which they sold in 1984 for $4,500 a front foot. Although he no longer owned a marina, Ray went on to fish for two more years before retiring.

Other early marinas were Gulf View Park at Caswell on Bay St. John operated by Clarence Walker. On Terry Cove Hudson Marina, owned and operated by captain and boat builder Jim Hudson; Callaway Marina, Trent Marina on the west side of Terry Cove operated by Captain Walter Trent (sold in 2004); Bear Point Marina on Arnica Bay and, of course, the original 'marina', the public dock on Bay La Launche.

Many marinas have been built to service the ever–growing charter and pleasure boat fleet. Some have gone out of business, some have dramatically expanded, and some are relatively new, but all have contributed to the growth of the Orange Beach charter fishing industry.

Tom Adam's Marina	Alabama Point Marina	Annan's Port
Bear Point Marina	Bill Landing	Bobby Walker Charter
Broadwater Charters	Brown Landing	Callaway Marina
Captain Ty's Landing	Cat–Cat Charters	Cotton Bayou Marina
Earl Griffith's Marina	Gulf View Park	Hudson Marina
Lauder Landing	Mess About Marina	Orange Beach Marina
Outcast Charter Dock	Pat's Marina	Perdido Pass Marina
Romar Harbor Marina	Roy Walker Marina	Safe Harbor Marina
SanRoc Cay Marina	Sportsman Marina	Sun Circle Marina
Sun Harbor Marina	Tradewind Charters	Trent Marina
	Zeke's Marina	

Dr. Garrett donated a total of eighteen acres at the mouth of Cotton Bayou and at Boggy Point to the State of Alabama in the 1950's for use as public launch ramps. The donation was based on his assumption that the proposed new bridge to Florida Point would be built from land at the entrance of Cotton Bayou or from Boggy Point. The bridge was built from Alabama Point instead, but two public launch ramps were still built on the donated land, one at the head of Cotton Bayou and one at Boggy Point and are still used extensively.

Wrecks and accidents

The Gulf of Mexico is no place for novice boat captains. The water can get rough in a hurry. Currents in the Gulf are constantly on the move and storms can blowup seemingly out of nowhere. Even with   experience things can happen on the Gulf; it's then that you want someone in command that knows what to do.

Before he built the *Dixie Maid*, Herman Callaway bought a captured 'rum–runner' from the Government. The boat was the *Kadi Did*, but after purchase it was renamed the *Irma*. While out on a fishing trip in the Gulf, the *Irma* was caught by a 'three sisters wave' (a group of three large waves) and was nearly capsized. The boat rode the first two waves, but the third one 'wrapped them up' according to his son Clifford. At the time there were the Captain and six fishermen on board. Though the wave blew out all fourteen windows in the boat, frames and all, the engine never quit. After making sure that all the passengers were safe, Herman calmly collected up all the window frames from the water and returned to port.

Dan Callaway was about three miles out in the Gulf with a party of eleven onboard the *Lady Lake*, when disaster struck. The bow of the '*Lady*' opened up in rough seas and the water started pouring in. They tried stuffing mattresses, and anything else they could find, into the hole, to no avail. Dan set a buoy so he could find the boat later and all took to the water in a small lifeboat. They were rescued by a passing boat and wound up in the hospital due to exposure. Dan went back to raise *Lady Lake* towing her to his dock. After removing the engine, she was deemed non–salvageable and was cut up to make bulk–heads. The engine on the *Lady Lake* was a 5–ton Fairbanks diesel.

James C. Callaway had a contract with the U. S. Lighthouse Service to service the navigation beacons along the Gulf coast. One of his sons, Dan Callaway, captained one of his father's schooners in that work. Beacons were used instead of todays buoys for navigational aids. Each beacon flashed its light at different intervals for locational identification. The beacon lights were powered by batteries that had to be checked frequently. Occasionally the batteries were replaced; at other times they just needed to have the acid replenished. On one particular day, Dan's son, Oscar, was servicing the batteries on a beacon when his hands

A typical lighthouse beacon in the Gulf of Mexico during the first half of the 20th century.

slipped allowing the glass battery to bang into the side of the schooner and splashed acid into his eye. Thinking quickly, Oscar dove into the water to wash the acid from his face, but the damage had already been done and Oscar lost one eye. After recovery, Oscar remained a seaman.

In an accident during April 1960, before the dredging of the Pass channel, Captain Rufus Walker, Jr., was returning from a charter fishing trip when a freak wave caught his boat, *Sea Duster*. The wave swung the *Sea Duster* around so fast that Rufus was knocked into the side of the boat and thrown overboard. It was later determined that his neck had been broken when he hit the side of the boat. His death was a great loss to this close–knit community.

Captain Clarence Walker was fishing for Bluefish one day when he struck a submerged wreck. An old steel hulled barque had sunk in the area sometime before. Clarence knew it was in the vicinity, but with shifting currents, the wreck had probably shifted position. He hit the wreck and knocked a hole in his boat. Quick action by the Captain allowed him to beach the boat with no harm to the passengers.

Perdido Pass was a dangerous place even for experienced captains. Prior to the routine dredging of the Pass channel and the building of the jetties there were numerous accidents in the Pass caused by shallow water, shifting currents, and sandbars.

Boat building today

Few fishermen build their own charter boats today. There are also few boat builders in the area. The primary reasons are cost and size; these two items are closely related.

Leon W. 'Buddy' Resmondo, who by the time of publication of this book will be over 80, established Resmondo Boat Works in 1956. Buddy built his first boat, a small dory, at age eight. Buddy's sons, Ronnie and Joey, now operate the boat works.

Several of today's fiberglass charter boats operating in the waters out of Orange Beach are Resmondo boats. Resmondo Boat Works also build wooden boat up to 78 feet long. Most of their wooden boats are built of Juniper wood.

A 'glass' boat in the 60–foot class, completely outfitted, will run in the one million–dollar range, pretty much out of reach of the single operator. Today, most charter boats are purchased with financial backers or partners, a far cry from the charter fleet of the 1950's.

Roland E. Walker and Artificial Reefs

The floor of the Gulf of Mexico in the bottom fishing areas is sandy and constantly shifting with the currents. Bottom feeding fish such as Snapper and Cobia (Ling) eat small crustaceans and fish which gather where grasses and seaweed grow. These areas, such as coral reefs and shipwrecks, grow plants and other organisms that attract the small crustaceans and fish, just the type places that charter fishermen love to fish. Normal underwater currents and storms cause these underwater features to be moved or covered by the shifting sand. All the fishermen knew about fishing large wrecks and knew where most of them were. However, as the charter fleet grew, there just were not enough wrecks to accommodate all the charter boats.

According to Roland Walker, Jr., during the 1950s, Roland, Sr., Ray, and Gladwin Walker, began thinking about making artificial reefs. Their first effort was to use the 'old barge' that had been used as the first canal bridge on Highway 59 at Gulf Shores. After completion of the first concrete bridge over the canal, the old concrete barge swing bridge was towed to the head of Cotton Bayou. The barge was considered 'derelict', so they and probably Neil Lauder and Ray Callaway towed the barge from the beach and out into the Gulf. They didn't make it very far though, when rough weather made them sink it where they were and get back to shore. That was the first successful artificial reef. At that point, they didn't know if size made a difference in attracting fish.

While the group experimented with everything from old car bodies, concrete pipe, etc., Captain Roland Walker began experimenting with the construction of smaller artificial 'reefs'. His first efforts consisted of tires, steel rods, and concrete, all tied together. These small reefs worked well, but were shortly covered with sand by the currents.

These were the days before Loran, GPS, and fish finders. To be able to find the site of a new reef, Walker would take Captain Roland Walker with one of the early artificial fishing reef he designed and built. compass readings on prominent land features and check the water depth with a lead line. One of the quotes from his boat log read, '7 pines at Romar & 3 pines to the east'; rather like hieroglyphics unless you knew what it meant.

The group's efforts continued by sinking twenty or more car bodies in a single place. They were larger and stayed longer and attracted more fish. Before today's environmental consciousness, all parts of the cars that contained fluids were removed along with anything else that would create problems in the environment. Jack Helmeyer, owner of an auto salvage yard in Foley, hauled cars for the artificial reefs.

By 1953, Roland Walker, Sr. was talking with Alabama Conservation Department Director, Bill Drinkard. He had fished with Walker over one of the artificial reefs and was impressed with the results. Drinkard then assisted in promoting State assistance for the reef program. His help made possible the State subsidized sinking in the Gulf of several mothballed World War II Liberty ships (locally known as the 'Ghost Fleet') that had been anchored in the Tensaw River. Researchers estimate that each of these ships produce about 5,000 pounds of sport fish per year.

Through his efforts, Roland E. Walker, Sr., became the 'spear head' for the group and is recognized as a pioneer in artificial reef building programs. Articles about his artificial reef building efforts have been published in 'The Reader's Digest', 'Sports Afield', and 'Field and Stream' magazines, as well as many newspaper articles across the country.

Today, the artificial reef program has grown and is strongly supported by the Orange Beach Fishing Association under their 'adopt–a–reef' program.

Roland's dream boat

One morning in 1965, Roland Walker, woke up after an incredible dream. His dream was complete with all details for a charter boat. When he told his wife about the dream that morning, she pointed out a couple of facts that he already knew: Roland already had a good boat, the *Sea Son*, which was serving him well; they really could not afford a new boat. Well, nothing stands between a fisherman and his dream. His new boat was built for him in Louisiana with Roland watching the construction as often as he could. The hull was constructed of cypress for durability. After 6 months, his 'dream' was a reality and *Perdido* was born.

Captain Roland Walker's *Perdido* under construction in Louisiana.

His boat, *Sea Son,* was passed to his nephew, LeeRoy Walker, once the *Perdido* was on the water. Roland used this boat for the rest of his life, even after retiring from the charter fishing trade. Roland E. Walker, Sr. passed away in 2003, at age 87. His sons have since moved the *Perdido* from Orange Beach to its new home at Ditto Landing in Huntsville, Alabama.

Anatomy of a Charter Boat
Building of the *Dixie Maid*

Herman Callaway was charter fishing as early as 1913. There was seldom a time when he did not have a boat under construction in the yard of his home on Highway 180 near Nancy Lane. Being inventive, innovative, and boat building were a few of the many things he had learned from his father, Captain James C. Callaway.

While we do not know the name of Herman's first boat, we do know that it was a 24 footer. His second boat, *Resolute* was a 26 footer. However, when people talk about Herman Callaway, everyone seems to remember the boat he designed and built by hand, the charter fishing boat *Dixie Maid*.

Construction of the nearly 40 feet long *Dixie Maid* began with collection of cypress logs that had been washed up and buried on the beach.

The *Dixie Maid* at dock.

This constant search of the beach after storms had other benefits to the Callaway family. Earlier, the wreck of the schooner *Bluefield* was discovered on Gulf Beach near the location of the old Pass. After several days of salvage, the *Bluefield* was stripped of most usable parts and lumber. Much of that lumber went into the construction of Herman's house, that of his brother Dan, and quite possibly was used on the *Dixie Maid.* During the days of the Great Depression through the 1930's and early 40's money was difficult to come by and one learned to become very self–reliant.

When a storm would uncover two suitable logs for use on the *Dixie Maid*, Herman and his boys would take his boat around to the beach. Landing the boys on the beach, they would dig the sand from around a log, swim out to the boat, drag a line back to the beach, and tie it to the log.

The wreck of the schooner *Bluefield.*

Herman in the boat would then drag it from the beach. The boys would ride the log as Herman towed it back around to the Orange Beach Hotel on Wolf Bay. It was then towed up the road to the house. Two such logs were found for use on the *Dixie Maid*, one being 65 feet long. The logs were then hauled to Bon Secour to be sawn into the necessary lumber.

Timber not found on the beach was cut on the property of Herman's home. The keel was cut from a Yellow Cypress tree at the back of the property. Cutting this tree caused problems with the adjacent property owner, D. R. Peteet. Peteet believed the tree had been on his property and threatened to have Herman arrested. Following a new survey of the Callaway property, Peteet gave up his protest, but never admitted his error...just another day of dealing with the 'hard nosed' D. R. Peteet. Normally cypress was not used for keel construction, but Callaway determined that the known strength and resistance to rot of Yellow Cypress, it would be a good selection and, besides, it was the only tree on his property that was the right size. The stump of that tree still protrudes

Although the Callaway property has been recently sold, the stump of the Yellow Cypress used for the Keel of the *Dixie Maid* is still there.

from ground in the back corner of the old Callaway property on Highway 180.

Actual construction of *Dixie Maid* began in 1937. After the keel (12 inches by 12 inches) and keelson (8 inches by 8 inches) were laid, Herman went in search of just the right natural shaped oak tree branch crooks to use for the connection of the ribs. Finding them on his property, he cut and

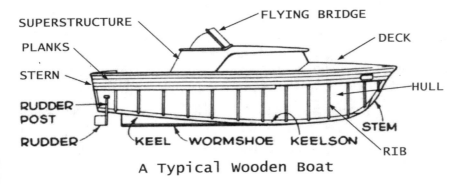

SUPERSTRUCTURE   FLYING BRIDGE
PLANKS   DECK
STERN   HULL
RUDDER
POST   STEM
RUDDER   KEEL WORMSHOE KEELSON
                                          RIB

A Typical Wooden Boat

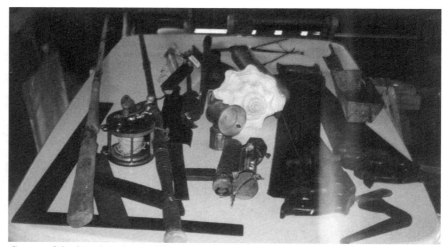

Some of the hand tools used by Herman Callaway to build the *Dixie Maid* along with some of the fishing equipment used on board.

hand–shaped them to their job. Other timber was felled and cut for hull and superstructure. Each plank was steamed and shaped by hand to fit the curve of the hull.

These were hard times even here at Orange Beach…there was not much money to buy things. It was a time to innovate with what you had on hand.

To fit out the *Dixie Maid,* Herman made, by–hand, all the brass fittings he had not already salvaged from shipwrecks. He developed a dual steering system to enable use of the wheel on deck or in the crow's nest without having to disconnect one to use the other…an innovation at the time. To provide outriggers for trolling, he purchased a radio antenna wire reel device from a deactivated military bomber and converted it into his outriggers. These were the first out–riggers used in Orange Beach and they worked very well. These outriggers can be seen today in the foyer of the Fish Camp restaurant on Highway 180 in Orange Beach… provided courtesy of Clifford Callaway. Herman Callaway developed his own deep–diving fishing lures from old metal flashlight cases. Some 'duster' lures were made with the addition of feathers ordered from Japan (to obtain the 'right' colors); later he made them from frayed rope.

Both Herman and his brother Amel made their own rods, reels, gaffs, etc.

The completed *Dixie Maid* still sat on cradle skids in his yard. In order to move her to the water, movable roller skids were placed under the boat.

A 1929 Chevrolet truck with one tire removed was used as a winch with the tow cable wrapped around the tireless rim of the right rear wheel and attached to the bow of the boat. A 'deadman' anchored the truck in front. The truck placed in gear wound the cable around the rim dragging the boat a short distance. The cable was then unwound and the process repeated many times. A slow process to be sure, but it worked. The *Dixie Maid* was drug down Nancy Lane, then east along the beach to his Brother Dan's place on Bay La Launche.

This photo from the 1950's shows Clifford Callaway and Andy Wenzel using the right rear wheel of a car to power the drilling of a water well. This was typical of the 'wheel powered' towing of the *Dixie Maid* to the water after construction at Herman Callaway's home on Highway 180.

Before launching, ballast was added along the keel using an assortment of railroad car couplings, rail and solid concrete blocks that were bolted to the keel and ribs.

The *Dixie Maid* was launched into the waters of Bay La Launche, at Dan Callaway's place; one year after construction was begun.

A solid brass rudder was added as a finishing touch to the *Dixie Maid*, possibly salvaged from a shipwreck on the beach. The boat's running lights were fueled by carbide (a common item used at the time...when a minute amount of water was added to the solid carbide, produced a gas that burned brightly, producing light). Herman used a headlight from a 1919 Cadillac as a fuel funnel and an old felt hat was stuffed inside it as a filter. That old headlight is in the personal collection of Herman's son, Nolan.

The sweep oar later used on the *Dixie Maid* had washed up on Gulf Beach and was eventually identified as from the sinking of the passenger ship *Robert E. Lee* off the coast of Louisiana during WWII. In recent research, it has been determined that the German submarine *U–166* had sunk the *Robert E. Lee* by torpedo. U–166 was sunk shortly thereafter from depth charge attack by the U. S. warship *PC–566*. The appearance of the sweep oar in the Orange Beach area is interesting, because the general Gulf currents move east to west, not west to east. The sweep oar is in the private collection of Clifford Callaway.

Herman leased docking facilities on Terry Cove from John Foley. He walked from his house to Terry Cove, stopping at Tillie Smith's Store to buy gasoline for his boat.

Retired lighthouse keeper Chester Williams, Herman's Father–in–law, introduced Herman to his friend Captain Green of Pensacola. Captain Green told Herman about the Dutch Bank, a small but ideal spot for bottom fishing, and how to locate it. The 'Bank' was only about 40 to 500 feet square and was located by its clay and gravel bottom with the use of a special 'sounder' designed and used by Herman. The 'sounder' was a hollowed out window sash weight tied to the end of a rope with the hollowed out center stuffed with Octagon soap. Octagon soap did not quickly dissolve and when the 'sounder' was lowered over the side of the boat and bounced on the bottom, the gravel, shells, and blue clay of the bank would stick in the soap.

After locating the 'Bank', Herman would mark the site with a weighted line and a floating gallon jug, but it seldom survived until his next trip, so the 'sounder' was regularly used.

This is the 'sounder' that was used by Herman Callaway to locate the Dutch Bank. The fishing spot that began charter boat 'bottom fishing'.

For an extended time no one went to the Dutch Bank except Herman and his son, Lloyd. Sometime later, they were joined by another son, Amel. The other charter captains ridiculed them until they realized that catching fish on every trip made for happy fishermen. According to Clifford Callaway, one evening, Roy Walker came to the porch of the Callaway home and asked, 'Mr. Herman can I follow you to the Dutch Bank tomorrow?' That was the beginning of year round fishing Industry in Orange Beach.

The *Dixie Maid* carried many fishermen on successful trips to the Gulf and to the Dutch Bank establishing the beginning of Red Snapper fishing by the Orange Beach fishing fleet. Prior to that time most charter fishing was done by trolling, as bottom fishing was considered 'trash' fishing. However, no boat lasts forever and *Dixie Maid* was no exception. She saw many years of hard productive work in the Gulf, but eventually she was no longer repairable. All usable parts were stripped, including her 90 HP Gray Marine gasoline engine. Many parts of his father's treasured boat are still lovingly cared for by his son, Clifford.

Captain Herman Callaway ultimately sold *Dixie Maid* to Foster Childress, and James Huff for $100 (the dry dock fee). The boat was to be sunk in the Gulf to form a new fishing reef. This was a fitting end to a charter fishing boat that had given such gallant service.

The actual deliberate sinking of the hulk of *Dixie Maid* is a whole other story. It seems that neither Foster nor James had any idea of the heavy railroad couplings or concrete blocks bolted to the keel and ribs for ballast in the *Dixie Maid*. Since the engine had been removed, they thought they needed to add more weight to help her sink. To the ballast already there, they added old washing machines, chunks of concrete, and even an old Corvair car body.

Buddy Moore and his friend Harry Brown rode on the *Dixie Maid* as the *Dark Thirty,* operated by Foster Childress, towed her to the location of her final resting–place. She was towed in the middle of the night to avoid anyone knowing the location of their soon to be new fishing reef. Buddy and Harry had a pump on board with them to keep the water level under control until ready for the sinking. So much for that idea!

The crew thought that the sinking would take several hours, but such was not the case. When they arrived at their chosen place south of Fort Morgan with eighty feet of water below them, the sea cocks were opened. *Dixie Maid* went down like a rock. Buddy and Harry were lucky to get off with the pump, before she went down. It was a scramble to cut the towrope tied to *Dark Thirty* in time to keep her from being pulled down by the rapidly sinking *Dixie Maid*. Arriving back at the dock much earlier than expected, they all told wild stories of their close call with disaster.

Boat and Fishing Photo Section

Above is the schooner *J S Murrow* of Captain James C. Callaway. Captain Callaway purchased the *J. S. Murrow* for freight hauling shortly after his arrival in Orange Beach, about 1875. After many years of service, the *Murrow* grounded in Wolf Bay during a storm and was severely damaged. She was salvaged and burned.

A view of the boat basin area on Bay La Launche, circa 1913. The schooner on left is the *Ellen C*, on the right *J .S. Murrow*. These ships were the primary means of shipping and receiving goods in the Orange Beach area and were owned and operated by Captain James C. Callaway.

Above is the schooner *Ellen C* of Captain James C. Callaway. The schooner was hand built in the shipyard at Sapling Point by Captain Callaway and his sons. The *Ellen C* spent most of its career in the lighthouse service, but also hauled freight throughout the Gulf of Mexico. After Callaway's death in 1917, the ship was sold into Mexico and was lost to history.

This 1895 photograph was taken on the deck of the schooner *Ellen C*. Note the large barrels of naval stores (Pine tree sap) and lumber on the deck. Between lighthouse service and freight hauling, Captain Callaway and his sons were kept quite busy.

The docks at Millview, Florida, on the east shore of Perdido Bay, not only shipped lumber from its many saw mills, they also were the pickup point for the U. S. Mail distribution into the area by contract mail boats. Photo from early 1900's.

Previous publications of this photograph stated this location as Orange Beach, but the authors believe the location to be Millview, Florida. This was one of the piers where the *J. S. Murrow* (shown here) loaded lumber from Millview's many saw mills for local use and export. Photo from 1917.

This photograph shows one of the early contract U. S. Mail boats (on the right). This particular boat is believed to be the mail boat of Captain B. T. Hudson, who had the mail contract before the Walker's. This photograph was taken on Wolf Bay about 1910.

This is the *Mexiwana* freight boat and may have been a contract mail boat. The *Mexiwana* was built by Leon McPherson of Josephine. McPherson bought Admiral Raphael Semmes home in Josephine after the Admiral moved to Mobile. McPherson converted the home into the Hotel Mexiwana, which he operated for several years. The boat was named after the hotel and probably based out of Semmes Bayou (now Robert's Bayou).

For many years, Captain Rufus Walker, Sr. and his family lived in Miflin at the head of Wolf Bay while he operated the U. S. Mail contract. His mail boat, the *Red Bird,* is shown here as it leaves the Josephine community, carrying mail, freight, passengers, and fresh baked bread to its next destination.

This photograph shows Captain Rufus Walker, Sr. (man in the center) at the Lillian Post Office during one of his many daily stops in the area. The other gentlemen are unidentified.

The *Edna* (U.S. Mail boat of Captain Rufus Walker, Sr.) shown at the head of Miflin Bay near where he and his family lived while he operated the mail service in the area.

This boat is an unidentified freight and passenger boat, possibly one of the early 'mail boats'. Boats of this type carried passengers and freight to the communities in the Perdido Bay area. This photograph, taken about 1918, shows a group of passengers ready to board at one of those 'in between' stops. The pole in the sand may have been a means to 'flag down' the boat.

At right is Captain James C. Callaway's schooner *Ellen C* at a sea beacon for routine maintenance. It was on a day such as this that Oscar Callaway, son of Captain Dan Callaway, lost his left eye in an accident.

As Oscar was removing one of the glass cased batteries to replenish the acid, it slipped from his hands, splashing acid in his eye. He immediately dove into the water to wash off the acid, but the damage was already done.

Oscar Callaway is shown in the photo on the left in October 1969, years after the accident.

179

During the early years of charter fishing in Orange Beach, some specially designed boats were built for bay and inland water fishing. The *Bertha Low* was a charter Tarpon boat. The fishermen shown here are holding a Crevalle, another specie taken in bay waters.

Gill netting has always been popular in the bays around Orange Beach. Several fish species run seasonally into bay waters with Mullet being the most popular. In the photo above, one of Rufus Walker, Sr.'s boys is standing on a dock watching the gill net boats getting ready for some fishing.

Above is Captain Herman Callaway's first charter boat. The boat was un–named and built by Captain Herman for bay and inshore fishing which was typical of the charter fishing done before the 1920's. Most charter fishing during that period was sport fishing for Tarpon and Bull Dolphin. When not charter fishing these boats were used for commercial and sustenance fishing.

Below is a photo from about 1956, showing the charter boats *Thelma Ann* of Captain Bob Walker, Sr. (on left) and the *Gloria June* of Captain Raymond Walker, as they start into Perdido Pass on their way to the Gulf of Mexico for a days fishing.

Captain Roy Walker (on right) with an unidentified fisherman showing a Tarpon taken on rod and reel. The photo was taken at Bear Point Marina in 1934.

The 1913 photo above was taken at Gulf View Park at Caswell. Hazel & Clarence Walker, Gulf View owners, are shown with Ted Joy (at right) who is credited with the first Tarpon taken on rod and reel in the Orange Beach area.

Following storms during the 19th and early 20th century it was common practice for seamen to search the beaches for ship wrecks. Herman Callaway is shown on the wreck of the schooner *Bluefield* that had washed up on Gulf Beach about 1921. Timber, fittings,and other items were salvaged from the *Bluefield.* These items saw many uses. Parts of the *Bluefield* were used in the construction of both Herman and Dan Callaway's homes, the Orange Beach Hotel, and in the construction of the charter boat *Dixie Maid.*

This is a view of the *Bluefield* as seen by the Callaway's prior to her salvage.

183

Above are two fishermen from the early 1900's with a fine catch of King and Spanish Mackerel.

Below is a photo of Captain Clate James of the *Condo Money*. He caught this nice swordfish while fishing with a friend aboard the *Sea Reaper* in 2003.

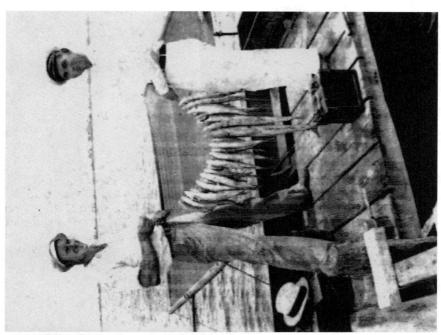

Above is a photo of Captain Rabun Walker, on boat, with an unidentified fisherman with his catch. Photo date unknown.

At right is Captain Rufus Walker, Jr. on the dock with and unidentified charter fisherman and a nice string of fish. Photo probably from the 1930s.

Above is Captain Roy Walker (on left) shown with two unidentified fishermen with their nice catch. Photo believed from the late 1940's.

The *Emma W,* charter boat of Captain Rabun Walker, is shown running on bay waters. The *Emma W* was originally owned by Captain Bob Walker, Sr. but, was sold to his older brother Captain Rabun.

Above is Captain Roy Walker's first charter boat, the *Buccaneer.* Captain Walker purchased the boat in New Orleans, Louisiana. in 1927.

The 38' charter boat *Elvira* was owned and operated by Captain Rabun Walker. This photograph, showing a fishing party on board, was taken in 1960.

These are members of the 1957 National Champion Auburn football team. Left to right: Bobby Lauder (son of Neil & Brownie Lauder), Jim Jefferies, Tommy Larino, and Jim Burson. From the photo, it looks like they had a great day of charter fishing aboard the *Duchess* of Captain Neil Lauder!

A group of Alabama County Agents brought by Ted Childress to Orange Beach for some Cobia (Ling) fishing in the late 1930's. Ted Childress (a County Agent in Conecuh County at the time) is pictured second from left. Ted Childress made many trips to Orange Beach during the 1930's and 40's to bring his 4H boys and other County Agents for a chance to fish in the waters of the Gulf of Mexico.

Now this is a catch! Captain Rabun Walker, on left, caught this beauty while snapper fishing with his brother Captain Roland Walker Sr. That is a 500 pound Warsaw Grouper. Caught in 1983.

The year of this photo was 1937. Showing off their catch for the camera are two unidentified fishermen . The young boy in the middle is Clifford Callaway, son of Captain Herman Callaway. Clifford was paid 50 cents a day to be Mate on his father's charter boat, the *Irma*.

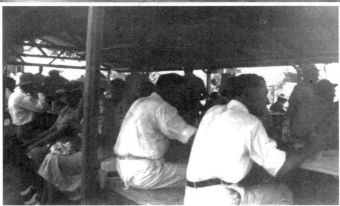

These three photographs are believed to be from the first Orange Beach Deep–Sea Fishing Rodeo held in July of 1938. The Rodeo was held on the east end of Terry Cove near where the Gulf Gate Lodge would be built.

Shown docked at Walker Marina are the *Sea Duster* (in foreground) of Captain Rufus Walker, Jr. and the *Emma W* (bow on) of Captain Bob Walker, Sr. April 1940.

On the left of the dock is the *Sea Duster*, which built in 1935 at Captain Rufus Walker, Jr's place in Orange Beach. On the right is the *Emma W,* Captain Bob Walker, Sr. (later sold to Rabun Walker). On display is a fine catch of Red Fish. Photograph believed taken in the 1940's.

At right is a 1945 photograph of Ella and Ray Callaway standing on the dock beside their charter boat *Elray.* A successful day of fishing on the Dutch Bank yielded 150 pounds of snapper.

Carlman Wilburn is shown standing on the dock in the background.

Above is the *Elray,* purchased in New Orleans, Louisiana, by Ray and Ella Callaway and Captained by Ray Callaway early in his career. This was Ray's first charter boat.

The 1946 photograph above shows Lauder Landing at the head of Cotton Bayou. Captain Neil Lauder owned and operated the Landing. His charter boat *Duchess* is seen at the dock. The long dark shape on the left is a World War II LST.

The photo below of Lauder Landing was taken in 1963. The number of boats at dock is a testament to the popularity of the Landing. Lauder Landing was one of the few early marinas in Orange Beach and the first one on Cotton Bayou.

"SEA-SON"
DEEP SEA TROLLING
ALL TACKLE FURNISHED
PARTIES OF SIX
ROLAND E. WALKER
ORANGE BEACH, ALA.

Deep Sea Fishing
ALL TACKLE FURNISHED
- PARTIES OF SIX -
AMEL CALLAWAY
ORANGE BEACH, ALABAMA
CONTACT BY WESTERN UNION

"REX"
DEEP SEA FISHING
- SIX PERSON PARTIES -
Tackle Furnished
OSCAR CALLAWAY
ORANGE BEACH, ALABAMA
CONTACT BY WESTERN UNION

Deep Sea Party Fishing
MAXIMUM SIX PERSONS
Tackle Furnished
RUFUS E. WALKER, JR.
Orange Beach, Ala. - Contact Western Union

Deep Sea Trolling
(6 PERSON PARTY)
ALL TACKLE FURNISHED
N. A. LAUDER
AT LAUDER'S LANDING
Orange Beach, Ala. - Contact Western Union

"EDNA W. OF CASWELL"
DEEP SEA and BAY FISHING
TACKLE FURNISHED
- PARTIES OF SIX PERSONS -
CROCKETT S. WHITE
ORANGE BEACH, ALABAMA
CONTACT BY WESTERN UNION

Above are typical advertisements for the charter boats of Orange Beach in 1949. Note that all ads specify contact by Western Union as telephones were not in operation in Orange Beach at the time. The reservations that came in from fishermen around the country by telegraph arrived in Foley and were hand delivered to the Captains in Orange Beach. Reservations today are received by mail, fax, telephone, Email, and internet web sites.

During the 1950's, the Orange Beach Fishing Association began experimentation in the building of artificial reefs to provide habitats for Gulf bottom fish such as snapper. Captain Roland Walker, Sr. was the spearhead for the program. The above photograph is a barge load of old car bodies destined for the Gulf to create artificial reefs as part of that program. The program grew to include concrete pipe as shown in the photograph below. Due to the effort of Captain Walker and others of the fishing association, the government ultimately released many decommissioned World War II Liberty ships for the creation of large reefs. Today, the reef program is promoted as the 'Adopt–a–Reef Program' and has been very successful in enhancing fishing resources in the Gulf of Mexico.

Above is the charter boat *Dolphin* of Captain Ray Callaway. The *Dolphin* was Captain Callaway's 2nd boat. He later sold it to Crockett White, Sr. Those were the days when there were so few boats on the water that you could troll on Cotton Bayou .

This is the charter boat *Lady Lake* of Captain Dan Callaway. The *Lady Lake* came apart at the bow and sank in rough weather in the Gulf with eleven passengers and crew on board. All were saved in a lifeboat. The *Lady Lake* was raised and towed back to Orange Beach, but was not repairable.

Above is the charter boat *Miss Kay,* the 38' charter boat of Captain Roy Walker. *Miss Kay* is shown in dry dock at Walker Marina. In many newspaper articles, *Miss Kay* was always referred to as Captain Roy's 'work horse'. She was built right here in Bay St. John on Walker Cay by Joe Pierce. She proudly carries a brass plaque for her three years service in the Coast Guard during WWII.

This is the *Gloria June,* Captain Ray Walker's first charter boat. The *Gloria June* was built in Bayou La Batre, Alabama. Charles Walker purchased the *Gloria June,* when Captain Ray bought the charter boat B*lue Chip*.

This portrait of Jerry Walker, son of Captain Roy Walker, was taken at Walker Marina in 1952, Jerry was 14 at the time. He literally grew up in and around the charter fishing industry in Orange Beach. Jerry has restored several of the early wooden charter boats.

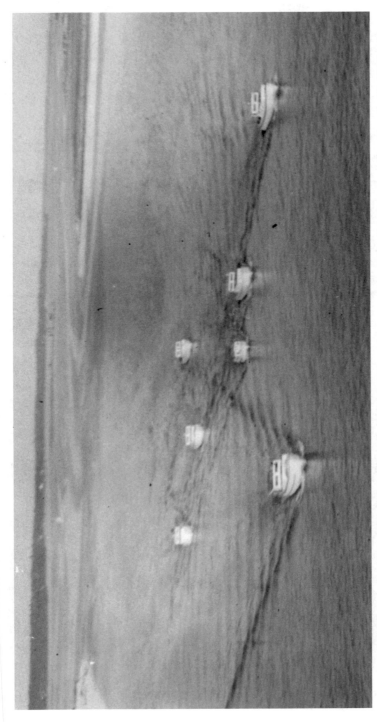

This is part of the Orange Beach charter fleet on a morning in 1952, as it moves through Perdido Pass, out–bound to the Gulf. The three boats in the background, left to right are *Miss Kay*, Captain Roy Walker; *Duchess*, Captain Neil Lauder; and *Gloria June*, Captain Ray Walker. The two boats in the center are *Emma W*, Captain Rabun Walker (boat bought from Bob Walker), and *Mildred C*, Captain Amel Callaway. The two boats in the foreground are *Sea Son*, Captain Roland Walker, Sr., and *Thelma Ann*, Captain Bob Walker, Sr.

199

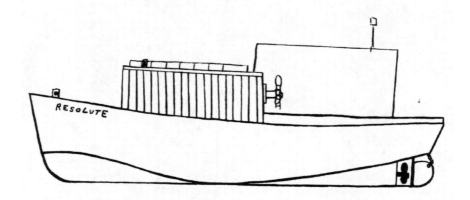

This sketch of the *Resolute* was drawn from memory by Nolan Callaway (son of Captain Herman Callaway) and was confirmed by his brother Clifford as correct. The *Resolute* was built by Captain Herman and was his second boat. She was named for a famous sailing schooner. At 26 feet, she was powered by a 4 cylinder Chevrolet engine. The steering wheel was later used on the charter boat *Dixie Maid.*

The charter boat *Dolphin* was Captain Ray Callaway's second charter boat. He began fishing with her April 1, 1953. Captain Ray later sold the *Dolphin* to Captain Crockett White, Sr., son–in–law of Captain Rufus Walker, Sr.

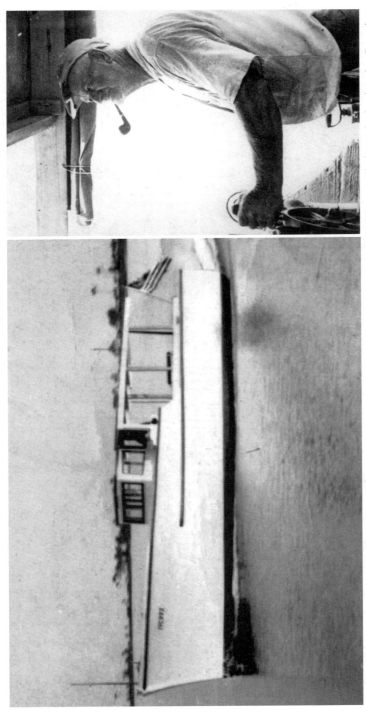

At right is Captain Herman Callaway at the wheel of the *Dixie Maid*. The *Dixie Maid*, at left, was built from the keel up by Captain Herman in the yard of his home on Highway 180 in 1938. Even the Yellow Cypress keel itself was cut on his property. The *Dixie Maid* took a year to build. This was Captain Herman's third charter boat and he knew what he wanted. Those items not salvaged from ship wrecks on the beach were made by hand. After his passing in 1974, she was salvaged and sunk as an artificial fishing reef...a fitting end for all her many years of gallant service.

Above is the *Dixie Maid,* the hand–built charter boat of Captain Herman Callaway, in dry dock. Built in 1938, the 40 foot *Dixie Maid* carried many folks to the Dutch Bank for a day of great fishing.

Below the *Dixie Maid* is shown at its dock on Terry Cove awaiting another group of fishermen. Photo taken circa 1940.

Left: Captain Herman Callaway pictured as a young man. Like his father before him, Herman was a man of many talents. He never bought anything that he could build.

Upper right is pictured the 'sounder' made and used by Herman Callaway to locate the famous Dutch Bank, one of the best of the early bottom fishing spots. The sounder had a hollowed out end which was loaded with Octagon brand soap. When the sounder hit bottom, the soap collected gravel and shells, indicating that you were over the Bank. Octagon soap was used due to its slow dissolving time.

At lower right: Clifford Callaway (son of Herman) at the old Callaway place on the Canal Road near Nancy Lane, is shown with the first outrigger that was used in Orange Beach, designed and built by his father. Made from parts of a military bomber, the outrigger was used on the charter fishing boat *Dixie Maid*, which was designed, hand–built and operated by Herman Callaway.

Above: Captain Herman Callaway (2nd from right) with a group of charter clients beside the *Dixie Maid* (on the right).

Below: A great days catch is displayed on the stern of the *Dixie Maid*. Captain Herman Callaway, with his distinctive pipe, looks on as his party shows off their catch. The large Jew Fish (Goliath Grouper) are now prohibited species.

At left is Captain Amel Callaway in the cockpit of his early charter boat, the *Red Wing*. The man behind Captain Callaway is unidentified, but that's a nice string of fish hanging from the canopy support. At right is a rare photograph of the *Red Wing* while running to the Gulf of Mexico for some charter fishing.

Above is a photo of charter and private boats in Cotton Bayou for protection from a storm. The protected areas of Cotton Bayou and Wolf Bay have and are still used to this day for protection of boats from hurricanes and tropical storms. Photo taken 1956.

This photo taken in February 2002 is in the area of Portage Creek on the Intracoastal Waterway where the first floating bridge was located. At the time, this bridge was the only road way in and out of Orange Beach. Prior to the opening of the Intracoastal Waterway, this area was also used by area boats for protection from storms.

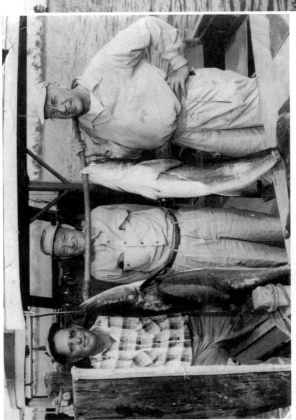

In the photo above from April 24, 1955, are Captain Roland Walker, Sr., on the left, on board *Sea Son* with fisherman, Urban Hughes, center, a biologist of Laurel, Mississippi, and Greer Williams, a writer for the *Saturday Evening Post* magazine from Chicago, showing off their catch. Many notable folks have and still do fish with the charter fleet of Orange Beach.

At right in this photo from April 1962, is Captain Ray Walker (standing) with several unidentified fishermen sorting their catch .

Above left: Earl Callaway, on the left, when he was Captain of the charter boat *Dottie Jo*. Earl is the son of Captain Ray Callaway. On the right, holding the fish, is Joey Garris. Earl was the only Callaway that held a Captain's license by the 1980's.
On the right: Earl Callaway, Ronnie Callaway (son of Ray and Ella Callaway), and Nancy Bagley as young children on the dock of Lauder Landing in 1954.

The charter boat *Sun Circle* (above and below) operated out of Sun Circle Resort located on St. John Bay. Tom Clark was Captain of this 40' charter fishing boat.

Captain Bob Walker, Sr. and his son, Captain Bobby, are shown onboard the *Thelma Ann* in 1963. This photograph was taken just a few months before Captain Bob died during a fishing trip.

Above is the charter boat *Thelma Ann* with Captain Bob Walker, Sr. at the helm. The *Thelma Ann* was built in Orange Beach by Jim Hudson and was inherited by Captain Bobby in 1963. The *Thelma Ann* was ultimately sold to Captain Bob's nephew, Jerry Walker, and has been lovingly restored. The *Thelma Ann* is one of the few early wooden charter boats to survive.

STAUTER BUILT BOATS

15-FOOT MOLDED PLYWOOD

Hull 3/16-inch thick, 54 inches wide and 28 inches deep. Bottom reinforced with oak keel. Motor suggested—10 H.P. to 33 H.P. Approximate weight 250 pounds.

SPEEDS. - Will make approximately 22 MPH with 10 HP motor, approximately 35 MPH with 22 HP motor and approximately 40 MPH with 33 HP motor.

14-FOOT SEMI-V-BOTTOM

3/16-inch thick, 3-ply, cypress bottom 3/4-inch thick. 50 inches wide with 18-inch sides. Motor suggested—5 H.P. to 16 H.P. Approximate weight 175 pounds.

SPEEDS. - Will make approximately 12 MPH with 5 HP motor, approximately 25 MPH with 10 HP motor and approximately 30 MPH with 16 HP motor.

Specifications

ALL BOATS.- These coats of marine paint outside, three coats of marine varnish inside, color sides, white bottom, green spar sail, black varnish inside and trim or green inside and varnish trim. Choice of other color combinations if desired. All fixtures brass or galvanized.

CHOICE - 6 Models to choose from priced from $97.00 up. Write for particulars.

STAUTER BOAT WORKS
—Located on Bay Bridge Causeway—
P. O. Box 575   Mobile 4, Alabama

Not all boats in Orange Beach are charter boats. Above, author Margaret Childress in her Stauter Built boat is shown towing Thurston Lauder on Cotton Bayou in 1964, the year she wrote the first short history of Orange Beach. This boat has been totally restored and is still in use. At left is a Stauter Built ad from 1949.

The photo above is of Captain Roland Walker's *Sea Son*, taken during the 1960's at his boat slip. Notice the typical docking conditions of the time, a far cry from the sophisticated convenience and safety of today's facilities.

Above is pictured the *Sea Rebel,* originally built for Captain Gladwin Walker by Jim Hudson. *Sea Rebel* was purchased by Captain Roland Walker, Sr. in 1960 and was captained by Billy and Roland, Jr. during 1960 and 1961. The *Sea Rebel* is one of the few remaining early wooden charter boats. The current owner is not known. Photo taken 2004.

This photograph shows the charter boat *Sea Son* in dry dock at Roy Walker Marina. *Sea Son* was built in Orange Beach by Jim Hudson in 1947. At the time of this photo, this was the primary charter boat of Captain Roland Walker, Sr. *Sea Son* was later sold to LeeRoy 'Lee' Walker.

This photograph shows the *Sea Son* of Captain Roland Walker, Sr. A family friend, Ann Clark of Point Clear, is shown with Captain Walker's children, Mary Nell and Roland, Jr., as they display a nice catch of fish, after returning from a fishing trip to Captain Walker's slip about 1953. Notice that there were not a lot of docking amenities in those days.

This photo taken at the ice house in Foley on December 21, 1956, shows a catch of 1800 pounds of snapper brought in by Captain Roland Walker, Sr. (on the left) of the *Sea Son.* Notice the pickup truck bed used as a trailer.

Above is Roland Walker, Jr. (seated in foreground) with a group of unidentified fishermen with a catch of Ling (Cobia) from charter fishing on Captain Roland Walker, Sr.'s *Sea Son.* This photo was taken April 10, 1949.

Above left is Captain Rufus Walker Jr. with his foot on the *Sea Duster* while talking to a group of men getting ready for a charter fishing trip. Captain Walker lost his life in an accident in Perdido Pass on April 26, 1961. A 'rogue wave' caught the boat slamming Captain Walker into the side of the cockpit breaking his neck and throwing him over–board. His death was a major shock to the community.

In the photo on the right is Captain Bob Walker, Sr. (on the right) with charter fisherman, Dudley L. Poe, Jr., and his catch. The photo was taken May 13, 1961.

Above are two photos of the charter boat *Blue Chip*, Captained by Ray Walker and later Charles Walker. The 40' *Blue Chip* has been fully restored by Jerry Walker.

In the early photo at right is Roy Walker on the dock with a good fish caught on rod & reel.

Below is a photo from the 1960's of Captain Roy Walker and his wife Eva Dietz Walker relaxing at their 'Walker Marina' on Terry Cove.

Captain Roland Walker, Sr. shown at the helm of his dream charter boat *Perdido*. The *Perdido*, (at right) was built in 1965 by Emmele DuPhrene in LaFitte, Louisiana. She served him well through many years of charter fishing and a few years of personal fishing after he retired. Captain Walker died in 2003, and the *Perdido* is now cared for by family in Huntsville, Alabama.

At left, Captain Roland Walker, Sr. is shown with his charter boat *Perdido* while under construction in Louisiana. At right is the *Perdido* nearing completion. The *Perdido* was built over several months during 1965 and was custom built to his exacting specifications with a length of 43 feet, a beam of 14 feet, and a draft of 4 feet.

Above is a photo from November 12, 1969, of Captain Rabun Walker with a 391 pound Warsaw Grouper caught while on his charter boat *Elvira.*

At right is a photo of the Roland Walker Family coming to dockside to see the catch of their friend, Joe Swinburn (in foreground). Joe fished with Captain Roland Walker Sr. on the *Sea Son* several times a year and became a close friend of the Family. The man behind Joe is Captain Roland Walker, Sr., then William Walker. Captain Walker's wife, Mary, is standing on the dock, the skirt of daughter, Mary Nell Walker, on top of the boat, others are unidentified. Date unknown.

The photo above of Captain Rabun Walker shows a nice catch from a fishing trip in 1958.

At left is Captain Earl Callaway with a large shark taken during the Orange Beach Fishing Rodeo in 1973.

The 38 foot charter boat *Elvira* is shown above at dockside in this 1977 photo. The *Elvira* was the second boat of Captain Rabun Walker.

Below is a family fishing scene aboard the charter boat *Perdido*. In the background is Captain Roland Walker, Sr., while his daughter Mary Nell Walker Hough is shown fishing for snapper.

The 1979 photo at left shows charter Captain Rabun Walker and an unidentified man, in coveralls, on the *Elvira* while at the dock at Walker Marina.

At right is a 1977 photo of Captain Rabun's daughter, Eva Marie Walker Springsteen, cutting bait while acting as first mate on her father's charter boat.

Above is the 40' charter boat *Rip Tide*, captained by Ray Callaway. This was Ray Callaway's third and last boat before he retired from charter fishing. That is Captain Ray standing on the bow with several fishermen in the background diligently fishing for delicious snapper.

In the photo below, the *Rip Tide* is shown coming into port. Note the Perdido Pass Bridge in the background.

Above is the 30' charter boat *On the Crosstie* of Captain Iris Etheridge. Captain Etheridge was the first woman captain in the Orange Beach charter fleet. For a decade, her First Mate was her husband Bill. Captain Etheridge also served on the Orange Beach City Council.

Alemite was built in 1946 and was operated by Captain Oscar Fell. Captain Fell had made a good living selling Alemite automotive products and thought it was a good name for his boat. Oscar Fell passed away in 2003. *Alemite* is currently owned and maintained by Jerry Walker.

Above is a nice display of an unidentified charter fisherman's catch at Captain Bobby Walker's 'Summer Breeze Charters' landing. Photo from 2004.

The photo above, from the 1950s, shows the dock at the Walker Marina on Terry Cove. The lady is Captain Ray Walker's wife, Mary Gene.

Above is the 55 foot, Resmondo built, charter boat *Summer Breeze I*. Originally captained by Bobby Walker, Jr., *Summer Breeze I* is now operated by Captain Sonny Alawine.

Above is the *Mildred C,* charter boat of Captain Amel Callaway headed out to the fishing grounds. This was the first boat built by Captain Amel. Photo from 1956.

Captain Bobby Walker, son of Captain Bob Walker, Sr., on the *Summer Breeze II* tied up along side the *Sea Rebel*. The *Summer Breeze II* is a 60' Resmondo built charter boat. Captain Bobby started his charter fishing career as a young man with the *Bobbi M*, a 38' boat, then, on the death of his father, he inherited the *Thelma Ann*. The *Summer Breeze I,* a 55' Resmondo built, was his first fiberglass charter boat.

Captain Bobby Walker is shown as the winning boat Captain in the Isle of Capri fishing tournament in 2001 out of Biloxi Mississippi., as his wife Bobbi (with the cup) gives congratulations.

Above is the 31 foot Sportfisherman, *Doug–Out* of Captain Bill Douglas. The *Doug–Out* is typical of many cruiser style charter boats currently in the Orange Beach charter fleet.

Above is (left to right) Clifford Callaway (son of Captain Herman Callaway), Tony Szczuka, Henry, Will, and Bill Littleton, and Jessie Lowery with their catch of 300 pounds of snapper caught while aboard the *Hot Spot* with Captain Nick Leiterman in 2003.

Above is a view south across the head of Cotton Bayou. The Charter boat cruising to its home port on the Bayou is the *Dark Thirty*. The *Dark Thirty* was originally owned by Foster Childress, brother of the author, but is now owned and operated by Captain Brooks and Captain Wesley Moore, the authors two sons.

Below is the *Dark Thirty* at its dock in Cotton Bayou. Captain Brooks also operates *Dolphin America*, a tour boat for Dolphin watching.

Author, Margaret Childress Long, is shown here with a nice catch at her home on Cotton Bayou. Margaret has been fishing the waters of Orange Beach since childhood. This photo taken in 1997.

Captain Wesley and Captain Brooks Moore are proudly showing a Ling (Cobia) they caught. The brother's boat, *Dark Thirty,* is docked at right. Photo on Cotton Bayou 2001.

Fishing is a rewarding experience. Above is Orange Beach resident, Jim Brown, who is shown with a check for $26,685 for catching the winning fish in his category while aboard the *Miss Celeste* of Captain Fitz Fitzsimmons during a fishing tournament in 2004.

Below is a photo from the early 1930's, before the big fishing tournaments, when fishermen could only enjoy the experience of fishing in the Gulf, showing–off their catch, and having a few great meals later.

From the very early days of Orange Beach the bays, inland waterways, and the Gulf of Mexico have beckoned pleasure boating. The sail boat above was one owned by the Walker family. The *Pursuit* outboard run–a–bout below is owned by Buddy Long (the author's husband) and stays tied to their pier on Cotton Bayou, always ready for a few hours touring on the water or for some serious fishing.

The portrait at left is of Gail Walker Graham, daughter of charter Captain Rabun Walker and manager of the Orange Beach Indian and Sea Museum. Having grown up in the Orange Beach fishing industry, Gail has a wealth of knowledge that she willingly shares with museum visitors. Gail was born Hilda Gail Walker, but changed her name when she married Captain Rickey Graham. The photo was taken in the museum in 2005.

At right is a photo of Rickey's fishing boat *Hilda G* as it sits on the ways for repair. Not all boats in the Orange Beach fleet are charter boats; some are commercial fishers. Rickey's *Hilda G* is a long–line boat that he 'single–hands' in the Gulf. Captain Rickey is shown on the right. The man on his left is his father, Captain Bill Graham

The photo above was taken after Hurricane Frederic in September 1979. It's hard to believe that this was the Callaway Marina of the photo below taken just a few years before. The damage of Hurricane Frederic was extensive, but the Orange Beach charter fishing industry came back bigger and better than ever.

Above is a photo of the Callaway Marina operated by Captain Ray Callaway and his wife Ella. The Callaway Marina was a busy place on Terry Cove. Photo taken in the early 1970's.

The Trent Marina (shown above) originally owned by Captain Walter Trent, was one of the early large marinas on Terry Cove. This photo was taken in September 2002. After many years of operation, Trent Marina was sold in 2004.

Charter captain and boat builder Jim Hudson, built his Hudson Marina on Terry Cove. Due to his handiwork and good service, Hudson Marina steadily grew to meet the ever expanding need. Notice the *American Star,* it is one of the many charter 'party' boats in Orange Beach.

Above is shown Zeke's Marina located on the south shore of Cotton Bayou. Zeke's was a popular marina for berthing charter boats, but in 2004, the marina was sold for private use. Zeke's Landing and Marina are named for Carl 'Zeke' Martin, one of the founders of Romar Beach. Photo from 2004.

Below is Sportsman Marina on the north shore of Cotton Bayou. Photo from 2004.

Above is 'SanRoc Cay Marina' on Cotton Bayou. The name was derived from the sand and gravel business of the owner, Robin Wade. Photo from 2004.

This Spring 2004 photo shows another of the marinas servicing all the boats in the area, 'Sun Harbor' located on Cotton Bayou, also offers dry storage. This is one of the older marinas, originally named 'Safe Harbor' marina. Sun Harbor Marina was destroyed by Hurricane Ivan in September 2004 and will not be rebuilt.

Pictured above is Ronnie Resmondo at the Resmondo Boat Works near Perdido Beach. Ronnie and his brother Joey operate the works. Their father, Leon 'Buddy' Resmondo now retired at 80, started the Boat Works in 1956.

Above is a view of the Resmondo Boat Works from the water taken in June 2004. The Resmondo Boat Works produces wood and fiber glass boats from small skiffs to 78 foot charter boats.

Where is Perdido Pass?

From at least 1830, the only pass from Perdido Bay to the Gulf of Mexico was south of Ono Island. Ono Island was not originally an island. It was Point Ornocor, a peninsula extending from what is now Alabama Point, that is until the 1906 Hurricane. In order to reach the Gulf of Mexico from Perdido Bay, fishermen were required to pass round the east end of the Point Ornocor (Ono Island) into Old River, then into the Gulf about the location of the present day Flora–Bama. This old pass was treacherous with a very narrow and constantly shifting channel.

When the *Ellen C* went to sea, she could only go through the pass on an out going tide and even then sometimes rowboats were used to guide her. The *J.S. Murrow* was in this pass when she was hit by a waterspout and laid on her side. Amel Callaway's wife, Mildred, was on board at the time and was injured.

Since the sea and fishing have always been of primary interest here, this circuitous route to the Gulf was wasted time away from fishing, freight delivery, or travel. So, early in 1906, Herman Callaway, probably his sons, and undoubtedly some of the Walker's (actual identities are lost to history) dug a shallow ditch by hand across the dunes to the Gulf at the current location of Perdido Pass. With the cut started, the hurricane of September 27, 1906, finished the job when its tidal surge blew open the channel. Thus was born, at the hands of man and nature, the Perdido Pass to the Gulf in the location we know it today. Over time, the course of Old River changed and the old pass was silted in. This new quick access to the Gulf was a real boom to the charter fishing business and boating in general.

To keep the new pass channel clear during the early days, Ed Frederick was paid by the Federal government to 'blow out' the channel. Frederick owned a powerful tugboat which he would anchor in the channel on an out flowing tide and 'kick' the sand out with the force of his propellers. Not the most effective way to clear a channel, but it worked.

Even this new pass was a dangerous place for the most seasoned captains. The channel was constantly shifting, filling with sand, and the bar that was formed was always a challenge. Like the old pass, there were no navigational aids other than the sharp eyes and seasoned minds of capable seamen. According to Roland Walker, Sr., when the tide was low you could easily run aground in the shifting channel. During Roland's lifetime, the pass moved west $\frac{1}{4}$ to $\frac{1}{2}$ mile. He stated that 'lots of times, if the Gulf was rough, you'd have to go to Pensacola to come home through the

Intercoastal (sic) Canal'.

Dredging of the Pass

During 1951 Roland Walker, Sr., Willard Morrill, and other members of the Orange Beach Fishing Association began a long crusade to get the channel of Perdido Pass marked and routinely dredged. In 1953, the State of Alabama Department of Conservation and the Baldwin County Commission entered into an agreement to dredge the pass. Also in 1953, the Alabama Department of Conservation and the State Highway

Department entered into an agreement with the Army Corps of Engineers for a study of beach erosion control at Perdido Pass. Although this study was presented to the Board of Engineers for Rivers and Harbors in Washington, DC in support of navigational improvements of the pass,

A typical dredge in operation.

it was rejected due to the relatively high costs of maintenance. In 1955, the Conservation Department dredged the pass across the bar. The State of Alabama again dredged the pass in 1959 and again in 1962. Most of this later dredging was done for the protection of the base of the newly constructed Perdido Pass Bridge.

As support information for a presentation to the U.S. Congress, Walker and the Orange Beach Fishing Association researched financial data of the local charter boat fleet. The data formulated for 1965 indicates a total of 53 boats operating out of Orange Beach; there were 30 charter boats with an average gross income of $6,000 per boat; 15 commercial fishing boats at $4,700 per boat and 8 commercial snapper fishing boats at $1,279 per boat. If an all weather Perdido Pass channel would be constructed, it was estimated that an addition of $2,000 per charter boat could be earned. Due to weather conditions affecting Perdido Pass, a total of 14 charter boats were forced to cancel 635 fishing trips, an average of 45 trips per charter. The report indicated that 14 charter boats lost 1,122 hours of fishing due to travel to the Pensacola Pass when Perdido Pass was too rough to run. Considering that the regular rate at the time was $6.50 per hour, this amounts to $520 per charter. Additionally, 8 charter boats consumed an additional 1,165 gallons of fuel per boat when forced to use the Pensacola Pass.

Bill Dickinson had remained a major supporter of the pass improvements since that first fishing trip with Roland Walker. When Bill Dickinson was elected as a Representative in Congress, things began going their way. During the early 1960's the first serious improvements to the pass were made.

An interesting sequence of events helped promote the building of the pass jetties and future dredging. Henry Sweet, who was the head of the Mobile District of the Army Corps of Engineers, built his house on land given to him by Amos Garrett at the end of Alabama Point in the 1950's. Hurricane Flossy, on September 24, 1956, hit the pass hard. Hard enough in fact, to significantly erode Alabama Point, removing the lake and much of the sand in front of Sweet's house. As a result, a steel–piling seawall and jetties were built, but most of the charter fishermen believed those seawalls and jetties to have been built incorrectly. It turned out that they were correct.

When Hurricane Betsy swept the area on Labor Day, September 8, 1965, the pass was hit hard once again. Sand eroded heavily behind the jetties and under the Sweet house, that left the jetties standing totally in the water. Part of the Sweet house was left hanging over the waters of the pass. Henry Sweet sued the State of Alabama for the loss of his house and won. It was not long after this that a new effort was made to solve the problems with Perdido Pass.

Shortly after Betsy did her damage, a new concrete seawall was constructed on Alabama Point, rock jetties put in, navigational aids were installed, and the channel was dredged to clear all the sandbars.

The Intracoastal Waterway
The Creation of 'Pleasure Island'

The Intracoastal Waterway in our area connects Pensacola and Mobile Bays. The waterway from the east passes through Perdido Bay, Arnica Bay, Bay La Launche, Wolf Bay, Portage Creek, Bon Secour Bay and into Mobile Bay. Area fishermen and those in the coastal barge business first discussed this waterway in 1908.

The waterway in our area became part of the Intracoastal Waterway system in 1932, when the U.S. Army Corps of Engineers dredged the necessary cuts. This waterway is used by commercial barges, fishing, and other pleasure boats connects Tampa Bay in Florida to Texas, and provides watercraft with protection from the open waters of the Gulf of Mexico.

The first dredge made its appearance in Perdido Bay approaching from the Florida side. There were four different dredges that worked on this section of the waterway: *Cafunsia*, *Pontchartrain*, *Sloat*, and *Texas*. The men that worked aboard the dredges were housed on a special multi–storied barge.

The work was hard and long. Several of the men from the area worked on the dredges, one of them was Neil Lauder, who lost an arm while working there. Another of the men, Corry Washington Rudd, came to the area on the dredges, stayed and married Frances Eleanor Callaway.

- Foley Onlooker newspaper – Orange Beach Community News – July 2, 1931:
  'The dredge 'Texas' is at last in Perdido Bay. Sunday, it was 100 yards out in the bay and it is said that the dredge will be at the head of Portage Creek by the end of this week, July 4. Clarence Walker of Caswell was the first to go to Pensacola through the new canal. Mr. Walker made the trip in his boat 'Jimmy' Saturday.'

The dredging of this canal created what is now known as 'Pleasure Island', separating it from the main land of Baldwin County. 'Pleasure Isle' as it is sometimes referred to, is composed of the land from Mobile Point at the mouth of Mobile Bay on the west to Alabama Point at Perdido Pass on the east, some 27 miles in length.

The Intracoastal Waterway along with the completion of the 'Causeway' across the northern end of Mobile Bay in 1927, the completion of Interstate Highways 10 and 65 during the 1980's, and the new bridges onto Pleasure

Island, have opened the Island to more visitors and new residents than ever.

It is not uncommon for the Island population to exceed 100,000, during today's summer season. Clifford Callaway, sitting on the porch of his family homestead, on Highway 180, during the summer of 2002, counted the passage of 300 cars in one hour on a week day…during the following Sunday afternoon, he counted 920 during the same hour of day. Clifford was born here in his family's home in 1923 and remembers a day in his youth when he walked all the way home from Highway 59 and never saw a car!

Education in Orange Beach

The first school building in Orange Beach was a log house located between the Walker and Johnson homes (now the Burkharts) in Caswell on St. Johns Bay. When the first school was established in the area (date unknown), the County paid for two months of school teaching and the parents of the young students hired a teacher for another month or two.

The first teacher was Mrs. Stewart Smith from Michigan, with her husband acting as principal. Another of the early teachers was Emily 'Bom' Cowan who lived with her husband in Caswell, about 1909. Mr. Cowan was a millwright at D. R. Peteet's sawmill. They had moved here from Wisconsin.

In 1910 the County built a new school building on Bay Circle. Mrs. Tilman was the first teacher in the new building. This building served until about 1930 when the school was consolidated with the Foley School. The building was purchased by the Baptist Church then

This is actually the second school in Orange Beach, but the first one built by the County. The building has seen a number of uses through its life and is now the Orange Beach Indian and Sea Museum.

donated to the City, the building is now located in the city complex on Hwy. 161. This same 'old school house' is now the Orange Beach Indian & Sea Museum, operated by Gail Walker Graham.

In 1930, a bus service to Foley was established for the students. The bus service was provided by Amel Callaway who bought the first school bus, a 1929 Chevy. The first drivers were his children, Billy, Lois, James, and Ray. The bus ran a route of fifty miles per day round trip; never exceeding 30 MPH (the bus had a governor that limited its speed). The bus would pick up the students around Orange Beach and Caswell then proceed to the

The first school bus. It was purchased by Amel Callaway and driven primarily by Lois Callaway, but also others of the Callaway family. Photo circa 1920.

pontoon bridge on their way to Foley. For safety, the children would disembark the bus, while the bus drove across the bridge. They would then walk across the bridge and stop for a drink at the artesian well on the other side. After a brief break, the young students would climb back on board and continue on to school.

As an example of how everything was used during the early days, that first school bus was used to haul the Callaway's pigs to and from the CCC camp that was at Gulf State Park. The CCC or Civilian Conservation Corps was a government program that put people to work during the Great Depression when jobs were scarce or nonexistent. It seems that the men at the Camp kept a pen for the pigs so they could dispose of their food scraps. The Callaways, of course, cleaned the bus well before carrying the children to school.

Using a newer bus (bus number 13) during the 1950s and 60s, Eleanor Lauder was one of the school bus drivers along with her nephews, Marion, Clifford, and Lloyd Callaway. Bus number 13 is remembered by many of today's residents. There were about sixty children from the area who rode the bus, including noted author and actress, Fannie Flagg, who lived in the area for about a year with her parents.

From 1930 to 1997, all Orange Beach children went to school in Foley.

The Orange Beach Elementary School opened in 1997 for students of

kindergarten through fifth grade. By 1999, a high school for grades ten through twelve was built in Gulf Shores to accommodate the growing populations of the Orange Beach and Gulf Shores area.

Orange Beach Elementary School opened in 1997.

Faulkner State Community College of Bay Minette opened its facility at Gulf Shores in 1993 on a 15 acre site on Highway 59. The Erie Meyer family of Gulf Shores donated the site and the facility was built by the City of Gulf Shores. With the resort atmosphere of 'Pleasure Island', this facilities' educational curriculum centers on the 'leisure services industry'. Classes and degree offerings are in Hospitality Services Management, Culinary Arts, Hotel/Restaurant Management, Travel/Tourism Management, Golf Course Management, and

Landscape Management and Operations. The facility also houses Frederic's, a state–of–the–art restaurant as a laboratory experience for students that is open to the public on a limited basis.

In 2002, Margaret Childress Long, as a former science teacher in the Baldwin County School System and long time resident with concern for the area's future, successfully ran for an elected school board position representing the district she loves.

Churches

Prior to the building of the 'new' school house in 1910, church services were held in private homes. After building of the school house on Bay Circle, religious Sunday schools and services were held there.

Sunday school in Orange Beach in 1919.

• Foley Onlooker – OrangeBeach community news 1929–1933: 'The regular weekly prayer meeting was held Sunday night at Mrs. Dietz' and was well attended, as it always is.'

Baptist Church services were held in the school house beginning in 1928. The church purchased the school house after the school was consolidated with Foley in 1930. Originally the Baptist Church in Orange Beach was a mission church of the First Baptist Church of Foley and was serviced by the pastors of the Foley Church. A new church was erected in 1953 and at that point Sunday school was held every Sunday. Church services however were held the first and third Sunday nights of each month.

Also in 1953 the local Orange Beach Presbyterian Church was organized. The Presbyterians held their Church services the second and fourth Sunday nights in the Baptist Church building. They broke ground on their own church in 1953 and added a major addition to the building in 1982.

Other denominations have since built churches in Orange Beach to serve the religious needs of the community. The following churches are now located here:

Christian Life Church (Assembly of God)
First Baptist Church of Orange Beach
Island Fellowship Baptist Church
Orange Beach United Methodist Church
Orange Beach Presbyterian Church
Peace Lutheran Church
Romar Beach Baptist Church
St. Thomas by the Sea (Catholic Church)

Non–denominational 'Easter Sunrise' services have been held in Orange Beach for many years. During the 1950's the service was held at the public beach area at Highways 161 and 182. It was then moved to Alabama Point and is now held on Florida Point.

Easter Sunrise service held on the public beach at the end of Highway 161 in 1953.

Community Activities

Until the growth spurt in the late 1940's, entertainment was, for the most part, home based. Couples visited each other or, on occasion, gathered in larger groups at private homes or at the Orange Beach Hotel. Sometimes families and friends would go on a 'busman's holiday' by going sailing in a group. Other forms of entertainment were a water borne visit to the 'honky–tonk' at Peterson's Point or a trip to Pirate's Cove to dance and enjoy friends. Other than that, it was fishing, picnics and swimming.

- Foley Onlooker – Orange Beach community news 1929–1933 – 'One of the best entertainment's, gotten up in a jiffy but good beyond compare with anything given here within the memory of the present population was had here last Friday evening. At first it was arranged as a musicale to be held at the home of Charles Rynd but owing to the fact that so many would be barred from the affair on account of small quarters, it was decided to have it at the "Pavilion" and to branch out a little and give the attendance a chance to do a little dancing. Charlie Dietz came down from Perdido Beach bringing his violin and cornet and Miss Rauchmann of Cullman an accomplished pianist were the chief actors and they certainly were the chief actors and they certainly were a whole orchestra in themselves to the mind of the assembled guests and we believe that included everybody within 2 miles for if anyone was missing it was their own fault and everybody was too busy to count noses. The music was grand and high class, the dancing was enjoyed by all participants and a light supper of coffee and cake topped off the evening.'

Of the more unusual activities, was an annual event held for several years during the 'wilderness' days, was a foxhunt. Mr. Hamilton, a Foley photographer, began the event by bringing in red foxes and dogs and before long the chase was on. Most of the residents had horses. They gathered up a few costumes and a full English style fox hunt was in process. The event didn't last for very many years, but during those years it did add excitement to the community.

One of the first clubs to form in the area was the Orange Beach Home Demonstration Club which organized September 1951 and was open to all women of Pleasure Island. Want to guess who organized this club...it was Dorothy Childress. The first membership roll had about twenty

members with both year round and summer residents. One of the club's dreams was to eventually purchase land and sponsor the building of a community center in Orange Beach.

The annual Community Picnic was started as a project of the Home Demonstration Club and has become an event enjoyed by residents and visitors alike. The club purchased land for the Community Center from Edna Walker White in 1959. Their dream became a reality in 1972 with the building of the OrangeBeach Community

Home Demonstration Club photo from 1954. The Orange Beach Home Demonstration Club was founded in 1951 by Dorothy Childress. The club was organized to provide activities for lady residents (permanent and summer) and to raise funds for the purchase of land for a community center. A goal which they achieved.

Center.The club disbanded on July 27, 1965. The annual Picnic they established turned into the Annual Barbecue and has continued ever since and is held on the second Saturday of June. For several years, Roy Blalock headed up the Annual Barbecue.

The Orange Beach Community Center organized September 10, 1959. It became inactive after March 1966, but was re–organized September 1968 and has stayed active on a monthly basis ever since.

Another club started by Dorothy Childress was the Scrabble–Rabble Club. A great club for ladies to get together and play Scrabble or other board and card games. The club is still active today with meetings rotating among member homes.

The Bear Point Civic Club puts on an annual 4th of July Picnic to accompany the annual 4th of July Fireworks display at the beach sponsored by the city.

The Orange Beach Fishing Association sponsors several annual activities. The Orange Beach Deep Sea Fishing Rodeo is held the entire month of October. This rodeo covers both offshore and inshore fishing.

Orange Beach World Championship Red Snapper Tournament held in the spring is unique in that all proceeds go to public artificial reef building, representation in Washington, D.C., or red snapper research. Another major event is the Orange Beach Billfishing Tournament held each July. All of these events have participants from all over the country and pass out lots of prizes.

The association also sponsors the annual Lighted Boat Parade during the Christmas season. This spectacular night time parade of boats of all shapes and sizes, cleaned up, dressed in their finery, and covered with lights is one to be seen. The Association actively promotes and supports the Adopt–A–Beach and Adopt–A–Reef programs. To find out more about these programs, just ask your boat captain or call the Orange Beach Fishing Association.

In March 1985, the Orange Beach Garden Club was organized with the stated goal 'To beautify our little piece of God's country'. Leona Thibodeaux was the first president. The club federated with the Alabama State Garden Club and the National Garden Clubs of America. In 1994, at the state District VIII fall meeting, Myrth Callaway, President 1993–1995, was

The Orange Beach Garden Club shown planting an Oak Tree from the Inspiration Oak in City Park with assistance of City workers.

made aware of a grant available to the clubs in Alabama. It was sponsored by Shell Oil Company and the National Garden Clubs. Jan Borum was the club grant chairman. Orange Beach Garden Club won $500, the top amount awarded in the state. The money was used in the clubs beautification projects.

The club sponsors an outdoors Christmas Decorating Contest, the Yard of the Month Award as well as the Arbor Day programs and plantings around the community. The club meets monthly on the fourth Tuesday at the community center.

Sailors will enjoy the Annual Lost Bay Regatta at Pirate's Cove.

Mardi Gras began in America in 1702, just up the road in Mobile. The first Mardi Gras society to form and parade in Orange Beach was the Crewe of Mystic Isle in 1994. Sylvia and Dean Howland and Earl Callaway were among its organizers. The Crewe of Mystic Isle paraded for several years before disbanding. The Orange Beach Mardi Gras Association currently has three Mystic Societies that parade on Mardi Gras Day (Shrove Tuesday) each year: Mystics of Pleasure, Sirens of the Sea, and Vontemps Cabrix (from Ono Island).

Add to those the numerous events like those sponsored by Flora–Bama Lounge, some that have become at least nationally famous like the Interstate Mullet Toss, the Mullet Triathlon, and the Sandstock Festival. The annual Frank Brown International Songwriters Festival, named for a long time denizen of the Flora–Bama, has expanded to venues throughout the area and is now one of the biggest festivals in Orange Beach.

A myriad of commercial activities and entertainment is available to both citizens and visitors that include everything from Dolphin watching, scuba diving and sailing, kayaking, para–sailing, treasure hunts, and a whole lot more.

But, the number one activity in Orange Beach was and still is charter fishing!

Utilities & Services

Electricity

Life in Orange Beach became considerably easier in 1948, when Baldwin Electric Membership Corporation established a local electric power grid to the area. This power grid replaced the kerosene and   carbide lighting, electric generators, and flashlights then in use. Roy Walker's house is believed to be the first to get electric lights.

Telephone

The sense of isolation ended a few years later in 1956, when John Snook of Gulf Telephone in Foley brought service to the community. This was no run of the mill phone service! The phones were connected to a 113 foot tall tower located on Highway 161 across from the new City Complex. The calls were wireless relayed to an antenna on the Foley water tower connected to the telephone exchange, much like today's cellular telephones.

This was the first system of its kind in the country.

The first lines were shared lines known as 'party' lines and each number had a special ring for identification.

Special 'first of its kind' communications tower by Gulf Telephone erected in 1956 on Highway 161 just south of Canal Road that brought telephone service to Orange Beach.

Calling out of Orange Beach was 'no charge', but anyone calling in, even from Foley, paid long distance rates and there was a strict limit of three minutes per call either way.

Newspapers and Television

The first newspaper regularly delivered to the area was the 'Foley – Onlooker', which began to arrive in 1977. Although the newspaper had begun publication on November 8, 1907, it was not delivered in Orange Beach due to the small population and the difficulty of transportation into the area.

As the area population grew, the 'Islander' began delivery, published by the 'Onlooker', but geared to happenings on Pleasure Island. Other newspapers, the 'Pelican' and the 'Mullet Wrapper', that are published in Florida, 'The Island Chronicle', and the 'Mobile Register – Baldwin Edition' are also available. With today's large tourist population, newspapers are available from around the country.

- Foley Onlooker – Orange Beach community news 1929–1933: 'The W. E. Baldwin's have purchased a radio and are getting good results. One doesn't feel as much out of the world with one of those installed.'

Radio was the evening companion of area residents until television was received in 1953, broadcast out of Pensacola. Cable television did not arrive until 1985, one of the benefits of city incorporation.

Fire protection

Before a volunteer fire service was established, what little fire protection there was came from the State Forestry Department stationed in Elberta and private citizens.

- Foley Onlooker – Orange Beach community news April 23, 1925 'A forest fire of considerable magnitude has kept us out fighting fire most all the week. Sunday, Stewart Smith was home from his school at Bon Secour and seeing the fire was about to do him great damage drove over to the beach and rallied all the available help, rushed back and with reinforcements saved all his property except his hog parlor.'

Orange Beach Volunteer Fire Service was established in 1961 through the efforts of Lawrence Bolton, a fireman at Brookley Field in Mobile, and with the active support of the late Fred Thrasher and Arthur Robinson, both of Bay Minette. By 1967 the fire service had a new building. Prior to that, the home built fire truck was kept at Roy Walker's marina.

Growing community need for water, sewer, and fire protection service was soon contemplated. The first meeting of the Orange Beach Water, Sewer and Fire Protection Authority was held in the home of Ted and Dorothy Childress on Cotton Bayou, September 18, 1968. The Baldwin County Commission appointed the first Board of Directors for this Authority, which consisted of Dr. Loren D. Moore, A. W. Robinson, Baldwin County Commission Chairman John B. Hadley, and Chairman Dorothy Childress.

Jerry Walker was the department's Chief by 1969 with about 10 officers and primary members plus volunteer fire fighters from around the community when needed. Lawrence Bolton was the group's technical advisor.

By 1992 the department had 4 full time firemen. Bill Addison was the first paid fireman...hired April 28, 1992. Fire Chief Mickey Robinson was hired a week later. Fire Chief Robinson retired in 2003. The volunteer fire service merged into the City of Orange Beach in 1994 and has grown to include 30 fire and rescue personal, an ambulance, two small fireboats, and one 30 foot fireboat for coastal marine fires. The Department has continued to expand to meet the needs of the rapidly growing City.

Water Service

After 2 years of construction and a FMHA low interest loan of $5,000,000, a public water system made its debut on January 15, 1974. Thus ending Dorothy Childress' weekly trip to haul water from the 'only faucet with good tasting water' near The Keg. This event made the local newspapers with a photo of Dorothy Childress at the old water tap.

As part of the water system, a 6 million–gallon storage tank was built near the head of Cotton Bayou to provide fire protection water for the coastal condominiums.

Sewer service

Pleasure Island Sewer Service began a sewer system for the new municipality in 1982 and operated a waste water treatment plant. After the city incorporation in 1985, Pleasure Island Sewer Service changed its name to 'Island Bay Utilities'. The system was foreclosed on by the Bank of Australia and the city eventually purchased the sewer treatment plant for $5,500,000 on January 28, 1991. Bob Carlton handled the negotiations for the city.

Wes Fallon was appointed as Public Works Director. The sewer system was rolled into the Governmental Utility Services Board (GUS Board) of the city. Eventually the GUS Board was dissolved and the City Utilities Department now runs the sewer system.

Police protection

In May 1985, the city established its first police force and appointed A.E. Cooper, a resident who had been a Police Chief in Opp, Alabama.

Today, the Police force has 36 offices and men, including one Fire Chief and one Assistant Chief, operating out of the municipal complex on Highway 161.

Incorporation of the City of Orange Beach

The construction boom, after Hurricane Frederic in September of 1979, included the building of many condominiums, resorts, marinas, restaurants, family dwellings, etc. The population expansion bringing with it all the problems that lack of local control can bring. However, gaining local control is not as easy as it might sound. Two different groups set about attempting to solve the problem by incorporation of the area into a city, but by different methods.

Joe Johnson, a retired pilot and engineer living in Orange Beach, and his friend Bob Milsap, a resident of Alabama Point, joined forces to begin negotiations with the City of Gulf Shores. This effort was trying to get the area south of State Park Drive or County Road 2, (now Marina Road) annexed to Gulf Shores. They did not believe that the residents of Orange Beach would be able to gain incorporation.

The other group headed by A. E. Cooper, a retired police chief living in Orange Beach, and his wife, Jean, were building a plan to incorporate Orange Beach as a city.

During the extended talks with Gulf Shores, Cooper called Joe Johnson asking him to review his plan for organizing the possible incorporation of Orange Beach as its own city. After joint review of Cooper's plan, Johnson suggested that if Cooper was not successful within two weeks that Cooper should join Johnson's plan. Cooper's effort took a little longer than two weeks, but the plan got under way and Johnson and Milsap joined forces with his local effort and discontinued their negotiations with Gulf Shores. Local community activists Dorothy Childress and Rose Williams joined the group.

The method chosen to gain incorporation was by general statute. Ack Moore, engineer with the water board, provided the group with section maps identifying potential voters.

As a result of the efforts of the group, a vote concerning the possible incorporation of the City of Orange Beach, Alabama, was held August 6, 1984. Although the referendum passed, some areas did not meet incorporation requirements. The areas of East Orange Beach, Bear Point, Terry Cove, Alabama Point, Romar Beach, and Ono Island along with a few other smaller areas did not vote to come into the city.

On September 11th, an election for Mayor and Council members was held with Dorothy Childress serving as the chief election official. Hazel Barnes and Mary Baker assisted Childress as election officials. This first election of city officers was conducted with the use of paper ballots.

The clear winners of the election were:
- Place 1: Rose Williams, a retired Bell telephone system manager
- Place 4: John F. 'Frank' Ellis, a former Opp, Alabama councilman

The other candidates required a runoff election on October 2nd. Candidates in the runoff election were:
- For Mayor: Ronald F. 'Ronnie' Callaway and A. E. Cooper
  Winner: Ronald F. Callaway, a civil engineer
- For Place 2: J. F. 'Jack' Govan and Marvin T. Robinson
  Winner: J. F. 'Jack' Govan
- For Place 3: William S. 'Steve' Garner and Bobbi Walker
  Winner: William S. 'Steve' Garner, a construction worker
- For Place 5: J. D. 'Jim' Snell and Bettye Brown
  Winner: J. D. 'Jim' Snell, a retired businessman

According to Dorothy Childress at the time, there were about 400 voters of 600 eligible voters who cast ballots in the run off election.

The newly elected officials were sworn into office by Baldwin County Judge of Probate Harry D'Olive in a ceremony held October 15, 1984 at the Community Center. Joseph L. 'Joe' Johnson was the Master of Ceremonies.

Frank Ellis was elected as Mayor Pro Tem and Beverly Callaway was appointed Historian of Orange Beach. The first City Attorney was Larry Sutley who had assisted A. E. Cooper and his group in the initial incorporation planning work.

With 1,010 residents, Orange Beach instantly became the sixth largest city in Baldwin County, Alabama. The City Council Chambers and the other offices of the city were located in one room of the Community Center. The City's first year budget was $60,000. Because of a small budget and no established credit, Councilmen Frank Ellis and Jim Snell personally guaranteed a loan to the city from First Alabama Bank (now Regions Bank) to allow the city to pay its first payroll. Another example of private assistance to the city was the purchase and donation by Bob Hall and Joe Johnson of an electric generator to keep the government operating during power outages.

Joe Johnson and Bob Milsap first used the motto 'Gem of the Gulf' in a campaign advertisement for Frank Ellis and Jim Snell during their run for seats on the first council. The motto was later adopted by the city.

At the councils first meeting the council members proposed a moratorium on building construction until a planning commission could be appointed and a zoning plan put in place. Mayor Ronnie Callaway did not agree with the proposed moratorium and left the meeting. The session continued under control of Mayor Pro Tem, Frank Ellis, and the moratorium was put in place.

At the time that the city government was finally in place, the sewer authority was brought into the city. The water board, however, was still under control of the county and they did not join the city. In fact, the county continues in control of the Water Board and control of board appointments, despite legal action by the city to gain control.

A planning commission was quickly established with Buzz Farias as chairman.

The City of Orange Beach immediately began annexation by legislation. The first area added to the city was Alabama Point from Highway 161 to the Florida line, excluding Ono Island. But the referendum was close with only 9 of the 17 votes cast in favor of annexation. East Orange Beach, Bear Point, and Terry Cove were added later.

The City of Gulf Shores tried to annex the Romar Beach area, but Orange Beach protested and the action was stopped in court. Orange Beach eventually added the area by what is referred to as 'lasso' annexation.

The first zoning action by the City Council was in May of 1985. The Orange Beach City Council adopted its first zoning ordinance on August 6, 1985. From that point, the adoption of the ordinance was a very contentious process and finally on April 22, 1991 was unanimously accepted by the City Council.

On October 17, 1985, a new municipal complex was begun on five acres of land on Highway 161, just south of Highway 180, donated by the late John McClure Snook and his wife, Marjorie, owners of Gulf Telephone Company in Foley. This modern municipal complex opened for city business in September of 1988. The complex cost $970,000 to build and was fully paid for when the city moved in as the city had derived a million dollars from the purchase of Island Bay Utilities.

The Snook's were very supportive of Orange Beach and donated land for the Marjorie Snook Park where the Indian and Sea Museum is located.

The land for the Orange Beach Post Office had been previously donated by the Snook's. After a new post office was built, the building was used for a short time as the second home of the city library and is now used as the Community Development building.

A plaque outside the municipal complex reads:
'The people of Orange Beach acknowledge with sincere appreciation and gratitude the generous donation of and for the site of the Municipal Complex by John McClure Snook and Marjorie Younce Snook. Purchased in 1950's by Ward H. Snook, Grace McClure Snook and J. M. Snook for future expansion of civic development and possible community service.'

In June of 1990, Orange Beach purchased 588 acres of land at a Meyer Foundation auction. The land that lay west of Orange Beach was purchased for $2,000 an acre. 396 acres of the land were classified as wet lands and discussions finally produced a land swap with Gulf State Park for some property adjacent to the Municipal Complex.

Ronnie Callaway was Mayor for the first eight years of the new city. The next election brought Councilman Frank Ellis as the cities second Mayor. Ellis had a stroke and a heart attack during his term and Bob Cauthen who was Mayor Pro–tem finished his term.

The next election for mayor went to Bert Krages, who never served due to improper filing of election paperwork. The same thing happened to an individual named Baker in the follow on election and Jerry Davidson assumed the position of Mayor for a few months until legal action removed him. Mike Shields was then elected Mayor Pro–tem and finally the city had a Mayor until a special election in 1996 elected Steve Russo. Russo was elected Mayor of Orange Beach for his third term in August 2004.

The Orange Beach Public Library, established in 1992, opened its doors to the public in the second City owned post office (near the City Complex) with three thousand books, but quickly out grew its home. The library then moved to the south wing of the new Municipal Complex. Demand for library services rapidly grew and a newly constructed library opened May 7, 2001, in its new home on the south shore of Wolf Bay.

In 1985, with a population of 1,010, the permanent population of Orange

Beach has steadily grown. Federal census records for 1990 show a population of 2,253, it jumped to 3,784 in the 2000 census. According to the Orange Beach Building Inspector's Office, commercial and residential construction permits were $76,786,298 in Orange Beach for the year 2000.

To provide controlled access to the island after evacuations for hurricanes, both Orange Beach and Gulf Shores issue 'Hurricane Decals'. For re–entry to the island a car must have the decal on their windshield.

All Orange Beach utility customers receive their decals every other year. Condo associations distribute decals to their property owners. Business owners must apply at the Fire Department. New residents to the area must provide proof of residence at the Orange Beach City Hall to receive their decals.

The Future

The city now covers approximately 15 square miles with numerous waterfront areas along the bays, bayous, and coves. From a census population of 2,300 in 1990 to 3,800 in 2000, it is obvious that the city has been 'discovered'. The summer time population reaches well over 40,000, as vacationers, fishermen, and summer residents come to 'get away', enjoy the water, fishing, and the cities relaxed lifestyle. To take care of the fishermen, 'winter' visiting 'snow birds', and the ever increasing summer tourists, Orange Beach now boasts over 8,000 condominium, hotel, motel, and rental home units for their convenience.

One of the prime attractions of the Orange Beach Community over the years has been the excellent fishing available in the bays and Gulf of Mexico right at the doorstep. The continued building of artificial reefs, modern conservation practices, and the overview of the National Marine Fishery – Gulf Council with local members on the board, the excellent fishing should continue into the future.

Where is Orange Beach headed for the future? The charter fishing industry is an extremely important part of the ever–growing tourist industry, which is the lifeblood of the community.

The true reality is that the 'island' environment is the draw. Maritime conservation programs such as the continued building of artificial fishing reefs, modern conservation of the fishery, and maintenance of clean water regulations in both the marine and land based ecology, are the keys to the continuation of the charter fishing industry and the Orange Beach charter fleet strongly supports these programs. Along with this is the continued expansion of police and fire protection, strong building codes and regulations, all with a strong eye toward the preservation of the environment, and remaining ever mindful of the potential of tropical storms and hurricanes.

For support of the tourist industry, the area continues to develop ecologically friendly entertainment facilities, housing concepts, and transportation to meet its family oriented growth. As a base for future growth, the city maintains a good balance between future growth and acknowledgement of the importance of its past.

There are few landmarks remaining that provide a connection with the beginnings of Orange Beach, but those are being preserved, such as the 'Indian and Sea Museum', the Orange Beach Hotel, the 'summer kitchen' post office, and several of the early charter fishing boats. With the dramatic increase of new population, historical highway and building signage is being discussed to help maintain our connection to the past and provide increased interest in the area for new comers.

Today, Ono Island remains outside the city, but Orange Beach provides police, fire, paramedic, water and sewer services on a contract fee basis.

Easy access to Orange Beach by the continued addition of bridges, the widening of access highways, as well as access to the area by water with the Intracoastal Waterway are but a few of the ways of getting here. Charter fishing, great food and housing, and its relaxing life style are good reasons to visit or stay. Orange Beach is indeed 'The Best Place to Be'!

Orange Beach – Summer 2004

Epilogue

'That's the price you pay to live in paradise'. If you haven't heard a local say that, stick around a few days, and you will. The comment refers to hurricanes and other storms, and Orange Beach has had its share.

As the writing of this book was nearing its end, Hurricane Ivan directly hit Gulf Shores, Alabama, on September 16, 2004. Ivan arrived as a high category 3 storm packing sustained winds of 130 miles per hour near the eye wall. Ivan was very large with a diameter of nearly 500 miles and tropical storm force winds extended out 100 miles from the eye. Orange Beach was in the northeast quadrant, the area of most severe damage, and took the brunt of a storm surge of 8 to 15 feet, with storm waves on top of that. It had been 25 years since Hurricane Frederic hit our area.

Ivan continued north, following Highway 59, leaving extensive damage in its wake. Trees and power lines were down everywhere, and many homes and businesses were destroyed, and most were damaged. Roadways were buried in sand and boats not secured in the back bays were damaged, sunk, or swept ashore. Beach erosion was severe and fishing reefs in the Gulf were covered with sand from the shifting currents. Orange Beach was however, spared loss of life.

While the area was still reeling from the effects of Ivan, Tropical Storm Arlene made landfall near Pensacola, Florida, with winds of 60 miles per hour and heavy rain on June 12, 2005. Then Tropical Storm Cindy hit southeast Louisiana, on July 6th and affected our area as a major rain event. An above average Atlantic Hurricane Season had been predicted for 2005, and it became obvious that the prediction was coming true. Hurricane Dennis followed on July 10th, and made landfall as another category 3 near Navarre, Florida, to our east...and caused extensive damage in northwest Florida and brought more rain to Orange Beach.

On August 29, 2005, Hurricane Katrina crossed the entrance to the Mississippi River southeast of New Orleans, Louisiana, and slammed into Waveland, Mississippi. Katrina hit as a category 4 storm and brought catastrophic damage to the Mississippi coast. Heavy damage extended eastward into south Mobile County and the west end of Pleasure Island. Storm surge flooding was severe in downtown Mobile, and along the western and eastern shores of Mobile Bay.

Then there was New Orleans! We have all seen the films and read the statistics about the failure of the 'protecting' levees that allowed catastrophic flooding to one of our major cities.

Hurricane Katrina is now considered the worst natural disaster in United States history.

We are all thankful that Orange Beach was spared the worst parts of the storm.

At the point of publication of this book, the 2005 Atlantic Hurricane Season is the most active season on record. The National Hurricane Center of the National Oceanic and Atmospheric Administration (NOAA), states that we are in a cycle of an above average number of storms which by historical records may last for a decade or more.

Although storms can and do cause damage, they also create opportunities. Opportunity can come when people are no longer willing to 'pay the price' for living in paradise and move on to other places. The sale of their land creates new opportunities for others. Rebuilding after major storm damage often is done under updated construction codes and with new techniques that provide stronger, more storm worthy structures. The city grows stronger after each such storm.

Modern weather and communication technologies allow advanced warning to those in the path of damaging storms to prepare for them or to get out of their way. Most natural disasters do not give such warnings.

The key to surviving hurricanes and tropical storms is preparedness. It is important to be ready before the storm season begins. See the appendix for storm preparedness information that is recommended by the American Red Cross and the Federal Emergency Management Agency (FEMA).

Restoration and maintenance of the beach front 'dune line' provides major protection from the damage of storm surge. During Hurricane Frederic, when most of the 'dune line' in Orange Beach was still intact, damage in Orange Beach was limited compared to other areas. However, the city is involved in dune and beach restoration that will, hopefully, provide continued protection to the beach area.

Controlled growth and maintenance of a vibrant resort area like Orange Beach is not an easy thing to balance. The growth and maintenance of Orange Beach as a city and especially as a destination resort city in just 21 years from its incorporation is a statement that it is doing many things right in maintaining that balance. As with most cities, the work to maintain that balance never quits.

Visitors and residents love Orange Beach, since it is such a beautiful place and the variety of fishing is so consistently good. Orange Beach is indeed a true family resort area and people will continue to come here, storms or no storms, to enjoy all we have to offer.

After all, it is 'The Best Place to be'!

Hurricane Ivan Photo Section

Above photograph of the popular Tacky Jack's restaurant on Cotton Bayou was taken from the water in Spring 2004.

The photograph taken below shows the destruction that Hurricane Ivan wrecked upon Tacky Jack's as the Hurricane swept Orange Beach on September 16, 2004.

Above is a photo taken of Sun Harbor Marina on Cotton Bayou in the Spring of 2004. Sun Harbor Marina was originally built as Safe Harbor Marina, but was sold and renamed. This marina was the only 'dry storage' boat facility in Orange Beach when it was built in the early 1960s.

Below is a photo of Sun Harbor Marina taken in the aftermath of Hurricane Ivan. The facility will not be rebuilt.

The photo above, viewed from the Gulf of Mexico, shows the damage along the beach front just to the west of Orange Beach. For the most part, the image shows the difference between newer and older construction codes and techniques. Below is a photo of the author's home on the north shore of Cotton Bayou. Margaret lost her pier and had other damage, but had little water in the house from the storm surge. The home has survived hurricanes since it was built in 1946.

These photos are of Zeke's Marina on the south shore of Cotton Bayou. Zeke's lost most of their docks and received water and wind damage to their water front buildings.

In the photo below, wind damage is evident to Zeke's dry boat storage building just to the west of their main docking area. Boats large and small were tossed about by wind and water. The dry boat storage building was damaged beyond repair and was torn down.

The photo above is of an unidentified fishing boat that broke its moorings during the storm and was washed ashore near the water tower at the head of Cotton Bayou.

Below is the charter boat *Rent It III* tied off and protected at the head of Cotton Bayou. The boat survived with little damage, as did other boats secured in this and other back bay areas.

Appendix

Cultural Chronology Periods of the Area

Dates	Cultural Periods
12500 – 8000 BC	Paleo–Indian
8000 – 6000 BC	Late Paleo–Indian/Early Archaic
6000 – 3500 BC	Middle Archaic (probably shell mounds)
3500 – 1000 BC	Late Archaic or Gulf Formation (earliest known shell mounds)
1000 BC – AD 200	Early Woodland (earliest known burial mounds)
AD 200 – 700	Middle Woodland
AD 700 – 1000	Late Woodland (adoption of maize cultivation)
AD 1000 – 1500	Mississippian (temple mounds)
AD 1500 – 1850	Historic

The photos above are of an archaeological dig at Caswell in the Spring of 2004. At upper left is Bonnie Gums, of the University of South Alabama, Archaeology Department, in charge of the project. She is shown pointing out artifacts in one of the excavation trenches. This is the site of the new Caswell Place development. The other photos show pottery shards, a volunteer at the washing tray, and two volunteers in one of the excavation pits. Hundreds of artifact were found of an early Native American summer fishing encampment.

Appendix

Flags over Orange Beach

Flags that did or could have flown over
Orange Beach or Baldwin County:

Early Flag of Spain (1507 – 1698)
Union Flag of Great Britain (1606 – 1814)
Flag of France (1698 – 1762)
Later Flag of Spain (1780 – 1800)
Bonnie Blue Flag (Flag of the Republic of West Florida
    Sept. 16 to Dec. 10, 1810) (later Flags of Texas Republic
    1836–1839 & Republic of Mississippi Jan. 6 to
    Jan. 26, 1861)
Star Spangled Banner: United States of America Flag (15 Star)
    during War of 1812
Flag of Mississippi Territory (1798 – 1818)
Flag of Alabama Territory (1818 – 1819)
Stars & Stripes: United States of America (1812 – 1861)
Alabama Republic Flag (Alabama Secession Flag) (January 11 to
    February 17, 1861)
CSA Stars and Bars – 1st Flag of Confederate States of America
    (March 4, 1861– May 1, 1863)
Southern Cross or Confederate Battle Flag – (Nov. 1861 – with
    variations to 1865)
CSA 2nd National – 2nd Flag of Confederate States of America
    (May 1, 1863 to March 4, 1865)
CSA 3rd National – last Flag of Confederate States of America
    (March 4, 1865 to present)
Stars & Stripes: United States of America (1865 – present)
Alabama State Flag – present
Flag of Baldwin County, Alabama – present
Flag of the City of Orange Beach, Alabama (1985 to present)
Jolly Roger (Skull & Crossed Bones)
    Flag of the Pirates that preyed out of this area on the gold
    filled Spanish galleons

Postmasters of Caswell, Alabama Post Office

Postmaster	Appointment Date
Alice L. Caswell	November 11, 1896
Mary Frances Strong 'Fanny' Walker	January 17, 1898
Winifred Walker Jones, Acting Postmaster	February 18, 1937
Winifred Walker Jones, Postmaster	February 19, 1937
Frances Walker Morrill, Acting Postmaster	November 24, 1942
Frances Walker Morrill, Postmaster	December 18, 1942

Editors note: Mail handling moved to Orange Beach Post Office September 30, 1954. Caswell Post Office closed October 1, 1954

Postmasters of Orange Beach, Alabama Post Office

Postmaster	Appointment Date
Elsie E. Diehl	March 5, 1910
Mina Callaway	April 4, 1918
Hilda G. Dietz (declined position)	March 23, 1920
Nancy B. West (declined position)	June 10, 1920
Charles H. Rynd	August 11, 1920
Philo S. Chappell, Acting Postmaster	April 1, 1926
Philo S. Chappell, Postmaster	May 26, 1926
Minnie Lee Callaway, Acting Postmaster	February 25, 1937
Minnie Lee Callaway, Postmaster	April 15, 1937
(Minnie Lee Callaway married Emmons Brown on December 8, 1937 changing her name to Minnie Lee Brown)	
Edna M. Callaway, Acting Postmaster	July 7, 1967
Edna M. Callaway, Postmaster	November 7, 1967
Sarah W. Taylor, Officer–in–charge	March 5, 1976
Sarah W. Taylor, Postmaster	January 15, 1977
Matt Bickers, Postmaster	February 1987 to present

Contract U.S. Mail Boats

Editors note: Early United States mail service in the Orange Beach/ Perdido Bay area was delivered to local Postmasters under private contract by boat. Those that are known are listed below:

Boat Name   Captain (contract holder)

Unknown – B. T. Hudson

Edna – Rufus Walker, Sr.

Holly Bird – Rufus Walker, Sr.

Red Bird – Rufus Walker, Sr.

Mexiwanna – Leon O. McPherson of Josephine

Above is the *Red Bird*, captained by Rufus Walker, Sr., a typical contract mail boat of the period. These boats hauled passengers and freight as well as the mail for the United States Postal Service.

Appendix

```
            Confederate.
   W  |      21      |   Ala.

        Lem   Walker
   Put., Co. F., 21 Reg't Alabama Infantry.

Appears on

            Company Muster Roll

of the organization named above,

for              Sep+Oct    , 186 3.

Enlisted:
When                 Sep 30, 1863 .
Where  St Clear
By whom  Capt Dade
Period  3 y or w
Last paid:
By whom  Never Pd
To what time                       , 186  .

Present or absent  Absent
Remarks  Detached to fish by Genl
Maury Sep 30, 63

Book mark:

(642)                  J S Douglas
                            Copyist.
```

This is a copy of Lemuel Walker, Jr.'s Confederate Muster Roll for September–October 1863. Note that the Department of the Gulf Commander Major General D. H. Maury officially sent Lemuel fishing for the Confederacy.

276

Lem Walker, Jr., Civil War pay record – 1862

I Certify that the within named .... _Lem Walker_ .... a .... _Private_ .... of Captain .... _B. H. Dunbar_ .... Company (.. _5_ ..) of the .... _21st_ .... Regiment of .... _Alabama Vols_ .... born in .... _Baldwin Co._ .... in the State of .... _Alabama_ .... aged .... _16_ .... years .... _5_ .... feet .... _9_ .... inches high, ... _fair_ .... complexion .... _blue_ .... eyes .... _dark_ .... hair, and by profession a .... _farmer, boy_ .... was enlisted by .... _Capt. McClesky_ .... at .... _Baldwin Co._ .... on the .... _13th_ .... day of .... _November_ .... eighteen hundred and sixty .... _one_ .... to serve for .... _five_ .... years, and is now entitled to a discharge by reason of .... _his being under age_ .... The said .... _Lem Walker_ .... was last paid by Paymaster .... _Maj. J. Barnwell_ .... to include the .... _30th_ .... day of .... _August_ .... eighteen hundred and sixty .... _two_ .... and has pay due from that time to the present date.

There is due him for travelling from .... _Choctaw Bluff_ .... to .... _Mobile_ .... being .... _110_ .... Miles at .... per Mile.

There is due him .... _nothing_ .... dollars on account of Clothing not drawn in kind.

There is due for Commutation of Horse .... day at .... per day.

He is indebted to the Confederate States .... _nothing_ ....

He is indebted to .... Laundress .... dollars.

Given in Duplicate at .... _Choctaw Bluff_ .... this .... _13th_ .... day of .... _October_ .... 1862.

.... _J. B. Branch, Lieut._ Commanding Company.

For pay from .... _1st_ .... of .... _Sept_ .... 1862 to .... _13_ .... of .... _Oct_ .... 186_2_ being .... _One_ .... months and .... _13_ .... days at .... _Eleven_ .... dollars per month, | 15.76

For pay for travelling from .... to .... being .... miles, at .... per mile |

For Clothing not drawn .... |

For Commutation of Horse .... days at .... cents per day, | 15.76

Amount, | 15.76

Balance Due, | 15.76

Received of .... _Alex. McVay Capt. & A.Q.M._ .... Paymaster, Confederate States Army, this .... _7th_ .... day of .... _Oct_ .... 186_2_ .... _Fifteen_ .... dollars and .... _Seventy Six_ .... cents, in full of the above account.

Pay .... _15.76_

Travelling allowance ....   (Signed in Duplicate.)

Clothing ....

For Commutation for Horse ....

Dollars .... _15 76_   _L. Walker_

277

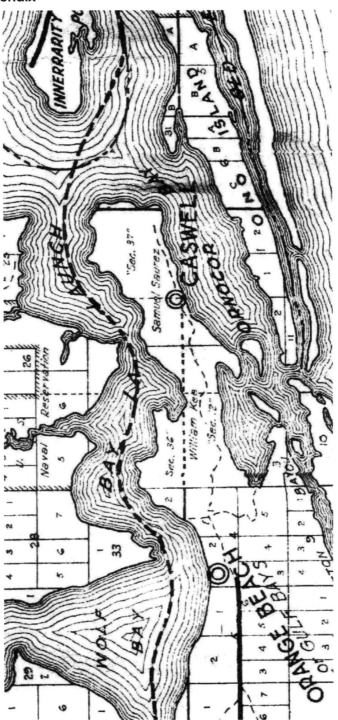

This map shows the location of the Samuel Suarez and William Kee Spanish Land Grants. These were the first Spanish Grants in Orange Beach.

Samuel Suarez Land Patent

Montgomery 011740   4—1040-B

The United States of America,

To all to whom these presents shall come, Greeting:

WHEREAS, There has been deposited in the General Land Office of the United States a Certificate of the Register of the Land Office at Montgomery, Alabama, whereby it appears that the private land claim of Samuel Suarez, being claim No.41 in a list by Commissioners Barton and Barnett of actual settlers in the district east of Pearl River, in Louisiana, prior to March 3, 1819 (American State Papers, Gales and Seaton Edition, Volume 3, Page 445), was granted as a donation by Section three of the Act of May 8, 1822 (3 Stat., 707), and that the said claim has been regularly surveyed and designated as Section thirty-seven in Township eight south and Section two in Township nine south all in Range five east of the St. Stephens Meridian, Alabama, containing five hundred fifty-nine acres and fifty-six hundredths of an acre, as shown by the township plats approved March 12, 1832 and April 4, 1832:

NOW KNOW YE, That the UNITED STATES OF AMERICA, in consideration of the premises, HAS GIVEN AND GRANTED, and by these presents DOES GIVE AND GRANT, unto the said Samuel Suarez, and to his heirs, the lands above described; TO HAVE AND TO HOLD the same, together with all the rights, privileges, immunities, and appurtenances, of whatsoever nature, thereunto belonging, unto the said Samuel Suarez, and to his heirs and assigns forever.

IN TESTIMONY WHEREOF, I,   Calvin Coolidge,

President of the United States of America, have caused these letters to be made Patent, and the Seal of the General Land Office to be hereunto affixed.

GIVEN under my hand, at the City of Washington, the **TWENTY-SIXTH**

(SEAL)   day of   **MAY**   in the year of our Lord one thousand

nine hundred and   **TWENTY-FIVE**   and of the Independence of the

United States the one hundred and   **FORTY-NINTH**

By the President: *Calvin Coolidge*

By   *Viola B. Pugh* , Secretary.

M. P. LeRoy

Recorder of the General Land Office.

RECORD OF PATENTS: Patent Number ____ **960055**

279

Appendix

William Kee Land Patent

Montgomery 011505.

4—1040-R

The United States of America,

To all to whom these presents shall come, Greeting:

WHEREAS, There has been deposited in the General Land Office of
the United States a Certificate of the Register of the Land Office at
Montgomery, Alabama, whereby it appears that the private land claim of
William Kee, being claim No.42 in a list, dated July 11, 1820, by the
Register and Receiver at Jackson Court House of actual settlers in the
district east of Pearl River in Louisiana, prior to March 3, 1819, who
have no claims derived from either the French, British or Spanish
Governments (American State Papers Duff Green Edition, Vol.3, page 393),
was confirmed by Section 3 of the Act of May 8, 1822 (3 Stat., 707), and
that said claim has been regularly surveyed and designated as Section
twelve in Township nine south and Section thirty-six in Township eight
south all in Range five east of the St. Stephens Meridian, Alabama,
containing five hundred sixty-seven acres and seventeen hundredths of
an acre, as shown by the Township Plats approved April 4, 1832 and March 12,
1832, respectively.

NOW KNOW YE, That the UNITED STATES OF AMERICA, in consideration of
the premises, HAS GIVEN AND GRANTED, and by these presents DOES GIVE AND
GRANT, unto the said William Kee, and to his heirs, the Lands above
described; TO HAVE AND TO HOLD the same, together with all the rights,
privileges, immunities, and appurtenances, of whatsoever nature, thereunto
belonging, unto the said William Kee, and to his heirs and assigns forever.

IN TESTIMONY WHEREOF, I, Calvin Coolidge,

President of the United States of America, have caused these letters to be made
Patent, and the Seal of the General Land Office to be hereunto affixed.

GIVEN under my hand, at the City of Washington, the FIFTH

(SEAL) day of SEPTEMBER in the year of our Lord one thousand

nine hundred and TWENTY-THREE and of the Independence of the

United States the one hundred and FORTY-EIGHTH

By the President Calvin Coolidge

By Dixla B Pugh , Secretary.

John O'Connell
Acting Recorder of the General Land Office.

RECORD OF PATENTS: Patent Number **916024**

6—3192

William Kee land grant affidavit – 1926

AFFIDAVIT
FILED   August 7th, 1926
DATED   June 16th, 1926
RECORDED   39 NS page 508

STATE OF ALABAMA.
BALDWIN COUNTY.

On this the 16th day of June, 1926, personally appeared before the undersigned authority, Lemuel Walker, who is personally known to me, who first being duly sworn doth depose and say: I am 80 years of age and have for 49 years resided on and in the vicinity of Perdido Bay. I was personally acquainted with the family of heirs of the original William Kee to whom has recently been patented what is known as the William Kee Grant on Bear Point on Perdido Bay and described as follows:

> Section 12 in Tp. 9 South, and Sec. 36 in Tp. 8 South all in Range 5 East of St. Stephens Meridian, Ala., containing 567.17 acres as shown by the township plats approved April 4th., 1832 and Mch. 12" 1832 respectively.

The heirs of said William Kee to whom said land was patented according to my knowledge and information gained from the family and the residents of this community during the 49 years I have resided here are as follows:

1. William Kee   4. John Kee, and
2. Isabella Villar, nee Kee   5. Virginia Yancey, nee kee.
3. Carmaleta Parrenot, nee Kee.

I have always understood that these were all of the heirs and that there were no others. It has always since I have been here for that 49 years been generally understood that there were these six heirs and that each heir and had inherited a one-sixth undivided interest in the above described William Kee Spanish Grant which was patented to said William Kee, deceased.

All of the six direct heirs of William Kee, decd., are now dead.

Lemuel Walker.

Sworn to before me this 16th day
of June , 1926.
                Claude Peteet
Notary Public, Baldwin Co., Ala.
My commission expires November 12th, 1927.

45

The above affidavit was sworn to by Lemuel Walker, Jr., June 16, 1926 regarding land sales and ownership of the William Kee land grant. It states the heirs of the William Kee grant. Note that the affidavit was taken by Claude Peteet, brother of D. R. Peteet. D. R. Peteet was an early developer in Orange Beach.

Appendix

Roscoe Clizbe Land Patent – 1906

The United States of America.

CERTIFICATE No. *27948* **To all to whom these presents shall come, Greeting:**

Whereas, *Roscoe J. Clizbe of Baldwin County, Alabama*

ha*d* deposited in the GENERAL LAND OFFICE of the United States a Certificate of the Register of the Land Office at *Montgomery, Alabama*, whereby it appears that full payment has been made by the said *Roscoe J. Clizbe*

according to the provisions of the Act of Congress of the 24th of April, 1820, entitled "An Act making further provision for the sale of the Public Lands," and the acts supplemental thereto, for *the East half of the North East quarter and the East half of the South East quarter of Section two in Township nine South of Range four East of St Stephens Meridian in Alabama containing one hundred and sixty acres and twelve hundredths of an acre*

according to the official plat of the survey of the said lands returned to the General Land Office by the Surveyor General, which said tract ha*d* been purchased by the said *Roscoe J. Clizbe.*

Now know ye, That the United States of America, in consideration of the premises, and in conformity with the several acts of Congress in such case made and provided, HAVE GIVEN AND GRANTED, and by these presents DO GIVE AND GRANT, unto the said *Roscoe J. Clizbe*

and to *his* heirs, the said tract above described: To HAVE AND TO HOLD the same, together with all the rights, privileges, immunities, and appurtenances, of whatsoever nature, thereunto belonging, unto the said *Roscoe J. Clizbe*

and to *his* heirs and assigns forever.

In testimony whereof, I *Theodore Roosevelt* PRESIDENT OF THE UNITED STATES OF AMERICA, have caused these letters to be made patent, and the seal of the General Land Office to be hereunto affixed.

[L. S.]

Given under my hand, at the City of Washington, the *thirtieth* day of *June*, in the year of our Lord one thousand eight *nine* hundred and *six*, and of the Independence of the United States the one hundred and *thirtieth*

BY THE PRESIDENT: *T. Roosevelt*

By *F. M. McKean* Secretary.

C. H. Brush Recorder of the General Land Office.

Perdido Bay Sailing Directions – 1908

GENERAL DESCRIPTION.

PERDIDO BAY*

empties into the Gulf of Mexico through Bayou St. John and a narrow pass located 13 miles westward of Pensacola entrance and 26¼ miles eastward of Sand Island lighthouse at Mobile Bay entrance. The bay is an irregularly shaped, shallow body of water, extending about 12 miles in a northeasterly direction, and at its head is entered by Perdido River, the bay and river forming part of the boundary between the States of Florida and Alabama. Millview, which is near the head of Perdido Bay, has lumber mills which are supplied by logs from the Perdido River; the lumber is shipped from Millview to Pensacola by rail. This is the only industry in this vicinity.

Bay La Launch and Wolf Bay extend westward and northward from the western end of Perdido Bay; they are of no importance, but at the head of Wolf Bay is the post village of Foley. The post village of Josephine is situated on the north shore, at the entrance to Bay La Launch.

The entrance from the gulf, between Florida Point on the east and Alabama Point on the west, is obstructed by a shifting bar which extends nearly ¼ mile seaward and over which there is a channel varying in depth from 5¼ to 12 feet, according to circumstances. In June, 1907, there were 8 feet in this channel. Occasionally a fisherman of 4 to 5 feet draft will cross the bar, but as there are no aids except local ones it requires a practiced eye to follow the channel among the shoals. In strong southerly winds the sea makes the bar impassable; strangers should never attempt to enter before sounding out the channel. Inside the entrance are numerous shoals, and these are continually shifted by the tidal currents which at times have great velocity and are caused principally by the winds. A vessel that crosses the bar and passes through the shoals in Bayou St. John can easily carry 7 feet of water to Millview, and 10 feet to Josephine and through Bay La Launch into Wolf Bay.

Sailing directions that would be of use to a stranger can not be given; it is hard to distinguish the entrance at a distance of 1 mile from shore, and the channel over the bar is liable to shift at any time.

Above is the description and sailing directions for Perdido Bay from the 1908 United States Coast Pilot – Atlantic Coast – Part VIII, book for the North Coast of the Gulf of Mexico, page 79. This was published just after the 'New' Perdido Pass was opened by the major Hurricane of 1906. The description of the Pass gives a small hint at the difficulties faced by the mariners of Orange Beach as they traveled back and forth to the Gulf in those early days. Today's pass can be difficult at times of rough weather, but with the placement of the jetties, the sea walls, and maintenance dredging of the channel, it is for the most part routine for both pleasure boaters and charter fishermen.

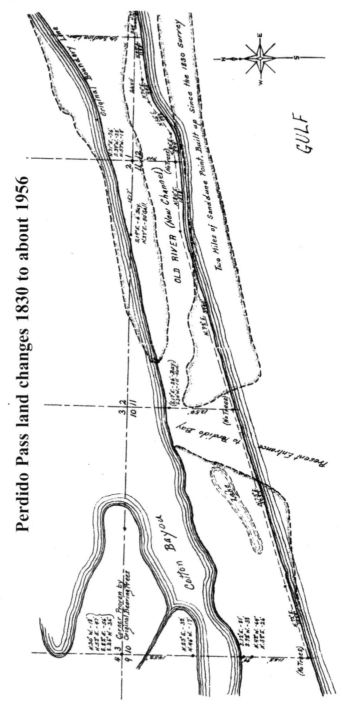

Perdido Pass land changes 1830 to about 1956

This survey map shows the changes in the area of the existing Perdido Pass from the boundary line of 1830 to about 1956. Notice several things on this map: 1) that prior to the existing pass, the land of what is now Alabama Point extended east to the old pass (not shown), this land was then called Point Ornocor; 2) the existing channel of Old River is referred to as the 'new' channel, since previously Old River entered the Gulf about where the Alabama State line is now and the 'new' channel formed after the 1906 hurricane; and 3) the lake on the western side of the existing pass was swept away by Hurricane Flossy, September 24, 1956.

Appendix

Early Orange Beach Fishing Boats
with Captains and builders – anotated where possible

Callaway Family Boats:

> unnamed – Herman Callaway – 24' – Herman's first boat– built by Herman
>
> *Dixie Maid* –Herman Callaway – 40'– built by Herman at his home – 1938 – this was Herman's 3rd boat
>
> *Dolphin* – Ray Callaway's 2nd boat – later purchased by Crockett White, Sr.
>
> *Dotty Jo* – Earl Callaway – owned by Joe Garris
>
> *Elray* –Ray Callaway – Ray's first boat
>
> *Irma* – see Kadi Did
>
> *Kadi Did* – Herman Callaway – a 'rum runner' purchased from Government and renamed *Irma*
>
> *Lady Lake* – Dan Callaway – a converted freight boat
>
> *Mildred C.* – Amel Callaway – 40' – first boat built by Amel
>
> *Minnie L.* – Dan Callaway – built by Hudie Ewing
>
> *Redwing* – Amel Callaway – 30'
>
> *Resolute* – Herman Callaway – 26' – 1920's and early 30's – Herman's 2nd boat
>
> *The Rex* – Dan Callaway (Dan's last boat) then Oscar Callaway – 30' –
>
> *Rip Tide* – Ray Callaway – 40' – Ray's 3rd boat – built by Resmondo

Walker Family Boats:

> *Blue Chip* – Raymond Walker & Charles Walker – 40'
>
> *Bobbi M* – Robert "Bobby' Walker, Jr. – 38'
>
> *Buccaneer* – Roy Walker's first boat – bought in New Orleans, LA in 1927
>
> *Capt. Lee* – Leroy Walker – 46'
>
> *Emma W* – Robert 'Bob' Walker's first boat – 28' later sold to Rabun Walker
>
> *Elvira* – Rabun Walker's second boat – 43'
>
> *Gloria June* – Ray Walker's first boat – later owned by Galen Walker– built in Bayou La Batre, AL
>
> *Gulf Rebel* – Gladwin Walker
>
> *Intruder* – Don Walker – 43' – later purchased *Sea Reaper II*
>
> *Jimmy* – first 'factory' built charter boat purchased and owned by J. D. Blacksher – Clarence 'Ted' Walker
>
> *Miss Kathaleen* – Leroy Walker – built in Bon Secour, AL by Joe Pierce

285

Miss Kay – Roy Walker – 38' – built on Walker Cay, AL
by Joe Pierce – served 3 years during WWII as a
Coast Guard Vessel

Perdido – Roland Walker – 43' – 14' beam – 4' draft

Ritz – Gladwin Walker – Gladwin's first boat

Sea Duck – Rufus Walker

Sea Duster – Rufus Walker, Jr. & Billy Walker &
Jerry Walker – built in Orange Beach at
Rufus Walker's place in 1935

Sea Reaper II – Don Walker

Sea Rebel – Gladwin Walker – built by Jim Hudson

Sea Son – Roland Walker later LeeRoy Walker –
built by Jim Hudson

Summer Breeze I – Robert 'Bobby' Walker, Jr. – 55' –
built by Resmondo

Summer Breeze II – Robert 'Bobby' Walker, Jr. – 60' –
built by Resmondo

Thelma Ann – Robert 'Bob' Walker, Sr. –
inherited by Robert 'Bobby' Walker, Jr. –
later purchased by Jerry Walker
Built by Jim Hudson

Tradewind – Gladwin Walker

Editors note: The following early boats were lovingly restored by Jerry Walker: Thelma Ann, Gloria June, Blue Chip, and the Alemite.

Other Early Charter Boats:

Albacore – Walter Trent – 47'

Alemite – Oscar Fell – later Jerry Walker – built in 1946

Bitsey –Ronald Lauder

Blue Bird – Horace L. Long Sr. – 32'

Boll Weevil – Gloyice Ard and Royce Ard – 38'

Bonita – Hudie L. Ewing

Borweed – Gloyice Ard – 38'

Castle I – Henry Parker – 47'

Dark Thirty – Foster Childress – later owned by
Brooks & Wesley Moore – 30' –
built 1974 by Buskin

Dealer – Frank Thompson – 42'

Delores III – John Stewart

Donald Frederick – Ed Frederick & Bruce Childress –
built by Ed Frederick

Dottie Joe II – Joe Garris – 48'

Doug Out – Bill Douglas
Duchess – Neil Lauder
Edna Lynn – Crockett 'CS' White, Jr.
Edna W. of Caswell – Crockett White, Sr.
Esther S. – Tom Adams
Fair Water – James 'Charles' Huff –40' – built by Resmondo
Fat Pat – John Turner
Gulf Rebel – Armand Annan – 44'
Gulf Stream – L. G. Carter & Bill Porter – 38'
Island Girl – Dan Negus – 50'
Maburn – Dr. Sibley Holmes – built by Herman Callaway
Mad Hatter – Charles Glazner
Miss Dot – Elbert White
Miss Edna W – Crockett White, Sr.
Mystery – Bud Moss – 31'
Nancy–D – Bubba Waltman
No*rth Star* – Pete Peters – 44'
Ono – Hugh Farr & Sonny Trimble
On the Crosstie – Iris Ethridge
Patti Ann – Bob Kostelecky
Peggy Lou – Jim Hudson – built by Jim Hudson
Perdido Maid – Willard Mall & Bill Morrill – later
          Louis Harms– built at Walker Cay, AL by Joe Pierce
Pompano – Hubert Low – later Carl McDuffie
          built by Jim Hudson
Pompano II – Hurbert Low – later Carl McDuffie –
          built by Hubert Low & Jim Hudson
R*ed Robin* – Ted Childress
Rookie – Allen Kruse – 47'
Sazerac – Kirk Williams – 32'
Sea Hunter – Rick McDuffie – 48' – Resmondo built
Sea Reaper – Earl Griffiths – 53'
Sporty Lady – Andy Platt – 34'
Summer Wind – George Carleton – 40'
Sun Circle – Tom Clark – 40'
Tanqueray – Deloy Lucas – 38'
The Sea Spook II – Frank ?
The Sportsman – Tom Adams
Viking – Walter Trent
War Eagle – Sonny Trimble – 35'
White Caps – Ty Fleming – 50'
White Caps II – Ty Fleming

Appendix

File No. I -1360

SERIAL NUMBER
A- 16890

Treasury Department

MB *Dixie Maid*

United States Coast Guard

ISSUE NUMBER
" NINE "

License to Operate or Navigate Motor Boats
Carrying Passengers for Hire

CANCELLED
DATE 3-7-52
FILE NO. I -1360
SERIAL NO. A-75717
ISSUE NO. -10-
* * * * * * HERMAN CALLAWAY * * * * * *

This is to certify that _____ HERMAN CALLAWAY _____

has given satisfactory evidence to the undersigned Officer in Charge, Marine In-

spection for the District of _____ MOBILE, ALABAMA _____, that he can safely be

intrusted with the duties and responsibilities of operator of motor boats as defined in

the Act of April 25, 1940, when carrying passengers for hire, on the navigable

waters of the United States, and is hereby licensed to act as such operator for the term

of five years from this date.

Given under my hand this _____ 26TH. _____ day of _____ MARCH _____, 19 51..

CHARLES C. PHILLIPS, lt. COMDR., USCG
OFFICER IN CHARGE, MARINE INSPECTION.
By direction of the OCMI

CG 861 (Rev. 9-40)

Captain Herman Callaway of the
charter boat *Dixie Maid.*

288

Perdido Pass Estimated Boat usage –1962
Data from 'Perdido Pass and Vicinity
A Report by John J. Patton, Chief Engineer ,
Alabama Department of Conservation
March 14, 1962'

Estimated boats using Perdido Pass by number and category:

Type	Length	Draft	Number
Area based Charter	28–40 ft.	2–4 ft.	24
Other Charter	28–40 ft.	2–4 ft.	7 to 10
Commercial Fishing	18–28 ft.	1–3 ½ ft.	51
Recreational	over 18 ft.	1–3 ft.	200
Recreational	under 18 ft.	1–2 ft.	200

On the left is the *Thelma Ann*, Captain Bob Walker, and *Gloria June*, Captain Raymond Walker, heading into Perdido Pass for a charter fishing trip into the Gulf of Mexico, about 1956.

Proposed Perdido Pass Changes
U. S. Army Corps of Engineers
1963

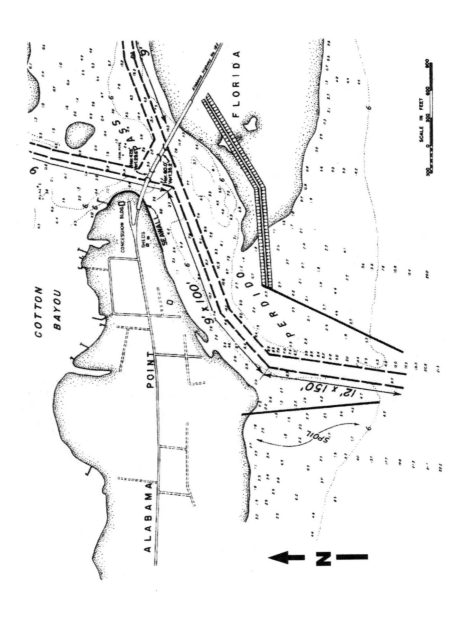

Appendix

Orange Beach Charter Boat Data – 1965

Editors note: The data presented here was gathered by charter boat Captain Roland Walker, Sr., in 1965 for presentation to the U.S. Congress in support of the Orange Beach Fishing Association's request for dredging, jetties, and navigational aids for Perdido Pass.

Estimated Gross Income:

> 30 Charter Boats – $180,000 an average of $6,000 per boat
> 15 Commercial Fishing Boats – $70,500 an avg. of $4,700 per boat
> 8 Commercial Snapper Fishing Boats – $10,234 an avg. of $1,279 per boat

With an adequate all weather Perdido Pass Channel:

> 15 Charter boats estimate they would have an additional annual income of $60,000 – an avg. of $2,000 (sic) per boat
> 8 Commercial Snapper Fishing Boats estimate they would have an additional income of $24,000 an avg. of $3,000 per boat

Because of weather conditions affecting Perdido Pass:

> 14 Charter boats were forced to cancel 635 fishing trips; an average of 45 trips per charter, for an estimated income loss of $31,750 – for an avg. income loss per charter boat of $2,267

Total estimated gross operating expenses:

> 14 Charter boats $76,410 – an avg. of $2,547 (sic) per charter boat per year
> 15 Commercial Fishing Boats $25,000 – an avg. of $1,666 per commercial fishing boat per year

Boats using Pensacola Pass because of weather conditions affecting Perdido Pass:

> 14 Charter boats lost 1, 122 hours fishing time due to travel to Pensacola Pass – an avg. of 80 hours per charter boat.

At the regular rate of $6.50 per hour this amounts to $520 per charter boat or a total of $7,260.

In addition 8 charter boats consumed an additional total of 9,320 gallons of gasoline or an additional consumption of 1,165 gallons per boat costing a total of $2,608 for an average of $326 per charter boat.

One large charter boat unable to use Perdido Pass at any time consumed 2,250 gallons of diesel fuel going into the Gulf of Mexico by way of Pensacola Pass as well as losing 450 hours of fishing time.

List of Major Accidents
Occurring in Perdido Pass – 1959 to 1965

Editors Note: Below is a listing of major accidents occurring in Perdido Pass. This listing was prepared by the Orange Beach Fishing Association in support of their efforts to get the Perdido Pass routinely dredged, seawalls placed, appropriate jetties built, and permanent navigational aids put in place.

According to information furnished by local navigation interests, numerous accidents have occurred to boatman attempting to navigate Perdido Pass at times when adverse wave and surf conditions rendered it hazardous for navigation. Narratives of a number of the major accidents, for which information is available, occurring since 1959, are given in the following paragraphs.

1. During the summer of 1959, the charter boat 'Dottie Lou' ran aground and sunk in Perdido Pass while trying to reach the protected waters of Perdido Bay after a squall rapidly developed in the offshore area. The operator and four passengers were   rescued without injury but damages to the boat, including the cost of raising, towing, and repairs totaled $2,135.

2. In April 1959, a charter boat operator rescued a 12–year old boy and his father from the waters of Perdido Pass after finding them at 6:00 o'clock in the morning hanging onto a boat that had   capsized in the Gulf entrance. The boat was salvaged, but the outboard motor and all fishing equipment were lost.

3. While engaged in commercial fishing activities in December 1959, the charter boat 'Sea Son' ran aground while trying to navigate Perdido Pass after being caught in the Gulf by a squall. The operator was fortunate in being able to free the vessel before it was a complete loss. Repairs to the boat, which required dry–docking to refasten parts of the keel, repainting, and a new motor, amounted to $1,230.

4. On 4 April 1959, the commercial fishing boat 'Magnolia' ran aground in Perdido Pass during bad weather while returning from a fishing trip. Due to the resulting structural damage sustained, the 'Magnolia' sank with 3,000 pounds of mackerel aboard. The market value of the fish lost was $390 and the cost of repairs to the boat amounted to $1,000. Several years prior to this accident, the same fisherman operating the snapper

boat 'Virginia Dare' ran aground in the Pass during bad weather. As a result of this accident, 4,000 pounds of snapper were lost and structural damages to the boat amounted to $364.

5. The rapid development of a squall in July 1960 caught a private cruiser in the waters of the open Gulf without enough fuel to reach either Pensacola or Mobile Bay entrance. The owner, knowing the dangerous conditions in Perdido Pass, was forced to seek refuge in Perdido Bay. While crossing the bar the boat fell into a wave trough, striking bottom, resulting in the loss of a wheel, strut, and shaft. Fortunately the cruiser had two engines and was able to reach safety under its own power. Damages to the boat as a result of this incident totaled $354.

6. In December 1960, the commercial snapper boat 'Barbara' ran aground in Perdido Pass while trying to reach the protected waters of Perdido Bay during bad weather. The accident happened at night and the boat and cargo were a complete loss. The estimated value of the boat was recorded by the U. S. Coast Guard at $17,000.

7. In April 1961, one of the most efficient and experienced charter boat operators lost his life while trying to navigate the Pass. The rapid development of a storm in the Gulf forced the return of the charter boat 'Sea Duster' with a party of four aboard. A heavy sea breaking across the shallow bar caught the boat, throwing the operator against a hard canopy and breaking his neck. One of the passengers was almost pulled into the water by the anchor rope as it fell overboard. Another boatman boarded the boat and brought it into port without injury to the other passengers. Damages to the boat amounted to about $200.

8. Due to the rapid development of a storm in the Gulf, a charter boat, engaged in commercial fishing activities during December 1961, tried to seek shelter through Perdido Pass. After reaching the pass, the boatman found the prevailing conditions too dangerous for navigation and consequently was forced to seek shelter through Pensacola Bay entrance. The heavy seas were from the southeast; or abeam, making the trip extremely difficult and hazardous. The vessel reached Pensacola Bay but waves breaking against the boat and cabin resulted in the requirement to dry–dock and repaint the boat.

9. On 5 July 1962, a pleasure cruiser was grounded while trying to return

through Perdido Pass during a sudden squall. Five persons were rescued but the boat, valued at $3,500, washed ashore about two miles east of the Pass and was a total loss. Rescue attempts by two boatmen failed when their vessel grounded in the heavy surf and was forced to turn back. Damages sustained by the vessel amounted to $250.

10.   Testimony presented at public hearings disclosed that during 1961 personnel from marinas located in the area rescued eight persons from the waters of Perdido Pass. The total vessel damages sustained as a result of these accidents amounted to $2,205.

11.   In 1965, the charter boat 'Oak Park' grounded in Perdido Pass and went to pieces endangering the lives of the five passengers and the skipper. The boat was a total loss.

Letter to Roland Walker about Perdido Pass – 1966

WILLIAM L. DICKINSON
2D DISTRICT, ALABAMA

OFFICE: ROOM 460
CANNON HOUSE OFFICE BLDG.
PHONE: 225-2901
WASHINGTON, D.C.

DISTRICT OFFICE:
ROOM 408 POST OFFICE BLDG.
PHONE: 263-7521, EXT. 453
MONTGOMERY, ALABAMA

Congress of the United States
House of Representatives
Washington, D.C. 20515

COMMITTEES:
GOVERNMENT OPERATIONS
HOUSE ADMINISTRATION

2D DISTRICT COUNTIES:
BALDWIN   CRENSHAW
BUTLER   ESCAMBIA
CONECUH   LOWNDES
COVINGTON   MONTGOMERY
PIKE

May 2, 1966

Captain Roland E. Walker
Orange Beach,
Alabama

Dear Captain Walker:

I want to personally express my sincere thanks to you for coming to Washington to testify before the Public Works Subcommittee on appropriations for Perdido Pass.

I frankly think it went well and although I have only talked with subcommittee members briefly following the hearings, I am encouraged at our prospects for obtaining these funds.

I thought you might like to have a copy of the picture taken while you were as a souvenir of your visit to Washington.

The girls all send their regards.

With kindest regards, I am

Sincerely,

Bill

WM. L. DICKINSON

WLD:em

Above is a letter from U.S. Representative Bill Dickinson to Captain Roland Walker, Sr. thanking him for his help in presenting support for navigational changes to Perdido Pass.

Appendix

DEPARTMENT OF THE ARMY
MOBILE DISTRICT, CORPS OF ENGINEERS
P. O. BOX 2288
MOBILE, ALABAMA 36601

IN REPLY REFER TO

SAMOP~O

2 June 1969

NAVIGATION BULLETIN NO. 69-44

PERDIDO PASS, ALA.

NOTICE TO NAVIGATION INTERESTS:

Construction of the Perdido Pass Channel project has been completed. Principal features of the project include a navigation channel 12 feet deep by 150 feet wide extending for a distance of 1,300 feet from the Gulf into the inlet, then 9 feet deep and 100 feet wide for 2,200 feet to the highway bridge where the channel branches into two 9-foot deep by 100-foot wide channels, one of which extends 3,400 feet into Terry Cove and the other 3,200 feet into the southerly arm of Perdido Bay.

Two converging rock jetties, one on each side of the channel, are provided to arrest the movement of sand across the Pass and thus reduce the tendency for the navigation channel to silt up. The west jetty extends from the west end of the seawall to about the 10-foot depth of water in the Gulf. The east jetty extends from Florida Point to the 12-foot depth in the Gulf and is provided with a low sheet-pile weir section with the top of the weir six inches below mean low tide. The 1,000-foot long weir section is provided to permit the predominantly westward movement of sand over the weir. A dredged deposition basin is provided between the weir section and the navigation channel to trap the sand before it reaches the channel.

The project will be maintained by periodic dredging to restore project depths where necessary in the channels and to remove accumulated material from the deposition basin. If the weir section had not been provided, the predominant movement of sand would be along the east jetty and across the channel at the outer end of the jetties. Maintenance of the project under such conditions would require dredging operations in unprotected waters of the Gulf and would be much more expensive and hazardous than the operations required for the project as built.

A plan of the project is shown on the reverse side of this bulletin. Channel markers shown on the plan are to be installed by the Coast Guard during the first week of June.

F. O. GAILLARD
Chief, Operations Division

Above is a notification letter to navigation interests issued from the Army Corps of Engineers regarding the completion of construction of a new Perdido Pass Channel.

Perdido Pass changes to Navigation – 1969

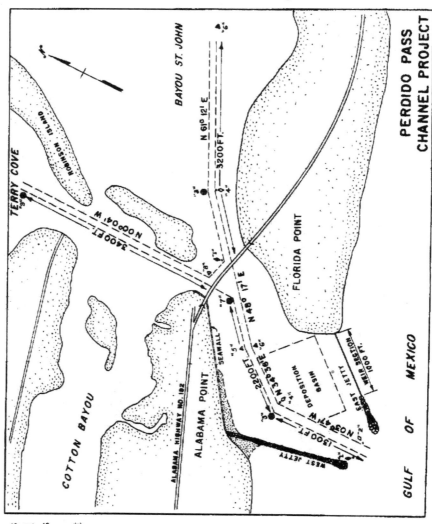

This chart shows the details of the Perdido Pass channel construction by Army Corps of Engineers in 1969. The design of this channel project is nearly identical to a channel project in Wilmington, North Carolina.

Appendix

Various Fishing Associations

Members
of the Perdido Pass Deep Sea Fishing Association

Editors note: The information in the following members list is from an advertisement in the 1939 issue of the 'Baldwin County Highlights and Highways' published by Goldenrod Studios.

Amel Callaway	Charles Huff	Dan Callaway
Bill Morrill	Herman Callaway	Bob Walker
Leroy Carson	Lee Walker	Al Dietz
Rufus Walker	H. L. Ewing	Roy Walker
B. T. Hudson	Rabun Walker	Jim Hudson
	Crockett White	

The First Officers of the 'Boatmen of Orange Beach'
June 1951
meeting held at home of Roland Walker, Sr.

Neil Lauder – President
Ray Callaway – Vice President
Roland Walker – Secretary
Hurbert Low – Treasurer

Name of the group was changed July 2, 1951 to
'Orange Beach Deep Sea Fishing Association'

Below is the current logo of the Orange Beach Fishing Association

Appendix

Orange Beach Fishing Association
2003–2004 Directory

Board of Directors
President: Mrs. Bobbi Walker
Vice–President: Captain Mike Rowell

Board Members

Captain Brian Annan	Captain Ben Fairey	Captain Mike Thierry
Captain Gloyice Ard	Captain Brian Lynch	Captain Skipper Thierry
Captain Randy Boogs	Captain Wynn Millson	Captain Bobby Walker
Captain Kathy Broughton	Captain Brian Nichols	Captain Don Walker
	Captain Dan Ratliff	

Captain's Directory

Captain	Boat Name	Boat data
Captain Alawine, Sonny	*Summer Breeze I*	55' Custom Resmondo 1–20 Pass.
Captain Andrews, John	*Therapy*	42' Sportfisherman 1–6 Passengers
Captain Annan, Donald	*Joyce*	40' Custom 1–6 Passengers
Captain Annan, Brian	*Gulf Rebel*	44' Custom 1–6 Passengers
Captain Ard, Tom	*Fairwater II*	40' Sea Harvester 1–22 Passengers
Captain Ard, Gloyice	*Boll Weevil*	38' Buskin 1–6 Passengers
Captain Arsenault, Dennis	*Miss Stephi*	20' Shoal Cat 1–4 Passengers
Captain Ballard, Claude	*Mar–T*	36' Topaz 1–6 Passengers
Captain Barron, James	*Movin On Up*	55' Ocean Sptfisher 1–6 Pass.
Captain Boggs, Randy	*Reek Surprise*	65' Custom Walk Around 1–60 Pass.
Captain Brackman, Robin	*Teacher's Pet*	27' Proline Ctr. Console 1–6 Pass.
Captain Broughton, Kathy	*Kittywake*	23' SeaPro 1–4 Passengers

300

Captain Brown, David	*Audrey II*	23' SeaPro 1–4 Passengers
Captain Brown, Jr., Mel	*Patti Ann*	30' Sportfish 1–6 Passengers
Captain Broz, Frankie	*Sea Spook II*	45' Sportfisherman 1–6 Passengers
Captain Bryant, Gary	Re*d Eye*	36' Topaz 1–6 Passengers
Captain Cappar, Dick	*Traveler*	38' Infinity 1–6 Passengers
Captain Chambliss, Jeff	*Baby Therapy*	22' Bay Quest 1–4 Passengers
Captain Cudworth, Jimbo	*Zeke's Lady*	62' Party Boat Up to 66 Passengers
Captain Daniels, Brian	*Limited Entry*	23' Sportcraft 1–6 Passengers
Captain Davis, Mike	*Albacore II*	44' Sportfisherman 1–6 Passengers
Captain Day, Chip	*Chipper's Clipper*	42' Custom Sptfisher 1–6 Pass.
Captain Douglas, Bill	*Doug–Out*	31' Sportfisherman 1–6 Passengers
Captain Eberly, Paul	*Reel Surprise*	65' Custom Walk Around 1–60 Pass.
Captain Ethridge, Iris	*On the Crosstie*	31' Sportfisherman 1–6 Passengers
Captain Fairey, Ben	*Necessity*	62' Resmondo 1–36 Passengers
Captain Fill, Peter	*Yankee Star*	38' Libby 1–6 Passengers
Captain Fitzsimmons, Fitz	*Miss Celeste*	100' Sportfisherman 1–66 Passenger
Captain Formwalt, Joe	*South Wind*	40' Commercial Marine 22 Passenger
Captain Foust, Steve	*Aquastar*	Gillman 57' 1–23 Passengers
Captain Frady, Troy	*Distraction*	42' Hatteras 6 Passengers
Captain Gaines II, Jack	*Adventure Quest*	46' Bertram 1–6 Passengers

Captain Garner, Chris	*Record Holder*	22' Offshore
		Up to 4 Passengers
Captain Gay, Wendell	*Job Site*	30' Black Watch
Captain Gams, Robin		1–6 Passengers
Captain Goodwin, Gary	*Jamie G*	36' Hatteras
		1–6 Passengers
Captain Greene, Johnny	*Itimidator*	65' Sportfisherman
		1–49 Passengers
Captain Grube, Neal	*Catch–It*	38' Sportfisherman
		1–15 Passengers
Captain Hardee, Michael	*Migration*	42' Bertram
		1–6 Passengers
Captain Harrison, Bob	*Pokey Jim II*	40' Chris Craft
		1–6 Passengers
Captain Hinz, Bill	*Wild Orange*	38' Sportfisherman
		1–6 Passengers
Captain Hollingshead, Johnny	*Miss Hollie*	38' Buskens
		1–6 Passengers
Captain Ivie, Patrick	*Intruder*	53' Sportfisherman
		1–28 Passengers
Captain Jimmerson, Scott	*Showtime*	45' Resmondo
		21 Passengers
Captain Johnson, Scott	*Aardvark*	23' Offshore
		1–6 Passengers
Captain Jones, Art	*Dana–J*	36' Custom
		1–6 Passengers
Captain Jones, Tom	*Jones Inshore*	22' Offshore
		1–6 Passengers
Captain King, Charles	*Wishbone*	39' Seaharvester
		1–22 Passengers
Captain Kostelecky, Bob	*Patti Ann*	30' Sportfish
		1–6 Passengers
Captain Kruse, Allan	*Rookie*	50' Custom Sportfish
		1–16 Pass.
Captain Lanier, Leonard	*Cutwater*	29' Open Sportfisher
		1–6 Pass.
Captain Lattof, Mitch	*Albacore II*	44' Sportfisherman
		1–6 Passengers
Captain Leiterman, Nick	*Hot Spot*	53' Sportfisherman
		1–28 Passengers

Captain Lynch, Brian	*Island Girl*	50' Gleen Young 1–20 Passengers
Captain Manthei, Erik	*Fish'n Fool*	44' Sportfisherman 1–20 Passengers
Captain McPherson, Don	*Getaway*	36' Hatteras 1–6 Passengers
Captain McDuffie, Rick	*Sea Hunter*	62' Resmondo Sptfish 1–35 Passenger
Captain Millson, Wynn	*Hey Boy II*	36' Topaz 1–6 Passengers
Captain Morgan, Darrell	*Ashley Reene*	40' Jersey 6 Passengers
Captain Murdoch, Ricky	*Fish Trap*	31' Island Hopper 1–6 Passengers
Captain Murphy, Kevin	*Good Times II*	42' Custom Sptfisher 1–22 Pass.
Captain Nash, Joe	*Cool Change*	46' Custom 1–20 Passengers
Captain Pfieffer, George	*C.A.T.*	40' Sea Harvester 1–30 Passengers
Captain Pruitt, Chad	*Reel Job*	24' Blazer Bay 1–6 Passengers
Captain Ratliff, Dan	*Shirley R., Too…*	34' Phoenix Express 1–6 Passengers
Captain Rowell, Mike	*Annie Girl*	62' Resmondo up to 40 Passengers
Captain Salley, Mike	*Sure Shot*	42' Sportfisherman 1–6 Passengers
Captain Shaver, Brent	*Captain Bligh*	23' Kenner 1–6 Passengers
Captain Shaver, Mo	*Mo Fishin*	23' Kenner Ctr. Console 1–6 Pass.
Captain Sightler, Dewitt	*C–Rose*	52' Sportfisherman 1–22 Passengers
Captain Smith, Russell	*Outcast*	65' Bonner 1–60 Passengers
Captain Smith, Sandy	*Misty*	52' Sportfisherman 1–6 Passengers
Captain Sowards, Grady	*Good Times I*	52' Harkers Island 1–20 Passengers

Captain Staff, Bill	*Sea Spray*	65' Resmondo
		1–43 Passengers
Captain Thierry, Mike	*Lady Ann*	60' Gillman
		1–19 Passengers
Captain Thompson, Eddie	*Showtime*	45' Resmondo
		21 Passengers
Captain Tillery, Donnie	*Robin Lynne*	45' Resmondo
		1–6 Passengers
Captain Trimble, Neil	*We'll See*	52' Custom Davis
		1–22 Passengers
Captain Tucker, Butch	*Shady Lady*	60' Sportfisherman
		1–42 Passengers
Captain Walker, Bobby	*Summer Breeze II*	60' Custom Resmondo
		1–30 Pass.
Captain Walker, Don	*Lady D*	62' Resmondo
		1–32 Passengers
Captain Walter, David	*Maranatha*	114' Reefmaker
		Work Boat
Captain Watts, Bryan	*Undertaker*	41' Sportfisherman
		1–6 Passengers
Captain Wheat, David	*Rip Tide*	45' Resmondo
		1–20 Passengers
Captain Wilhite, Alfred	*Summer Hunter*	39' Sportfisherman
		1–6 Passengers
Captain Wilson, Seth	*Jaclyn Rose*	38' Bertram
		1–6 Passengers
Captain Wise, Troy	*4 Seasons Outfitters*	24' Carolina Skiff
		1–6 Passengers
Captain Woodruff, Dale	*Class Act*	52' Miller
Captain Woodruff, Ron		

Charter Trip Etiquette
from
2003–2004 Orange Beach Fishing Association Directory

1. Dress for comfort. Bring sunglasses, soft sole light colored shoes, sunscreen and a camera.

2. Avoid heavy rich foods and alcohol the night before. Eat a light breakfast that morning. If taking motion sickness medication follow its directions.

3. It is customary to bring lunch for the crew. Bring an ample supply of eats and drinks.

4. Respect the boat and equipment. Your Captain and Crew have a lot of respect and pride in their vessels. Equipment can be costly to you if damaged or lost overboard.

5. Deckhands work hard for you and have pride in your catch. Their day starts several hours before your trip and extends hours after you are gone. We recommend a 15% tip over and above a fish cleaning fee.

6. Trips from 4 hours to 3 days are available. Choose a trip that suits you. Always inquire about payment method, cancellation and bad weather policies.

List of Saltwater fish species

Black Grouper
Bluefish
Cobia (Ling)
Crocker
Dolphin
Florida Pompano
Flounder
Gag Grouper
Gray Snapper (Mangrove,
   Black)
Gray Triggerfish
Greater Amberjack
Jack Crevalle
King Mackerel
Lane Snapper
Marlin
Red Fish (Red Drum)
Red Grouper
Red Snapper
Sailfish
Scamp
Shark
Sheepshead
Snapper (Red, Vermilion or
   Beeliner, Lane Gray,
   Mutton, Yellowtail)
Spanish Mackerel
Spotted Seatrout
Striped Bass
Swordfish
Tarpon
Tripletail (Blackfish)
Tuna
Vermillon Snapper (Beeliner)
Wahoo
Yellowfin Grouper

Prohibited fish species:
Goliath Grouper (Jewfish)
Nassau Grouper
Ray:
   Atlantic Manta
   Spotted Eagle
Shark:
   Atlantic Angel
   Basking
   Bigeye
   Thresher
   Duskey
   Long Mako
   Sand Tiger
   Whale
   White
   Nurse
   Smalltail
Smalltooth Sawfish
Largetooth Sawfish

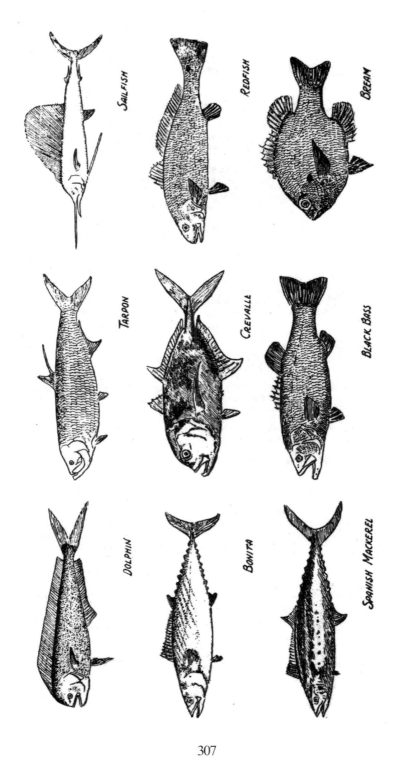

SAILFISH

REDFISH

BREAM

TARPON

CREVALLE

BLACK BASS

DOLPHIN

BONITA

SPANISH MACKEREL

11ᵗʰ Annual

WHO IS ELIGIBLE?
Any full paying passenger fishing aboard a member Orange Beach Fishing Association Charter Boat from October 1 through October 31, 2004. There are no additional entry fees.

HOW TO ENTER
Contact any boat in this directory or visit our website at www.gulffishing.net and click on Captain's Directory for a listing of boats.

DIVISIONS
This year's rodeo offers separate divisions for "inshore" and "offshore" fishing.

PRIZES
Cash and prizes will be awarded in each category. Weekly prizes will be awarded for the largest Red Snapper.

MANY THANKS TO OUR 2003 SPONSORS
Alabama Gulf Coast Area Chamber of Commerce, Blue Water Ships Stores, C-Sharpe Co., LLC, Island Wide Marine Agency, J&M Tackle, Resmondo Boat Works, Inc., Sam's, SanRoc Cay, Saunders Yachtwoks, Smith Outdoors, Top Gun Tackle, Vision Bank, Whitney Bank, and Zeke's Landing Marina.

Contact
The Orange Beach Fishing Association for Official Rules
Results are updated weekly on our website at www.gulffishing.net
P.O. Box 1202 • Orange Beach, AL 36561 • (251) 981-2300
Rodeo still being planned at time of printing. Information subject to change.

Above is a 2004 advertisement for the annual Orange Beach Fishing Rodeo held the full month of October each year by the Orange Beach Fishing Association .

Appendix

Above is an advertisement for the annual Orange Beach World Championship Red Snapper Tournament of the Orange Beach Fishing Association for the year 2005. All proceeds go to building public artificial reefs, representation in Washington, DC, and funding red snapper research.

GULF COAST CHALLENGE
BILLFISH TOURNAMENT
ORANGE BEACH, ALABAMA

SPONSORED BY

THE ORANGE BEACH FISHING ASSOCIATION

JULY 5 - 6

SPORTSMAN MARINA

ENTRY FEE $2500

CONTACT

THE ORANGE BEACH FISHING ASSOCIATION

FOR OFFICIAL RULES AND REGISTRATION FORMS

251-981-2300

PRIZES AWARDED IN FOUR CATEGORIES

BLUE MARLIN, TUNA, DOLPHIN AND WAHOO

[Above is the flyer for the annual July Orange Beach Bill Fishing Tournament of the Orange Beach Fishing Association for the year 2002.]

This is a copy of a stock certificate that belonged to Ted Childress for 31–1/2 shares in the South Baldwin Oil Company, Inc. This company drilled the first and only known oil well in Orange Beach in 1952. The well was a 'dry well'; i.e., finding no oil or gas. The well was located just east of Highway 161, about a block south of Marina Road.

After the well was dismantled, the area was used as a community trash dump for many years.

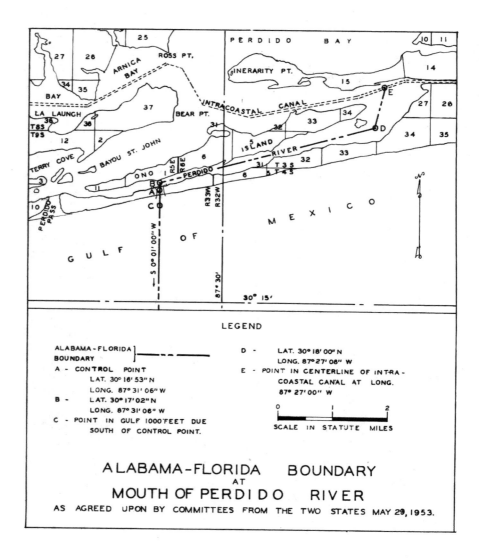

LEGEND

ALABAMA-FLORIDA
BOUNDARY
A - CONTROL POINT
     LAT. 30° 16' 53" N
     LONG. 87° 31' 06" W
B - LAT. 30° 17' 02" N
     LONG. 87° 31' 06" W
C - POINT IN GULF 1000 FEET DUE
    SOUTH OF CONTROL POINT.

D - LAT. 30° 18' 00" N
     LONG. 87° 27' 08" W
E - POINT IN CENTERLINE OF INTRA-
    COASTAL CANAL AT LONG.
    87° 27' 00" W

SCALE IN STATUTE MILES

ALABAMA-FLORIDA   BOUNDARY
AT
MOUTH OF PERDIDO   RIVER
AS AGREED UPON BY COMMITTEES FROM THE TWO STATES MAY 29, 1953.

312

Appendix

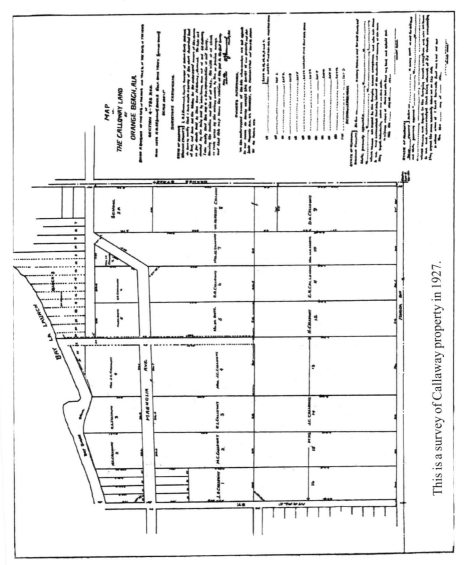

This is a survey of Callaway property in 1927.

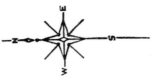

313

Walker Family Property

This is a 1953 survey of the subdivision of the G. C. Bill Estate. This property was originally part of the William Kee Spanish Land Grant. This survey does not include the Lemuel Walker, Sr. or Jr. property.

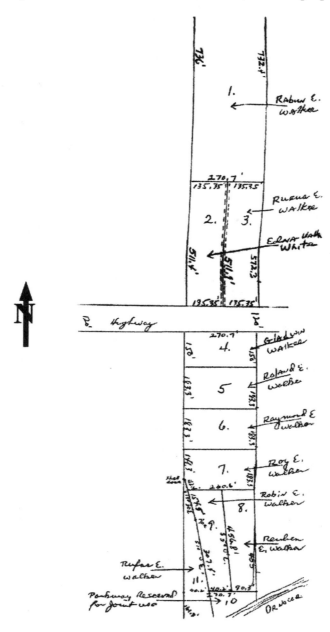

Appendix

Descendants of James Clifford Callaway

1	James Clifford Callaway	1854 – 1917	
..	+Nancy Ellen Childress	1857 – 1942	
....	2	Anna Caroline Callaway	1876 – 1935
....		+Frank Hannibal Parker	1871 – 1960
....	3	Ethel Ruth Parker	Unknown – Unknown
....		+Bill Korte	Unknown – Unknown
....	3	Louisa Antionette "Nettie" Parker	1896 – 1994
....		+Irvin Adolph Knopp	Unknown – Unknown
....	3	Carrie Maebelle Parker	Unknown – Unknown
....		+John Robert Davis	Unknown – Unknown
....	3	James Hannibal Parker	Unknown – Unknown
....		+Irma Amelia Rudnik	Unknown – Unknown
....	3	Frances Ellen Parker	Unknown – Unknown
....	3	William Earl Parker	Unknown – Unknown
....		+Willadean "Billie" Lewis	Unknown – Unknown
....	3	Gladys Christine Parker	Unknown – Unknown
....		+Frank Jones	Unknown – Unknown
....	3	Opal Eunice Parker	Unknown – Unknown
....		+George Shoemaker	Unknown – Unknown
....	3	Donald Weller Parker	Unknown – Unknown
....		+Ethel Hazel Lewis	Unknown – Unknown
....	3	Mary Anna Parker	Unknown – Unknown
....	2	Wiley A. Callaway	1880 – 1881
....	2	Willie 'Florence' Callaway	1877 – 1947
....		+Hendrich Detter Harms	1877 – 1953
....	3	Cresie Grey Harms	Unknown – Unknown
....		+James Terry Snow	Unknown – Unknown
....	3	Rudolph William Harms	Unknown – Unknown
....		+Leona H. Beyers	Unknown – Unknown
....	3	Herbert Oscar Harms	Unknown – Unknown
....		+Helen Johnson	Unknown – Unknown
....	3	Louis Ralph Harms, Sr.	Unknown – Unknown
....		+Mable Beyer McGrew	Unknown – Unknown
....	3	George Frederick Harms	Unknown – Unknown
....		+Ethel Mae Nelson	Unknown – Unknown
....	3	Baby Harms	Unknown – Unknown
....	3	Leon Langdon Harms	Unknown – Unknown
....		+Doris Alene Potts	Unknown – Unknown
....	2	William Herbert "Uncle Hurbert" Callaway	1883 – 1953
....		+Laura Alabama Ewing	1888 – 1982
....	3	Harvey Heindinmire Callaway	1908 – 1933
....	3	Myrtle Yonne Callaway	1910 – 1963
....		+Samuel White Oliver	1912 – 1963
....	4	Samuel White Oliver, Jr.	1929 – 1970
....		+Joyce Louise Mathews	Private –
....	4	Leo Clifton Oliver	Private –
....		+Ann E. Stellhorn	Private –
....	4	Jewell Carolyn Oliver	Private –
....		+Charles Edmond Dunnam	Private –
....	3	James George Callaway	1912 – 1920
....	3	Lilly Callaway	1913 – 1969
....		+Herman Williams	Unknown – Unknown
....	3	Meigs Childress Callaway	1915 – 1917
....	3	Jess Willard Callaway	1917 – 1922

	Gen	Name	Dates
....	3	Jack Dempsey Callaway, Sr.	1919 – 1998
....		+Louise Mildred McIntyre	1920 – Unknown
....	4	Carolyn Louise Callaway	Private –
....		+Francis Edward Lake	Private –
....	4	Jack Dempsy Callaway Jr.	Private –
....		+Donna Sue Unknown	Private –
....	4	Myrtle Yvonne Callaway	Private –
....		+Phillip Mathers	Private –
....	4	Pamela Dale Callaway	Private –
....		+Terry Mitchell Poiroux	Private –
....	2	Daniel 'Dan' Oscar Callaway, Sr.	1885 – 1967
....		+Molly Ewing	1890 – 1969
....	3	Frances Eleanor Callaway	1908 – 1979
....		+Corry Washington Rudd	1895 – 1972
....	4	Merle Eleanor Rudd	Private –
....		+Corry Deeter Harms, Sr.	Private –
....	3	Vallie Callaway	1909 – 1989
....		+Buford Marion Williams, Sr.	1900 – Unknown
....	4	Buford Marion Williams, Jr.	Private –
....		+Bevery Rae Brown	Private –
....	3	Minnie Lee Callaway	1911 – 1981
....		+Emmons 'Em' Durell Brown	Unknown – 1978
....	3	Daniel 'Oscar' Callaway, Jr.	1914 – 1987
....		+Edna Mary Broussard	1913 – 1983
....	4	Beverly Ann Callaway	Private –
....		+John Edward Kountz	Private –
....	4	Robert Allen Callaway	Private –
....		+Joyce Thomas	Private –
....	2	Elver Rix Callaway, Sr.	1887 – 1955
....		+Mina Laura Wilson	1886 – 1960
....	3	Ellen Lousia Callaway	1914 – Unknown
....		+John Arthur Walter	Unknown – Unknown
....	4	Robert Russell Walter	Unknown – Unknown
....	3	Elver Rix 'Cal' Callaway, Jr.	1918 – 1999
....		+Kathryn Mae Nelson	Private –
....	4	Rix Leon Callaway	Private –
....		+Denise 'Dede' Lynn Bowen	Private –
....	4	Christine Callaway	Private –
....	3	Elsie Elizabeth 'Betty' Callaway	1924 – 1988
....		+Joseph Burl Shouldis	1920 – 1988
....	4	Ann Austin Shouldis	Private –
....		+Robert Herald Massey	Private –
....	4	James Frederick Shouldis	Private –
....		+Laurie Jean Bryars	Private –
....	4	John Shouldis	Private –
....	2	James 'Amel' Callaway	1890 – 1974
....		+Mildred Hubbard	1892 – 1984
....	3	Eva 'Lois' Callaway	1911 – 1990
....		+Chester"Chet" Bessette	1907 – 1969
....	4	Mildred Dora Bessette	Private –
....	4	Edward Gary Bessette	Private –
....		+Susan Lee Martin	Private –
....		*2nd Wife of Edward Gary Bessette:	
....		+Kathy Jean Mirabile Smith	Private –
....		*3rd Wife of Edward Gary Bessette:	
....		+Lynn Wunnenberg	Private –

	Level	Name	Dates
....	3	Marian 'Eleanor' Callaway	1914 – Unknown
....		+Ronald James Lauder	1908 – 1971
....	4	Mildred Marie Lauder	Private –
....		+Eldred Burder Tedgew, Jr.	Private –
....	4	Marion Eleanor Lauder	Private –
....		+Thomas Wayne Richburg	Private –
....	3	Katherine Riley 'Brownie' Callaway	1917 – 1996
....		+Neil Anderson Lauder	1912 – 1995
....	4	Robert 'Bobby' Neil Lauder	1938 – 1974
....		+Peggy Jo Forehand	Private –
....	4	James Amel Lauder	Private –
....		+Frances Skipper	Private –
.... *		*2nd Wife of James Amel Lauder: unknown	
....		+Elaine Benick	Private –
....	4	David Thurston Lauder	Private –
....		+Margaret Miller	Private –
....	3	William Ashbel 'Billy' Callaway	1920 – 1998
....		+Elinor Hanson	Private –
....	4	Richard Murray Callaway	Private –
....		+Frances 'Mitsy' Whalen	Private –
....	4	Melissa Lynn Callaway	Private –
....		+Edward Moody	Private –
....		*2nd Wife of William Ashbel 'Billy' Callaway:	
....		+Muriel Hamlin	Unknown – Unknown
....	4	William Raymond Callaway	Private –
....	4	Kenneth David Callaway	Private –
....	3	James Dudley Callaway, Sr.	1922 – 1995
....		+Mary Ann Turner	Unknown – 1982
....	4	James Dudley Callaway Jr.	Private –
....	4	Judy Ann Callaway	Private –
....		+Randall Carroll Hartley	Private –
....	4	Amanda Sue Callaway	Private –
....		+Jack Nevitt	Private –
....	4	Scott Amel Callaway	Private –
....	3	Raymond 'Capt. Ray' Dudley Callaway	1925 – 1998
....		+Ella Rose Hutchinson	Private –
....	4	Earl Raymond Callaway	Private –
....		+Julie Marie DePetro	Private –
....	4	Roland Arthur Callaway	Private –
....	3	David Hubbard Callaway	Private –
....		+Ellen Henrietta Rummel	Private –
....		*2nd Wife of David Hubbard Callaway:	
....		+Marie Beyers Feuchfinger	Private –
....	4	Susan Ellen Callaway	Private –
.................:...............		+John David Kramer	Private –
....	4	Debra Dawn Callaway	Private –
....		+Charles Curtis Finch, Jr.	Private –
....	4	Reed Ashley Callaway	Private –
....		+Charlotte Thames	Private –
....	3	Macklin Neil Callaway	Private –
....		+Jacquline Groff	Private –
.... 2		Herman Heinburg Callaway	1891 – 1974
....		+Elma Lucretia Williams	1897 – 1970
....	3	Arvin Williams Callaway	1914 – 1980
....		+Irene Green	1914 – 1988
....	4	Walter 'Wally' Williams Callaway	Private –

	+Karen Walch	Private –
3	Lloyd Tabar Callaway	1917 – 1990
	+Loraine Rodguies	Private –
4	Dianna Callaway	Private –
3	Marion Leslie Callaway	Private –
	+Helen Wagner	Private –
4	Steven Leslie Callaway	Private –
	+Janet Gail	Private –
4	Todd Rawlin Callaway	Private –
	+Linda K. Unknown	Private –
3	Herman 'Clifford' Callaway	Private –
	+Jean Antoinette Powers	1925 – 1999
4	Gary Wayne Callaway	Private –
	+Debra Coco	Private –
4	Donna Marie Callaway	Private –
	*2nd Wife of Herman 'Clifford' Callaway:	
	+Lee Ella Conlay	1923 – 1988
4	Rita Jean Callaway	Private –
	*3rd Wife of Herman 'Clifford' Callaway:	
	+Cornelia 'Myrth' Graham Fuller	Private –
3	Hazel C. Callaway	1925 – 1975
	+O. Donald 'Andy' Wenzel	Private –
4	O. Donald "Donnie" Wenzel, Jr.	Private –
	+Beverly Unknown	Private –
4	Rebecca "Becky" Wenzel	Private –
	+William "Bill" Paul	Private –
3	Nolan Chester Callaway	Private –
	+Kathleen Collette Dorsey	Private –
4	Robert Lester Callaway	Private –
4	David Lynn Callaway	Private –
4	Debra Allen Callaway	Private –
4	Carolyn Sue Callaway	Private –
	*2nd Wife of Nolan Chester Callaway:	
	+Kathryn Laverne 'Kitty' Barchard	Private –
2	Minnie Childress 'Chip' Callaway	1894 – 1966
	+Dorothy Beatrice Orr	1905 – 1989
3	Betty Jean Callaway	Private –
	+Elmer George Schuchmann, Jr.	Private –
	*2nd Husband of Betty Jean Callaway:	
	+Oliver Wilbert Perkins	Private –
3	Doris Faye Callaway	Private –
	+Oliver Hanson Hall, Jr.	Private –
3	Mary Louise Callaway	Private –
	+Donald Howard Ziegler, Sr.	Private –
2	Hilda Gulli Callaway	1896 – 1985
	+Edward George Dietz	1873 – 1931
3	Alazarian Edward Dietz	1914 – 1977
	+Mary Bernadine Ray	1915 – 1980
4	David Ray Dietz	Private –
3	Evalyn "Eva" Gray Brasher Dietz	1913 – 1996
	+Roy Elwood Walker	1909 – 2001
4	LeeRoy Walker	Private –
	+Stephnie Fun	Private –
4	Warren Elwood Walker	1935 – 1999
	+Molly Brown	Private –
4	Jerry Rex Walker	Private –

....		+Betty Marie Springsteen	Private –
....	3	Alma May Brasher Dietz	1915 – 1997
....		+Rabun Earl Walker	1912 – 1986
....	4	James Kenneth Walker	1936 – 1999
....		+Loretta Unknown	Private –
....	4	Abbie Yvonne Walker	Private –
....		+Rex David Bullard, Jr.	Private –
....	4	Sidney Earl Walker	Private –
....		+Ann Johnson	Private –
....		*2nd Wife of Sidney Earl Walker:	
....		+Sarah Wilson	Private –
....	4	Eva Marie Walker	Private –
....		+Julian Raymond Springsteen	Private –
....	4	Hilda Gail Walker	Private –
....		+Richard Allen Graham	Private –
....	2	Raphael 'Leon' Callaway	1899 – 1977
....		+Forrest Estella Waldrop	1903 – Unknown
....	3	Maxine Marie Callaway	1923 – 1923
....	3	Rex Leon Callaway	Private –
....		+Carol Evans	Private –
....	3	Ronald Forrest "Ronnie" Callaway	Private –
....		+Margaret Wooley	Unknown – Unknown
....		*2nd Wife of Ronald Forrest "Ronnie" Callaway:	
....		+Mary Unknown	Private –

319

Descendants of Lemuel Walker, Sr.

```
1  Lemuel Walker, Sr.              1817 – 1896
..  +Rosine Patterson Gabel         1839 – 1878
........      2        Juliet Walker           1862 – Unknown
........      2        William B. Walker       1868 – 1886
        *2nd Wife of Lemuel Walker, Sr.:
..  +Lovey Styron                   1816 – 1860
........      2        Sammy or Larry Walker       1840 – Unknown
........      2        Elizabeth Missouri Walker   1844 – Unknown
............           +Josuiah W. Mathis          Unknown – Unknown
........      2        Lemuel "Lem" Walker, Jr.    1846 – 1934
............           +Mary Frances "Fanny" Strong   1849 – 1941
................           3    Charles Warren Walker       1867 – 1953
.....................            +Susie Jane Nobles          Unknown – Unknown
.....................      4     Claudia Walker              1892 – 1894
.....................      4     Stella Mae Walker           1894 – Unknown
.........................        +James Richard Goodykoontz  Unknown – Unknown
.........................  4     Annie Casseline Walker      1895 – 1905
.........................  4     Clara Juanita Walker        1898 – Unknown
.........................        +Ray T. Hallmark            Unknown – Unknown
.........................  4     Charles Albert Walker       1900 – Unknown
.........................  4     William Lemuel Walker       1903 – Unknown
.........................        +Vera E. Green              Unknown – Unknown
.........................  4     Susie Lucille Walker        1906 – Unknown
.........................        +Leroy Dozier               Unknown – Unknown
.........................  4     Frances I. Walker           1908 – Unknown
.........................        +Everett C. Skinner         Unknown – Unknown
.........................  4     Charles Warren Walker, Jr.  1914 – Unknown
.........................        +Doris Unknown              Unknown – Unknown
................           3    Albert Walker               1869 – 1876
................           3    Lemuel LeeRoy 'Lee' Walker  1871 – 1946
.....................            +Dory B. Ely                Unknown – Unknown
................           3    Wilmer Walker               1873 – 1953
.....................            +Ellen Nora Lee Poidevant   Unknown – Unknown
.........................  4     Ethel Frances Walker        1902 – Unknown
.........................        +Wilmer Hallmark            Unknown – Unknown
.........................  4     William Douglas Walker      1904 – Unknown
.........................        +Unknown Haze               Unknown – Unknown
.........................  4     Wilmer Walker, Jr.          1906 – Unknown
.........................        +Alma Brewton               Unknown – Unknown
.........................  4     Lois Lee Walker             1908 – Unknown
.........................        +Julin Murphy               Unknown – Unknown
.........................  4     Catherine M. Walker         1910 – Unknown
.........................        +Unknown Altman             Unknown – Unknown
.........................  4     Oliver Rabun Walker         1912 – Unknown
.........................        +Wilma Unknown              Unknown – Unknown
.........................  4     Maurice Franklin Walker     1918 – Unknown
.........................        +Regina K. Unknown          Unknown – Unknown
................           3    Virginia Walker             1875 – 1882
................           3    Rufus Edward Walker, Sr.    1878 – 1950
.....................            +Abbie M. Bill              1885 – 1931
.........................  4     Willie Edwin Walker         1901 – 1901
.........................  4     Edna Abbie Walker           1902 – 1987
.........................        +Crockett Stapleton White   1891 – 1966
```

.... 5	Crockett Stapleton 'CS' White, Jr.	1924 – 1998
....	+Patricia Hern	Unknown – Unknown
.... 6	Bethney Crickett White	Private –
....	*2nd Wife of Crockett Stapleton White, Jr.:	
....	+Mary Helen 'Tiny' Ezell	Unknown – 2002
.... 6	Edna Lynn White	Private –
.... 6	Cheryl Ann White	Private –
.... 6	Eric White	Private –
.... 5	Elbert Edmondson White	1927 – 1984
....	+Dorothy Sawyer	Private –
.... 6	Elbert Gordon White	Private –
.... 6	Thomas Gilman White	Private –
.... 6	Steven Timothy White	Private –
.... 6	Jeffery Dean White	Private –
.... 6	David Mark White	Unknown – 1984
.... 6	Angelia Renee White	Private –
.... 4	Lida Alice Walker	1904 – 1909
.... 4	Rufus Edward Walker, Jr.	1907 – 1961
....	+Emma Willis	1910 – 1993
....	5 Rufus Edward "Bo" Walker III	1933 – 1962
....	5 Willard Eugene "Billy" Walker	1937 – Unknown
....	+Lois Gail Stedam	1940 – Unknown
.... 4	Roy Elwood Walker	1909 – 2001
....	+Evelyn Gray Brasher Dietz	1913 – 1996
....	5 LeeRoy Walker	Private –
....	5 Warren Elwood Walker	1935 – 1999
....	5 Jerry Rex Walker	Private –
....	+Betty Marie Springsteen	Private –
.... 4	Rabun Earl Walker	1912 – 1986
....	+Alma May Brasher Dietz	1915 – 1997
....	5 James Kenneth Walker	1936 – 1999
....	+Jo Ann Helton	Private –
....	*2nd Wife of James Kenneth Walker:	
....	+Betty Yarbrough	Private –
....	*3rd Wife of James Kenneth Walker:	
....	+Loretta Garrett	Private –
....	5 Abbie Yvonne Walker	Private –
....	+Rex D. Bullard	Private –
....	5 Sidney Earl Walker	Private –
....	5 Eva Marie Walker	Private –
....	+Julian Springsteen	Private –
....	5 Hilda Gail Walker	Private –
....	+Richard Graham	Private –
.... 4	Robert Earnest " Bob" Walker	1913 – 1963
....	+Liza Stewart	1920 – 2002
....	5 Thelma Inez Walker	Private –
....	+Robert Lee Lane	Private –
....	*2nd Husband of Thelma Inez Walker:	
....	+Douglas Frank	Private –
....	5 Robert Ernest "Bobby" Walker, Jr.	Private –
....	+Martha Jane Buskin	Private –
....	*2nd Wife of Robert Ernest "Bobby" Walker, Jr.:	
....	+Bobbie Morris	Private –
....	5 Brenda Walker	Private –
.... 4	Roland Erwood Walker, Sr.	1916 – 2003
....	+Mary A. Gallway	1918 – 1974

....*2nd Wife of Roland Erwood Walker, Sr.:		
.... +Margaret Gallway	Private –	
.... 5 Roland Erwood "Roly" Walker, Jr.	Private –	
.... +Peggy McCormick Skilling	Private –	
.... 5 Mary Nell Walker	Private –	
.... +Marvin Hough	Private –	
.... 5 William H. Walker	Private –	
.... +Jeanne Ruth Henry	Private –	
.... 4 Rex Edward Walker	1918 – 1933	
.... 4 Raymond Elmer Walker	1923 – 1985	
.... +Mary Gene Gammon	Private –	
....5 Raymond Charles Walker	Private –	
.... 4 Ruben Emmons Walker	1925 – 1978	
.... +Cornelia Vinson	Private –	
....5 Gala Susan Walker	Private –	
.... *2nd Wife of Ruben Emmons Walker:		
.... +Blanch Unknown	Private –	
....5 Janet Irene Walker	Private –	
.... *3rd Wife of Ruben Emmons Walker:		
.... +Katerine Matson	Private –	
.... 4 Richard E. Walker	1926 – 1927	
.... 4 Gladwin Charles Walker	Private –	
.... +Nora Vinson	Private –	
.... 5 Galen Walker	Private –	
.... +Penny Vickery	Private –	
.... 5 Terry Walker	Private –	
....+Mary Roberson	Private –	
.... 5 Don Walker	Private –	
....+Patsey Smith	Private –	
.... 3 Julia Cassline Walker	1880 – 1916	
.... +Charles Mann	Unknown – Unknown	
.... 3 Clarence Dean "Uncle Ted" Walker	1883 – 1971	
.... +Hazel Low	Unknown – Unknown	
.... 4 Bertha Ruth Walker	Private –	
.... +William Robinson	Unknown – Unknown	
.... 4 Infant Walker	Unknown – Unknown	
.... 3 Mary E. Walker	1886 – 1968	
.... +Alvin Thiel	Unknown – Unknown	
.... 4 Alvin Thiel, Jr.	Private –	
.... *2nd Husband of Mary E. Walker:		
.... +Unknown Grant	Unknown – Unknown	
.... *3rd Husband of Mary E. Walker:		
.... +Unknown Wilkie	Unknown – Unknown	
.... *4th Husband of Mary E. Walker:		
.... +Raymond Chaney	Unknown – Unknown	
.... 3 Frances "Aunt Frank" Walker	1889 – 1954	
.... +Willard " Bill" Morrill	Unknown – Unknown	
..........................4 Infant Morrill	Private –	
..........................4 Betty Ann Morrill	Unknown – Unknown	
..........................4 Joy Morrill	Unknown – Unknown	
.... 3 James Edmond Walker	1891 – 1966	
.... +Helen Unknown	Unknown – Unknown	
.... *2nd Wife of James Edmond Walker:		
.... + Unknown Glow	Unknown – Unknown	
.... 3 Wenefred Walker	1895 – Unknown	
.... +James Auston Jones	Unknown – Unknown	

....	4	James Auston Jones, Jr.	Private –
....	4	Jean Frances Jones	Private –
....		*2nd Husband of Wenefred Walker:	
....		+Lawrence Denehie	Unknown – Unknown
....	2	Horatio Walker	1849 – 1909
....		+Julia Ann Strong	1851 – 1882
....	3	Samuel Walker	Unknown – Unknown
....	3	Claudia Walker	Unknown – Unknown
....	3	Norman Walker	Unknown – Unknown
....	3	Rhetta Walker	Unknown – Unknown
....	3	James Walker	Unknown – Unknown
....		*2nd Wife of Horatio Walker:	
....		+Adeline Hall Nelson	1865 – Unknown
....	2	Kitty A. Walker	1851 – Unknown
....	2	Epsey Walker	1854 – 1924
....		+Elisha Gilbert Strong	Unknown – Unknown
....	2	James Walker	1856 – Unknown

Orange Beach Water and Sewer Board

The Baldwin County Commission on September 6, 1968, appointed the first Board of the Orange Beach Water and Sewer Board. John B. Hadley was Chairman of the Commission at the time and was a local resident.

Board members: Dorothy Childress – Chairman
                  Loren D. Moore
                  A. W. Robinson

Appendix

Orange Beach Incorporation – First City Officers

Orange Beach held its referendum for possible incorporation on September 11, 1984. The initiative passed. Baldwin County Probate Judge Harry D'Olive declared the City of Orange Beach an incorporated municipality and Baldwin Counties sixth largest city on August 1, 1984.

The first officers of the city were elected on September 11, 1984 or in the run–off election October 2, 1984:

Mayor: Roland F. 'Ronnie' Callaway
Council Place 1: Rose Williams
Council Place 2: J. F. 'Jack' Govan
Council Place 3: William S. 'Steven' Garner
Council Place 4: John F. 'Frank' Ellis – Mayor Pro Tem
Council Place 5: J. D. 'Jim' Snell

The first City Council of Orange Beach, was sworn–in by Baldwin County Probate Judge Harry D'Olive (seen at far left), October 15, 1985, at the Orange Beach Community Center. From left to right are City Officers: J. F. 'Jack' Govan, William S. 'Steven' Garner, Ronnie Callaway, J. D. 'Jim' Snell, Rose Williams, and John F. 'Frank' Ellis.

Climate and Weather information

Temperature data from Alabama Gulf Coast magazine 2003:

Month	Daily Max.	Daily Min.	Monthly Avg.	Water
January	57.5	43.5	50.5	55
February	60.4	46.3	53.4	57
March	66.7	54.3	60.5	64
April	74.4	62.7	68.5	69
May	81.3	69.7	75.5	76
June	86.5	75.3	81.1	82
July	89.0	76.6	82.8	84
August	88.6	76.9	82.8	85
September	85.4	73.8	78.6	81
October	77.5	64.8	71.2	74
November	69.1	55.8	62.5	65
December	61.7	48.2	55.0	57

Editors note: A hard–freeze destroyed citrus and tobacco crops across the Deep South in the winter of 1916–1917. This freeze destroyed commercial Orange growing in the Orange Beach area.

Tropical Weather Information

Courtesy of National Weather Service & Emergency Management Agency
– Mobile Office

Small Craft Advisory	**Gale Warnings**	**Storm Warning**	**Hurricane Warning**
Sustained conditions hazardous to small boats (18 knot winds)	Forecast winds of 34 to 47 knots	Forecast winds above 48 knots (48–63 knots when associated with a hurricane)	Issued in connection with a hurricane (64 knots and above)

Tropical Weather Information: Weather flag system (above):

Small Craft Advisory – sustained winds 38 mph (33 knots)
Gale Warnings – Forecast winds 38 to 54 mph (34 to 47 knots)
Storm Warning – Forecast winds 55 to 73 mph (48 to 63 knots)
Hurricane Warning – Forecast winds 74 mph and above

General information and definitions:

The tropical weather season runs from June 1 to November 30 with the month of September generally the most active.

A **Tropical Depression** is an area of disturbed weather with counterclockwise rotation of winds with maximum wind speeds of 38 MPH or less.

A **Tropical Storm** forms from a tropical depression when sustained winds reach 39 to 73 MPH.

A **Hurricane** forms from a tropical storm when sustained winds reach 74 MPH or more.

Hurricanes are ranked by category or class of sustained winds:
Category **1**: winds 74 to 95 mph (62 to 82 knots)
2: winds 96 to 110 mph (83 to 95 knots)
3: winds 111 to 130 mph (96 to 113 knots)
4: winds 131 to 155 mph (114 to 135 knots)
5: winds above 155 mph (over 135 knots)

Watches and Warnings:

A **Hurricane Watch** is posted when there is a threat of hurricane conditions within 24 to 36 hours.

A **Hurricane Warning** is posted when hurricane conditions are expected in 24 hours or less.

Hurricane Preparedness Information

Editors note: The following information is supplied by the Federal Emergency Management Agency (FEMA) of the Department of Homeland Security, and the American Red Cross.

Before the Hurricane Season begins
(season June 1 to November 30):
* Develop a Family Disaster Plan
* Create a Disaster Supply Kit
* Determine a place to go for evacuations
* Determine how to Secure your home
* What are you going to do with your pets (most evacuation centers do not take pets)

Family Disaster Plan:

* Discuss the type of hazards that could affect your family. Know your home's vulnerability to storm surge, flooding, and wind.

* Locate a safe room or the safest areas in your home for each hurricane hazard. In certain circumstances the safest areas may not be your home, but within your community, or evacuation.

* Determine escape routes from your home and places to meet.

* Have an out–of–state friend as a family contact, so all your family members have a single point of contact.

* Make a plan now for what to do with your pets, if you need to evacuate.

* Post emergency telephone numbers by your phone and make sure your children know how and when to call 911.

* Check your insurance coverage – flood damage is not covered by homeowners insurance...only the National Flood Insurance Program covers floods.

* Stock non–perishable emergency supplies and a Disaster Supply Kit.

* Use a battery operated radio that will receive local emergency management information or the NOAA weather station. Keep an extra supply of batteries for the radio.

* If possible take a First Aid, CPR, and disaster preparedness classes.

Red Cross Disaster kit info

There are six basics you should stock for your home: water, food, first aid supplies, clothing and bedding, tools and emergency supplies, and special items. Keep the items that you would most likely need during an evacuation in an easy–to carry container...suggested items are marked with an asterisk(*). Possible containers include a large, covered trash container, a camping backpack, or a duffle bag.

Water

    * Store water in plastic containers such as soft drink bottles. Avoid using containers that will decompose or break, such as milk cartons or glass bottles. A normally active person needs to drink at least two quarts of water each day. Hot environments and intense physical activity can double that amount. Children, nursing mothers, and ill people will need more.

    * Store one gallon of water per person per day.

    * Keep at least a three–day supply of water per person (two quarts for drinking, two quarts for each person in your household for food preparation/sanitation).*

Food

    * Store at least a three–day supply of non–perishable food. Select foods that require no refrigeration, preparation or cooking, and little or no water. If you must heat food, pack a can of Sterno. Select food items that are compact and lightweight. Include a selection of the following foods in your Disaster Supplies Kit:

    * Ready–to–eat canned meats, fruits, and vegetables
    * Canned juices
    * Staples (salt, sugar, pepper, spices, etc.)
    * High energy foods
    * Vitamins
    * Food for infants
    * Comfort/stress foods

First Aid Kit

Assemble a first aid kit for your home and one for each car.

    * (20) adhesive bandages, various sizes.
    * (1) 5" x 9" sterile dressing.
    * (1) conforming roller gauze bandage.
    * (2) triangular bandages.
    * (2) 3 x 3 sterile gauze pads.
    * (2) 4 x 4 sterile gauze pads.
    * (1) roll 3" cohesive bandage.
    * (2) germicidal hand wipes or waterless alcohol–based hand sanitizer.
    * (6) antiseptic wipes.
    * (2) pair large medical grade non–latex gloves.
    * Adhesive tape, 2" width.

* Anti–bacterial ointment.
* Cold pack.
* Scissors (small, personal).
* Tweezers.
* CPR breathing barrier, such as a face shield.

Non–Prescription Drugs
* Aspirin or non–aspirin pain reliever
* Anti–diarrhea medication
* Antacid (for stomach upset)
* Syrup of Ipecac (use to induce vomiting if advised by the Poison Control Center)
* Laxative
* Activated charcoal (use if advised by the Poison Control Center)

Tools and Supplies
* Mess kits, or paper cups, plates, and plastic utensils*
* Emergency preparedness manual*
* Battery–operated radio and extra batteries*
* Flashlight and extra batteries*
* Cash or traveler's checks, change*
* Non–electric can opener, utility knife*
* Fire extinguisher: small canister ABC type
* Tube tent
* Pliers
* Tape
* Compass
* Matches in a waterproof container
* Aluminum foil
* Plastic storage containers
* Signal flare
* Paper, pencil
* Needles, thread
* Medicine dropper
* Shut–off wrench, to turn off household gas and water
* Whistle
* Plastic sheeting
* Map of the area (for locating shelters)

Sanitation
* Toilet paper, towelettes*
* Soap, liquid detergent*
* Feminine supplies*

* Personal hygiene items*
* Plastic garbage bags, ties (for personal sanitation uses)
* Plastic bucket with tight lid
* Disinfectant
* Household chlorine bleach

Clothing and Bedding
*Include at least one complete change of clothing and footwear per person.
* Sturdy shoes or work boots*
* Rain gear*
* Blankets or sleeping bags*
* Hat and gloves
* Thermal underwear
* Sunglasses

Special Items
* Remember family members with special requirements, such as infants and elderly or disabled persons

For Baby*
* Formula
* Diapers
* Bottles
* Powdered milk
* Medications

For Adults*
* Heart and high blood pressure medication
* Insulin
* Prescription drugs
* Denture needs
* Contact lenses and supplies
* Extra eye glasses

Entertainment
* Games and books

Important Family Documents
* Keep these records in a waterproof, portable container:
    Will, insurance policies, contracts deeds, stocks and bonds
    Passports, social security cards, immunization records
    Bank account numbers
    Credit card account numbers and companies
* Inventory of valuable household goods, important telephone numbers

* Family records (birth, marriage, death certificates)

* Store your kit in a convenient place known to all family members. Keep a smaller version of the supplies kit in the trunk of your car.

* Keep items in airtight plastic bags. Change your stored water supply every six months so it stays fresh. Replace your stored food every six months. Re–think your kit and family needs at least once a year. Replace batteries, update clothes, etc.

*Ask your physician or pharmacist about storing prescription medications.

When a **Hurricane Watch** is issued **YOU SHOULD**:
        *Check your Disaster Supply Kit.
Make sure nothing is missing. Determine if there is anything you need to supplement your kit. Replenish your water.
        *Activate your Family Disaster Plan.
Protective measures should be initiated, especially those actions that require extra time (for example, securing a boat or leaving a barrier island).

When a **Hurricane Warning** is issued **YOU SHOULD**:
        *Ready your Disaster Supply Kit for use.
If you need to evacuate, you should bring your Supply Kit with you.
        *Use your Family Disaster Plan.
Your family should be in the process of completing protective actions and deciding the safest location to be during the storm.

To protect your property
Before the storm comes…Hurricanes can be killer storms. Follow the advice of local emergency management officials.

Put 1/2 inch plywood or storm shutters over big windows.

Pickup and store loose things in the yard – toys, lawn chair, tools, etc.

If you live in a flood prone area consider evacuation…as hurricane storm surge is extremely dangerous.

Store water in plastic containers such as soft drink bottles. Avoid using containers that will decompose or break.

Check your Disaster Kit

Double check your Disaster Plan.

Fill all your vehicles and power tools, such as chain saws, etc., with gasoline

When the storm arrives…

1. Activate your Disaster Plan
2. Have your Disaster Kit at hand.
3. Stay indoors – flying debris, falling trees, and downed power lines are serious hazards.
4. Stay tuned to your radio or television for current local weather information
5. Beware of the eye of the storm...a hurricane is a big doughnut of winds with a calm section in the middle...that's the eye of the storm. The whole hurricane could be hundreds of miles across. The calm center may last for several minutes to an hour or more. The sun may come out and you think the storm is over. But it isn't! As the hurricane moves, winds will blow just as hard as they did, but from the opposite direction.

Appendix

Tropical Weather Systems affecting the area

Information courtesy of National Weather Service & Emergency Management Agency – Mobile Office and NOAA, (National Oceanography and Atmospheric Administration) – WKRG TV5 of Mobile, Alabama.

*Editors note: Dates in **BOLD** are considered major storms with accompanying damage.*

Date		Land fall area with notes
1559 September 15	—	Coast near present day Mobile & Pensacola (Damaged de Luna's fleet)
————————	—	Coastal storms during this period were not recorded
1732	—	Mobile
1736	—	Pensacola – Village destroyed
1740 September 12	—	SE Mississippi to NW Florida
1766 October 22	—	Pensacola
1772 September 4	—	SE Louisiana to SW Alabama
1813 August 19	—	Gulf coast
1819 August 27–28	—	Mississippi & Alabama
1822 July 11	—	Mobile
1852 August 23	—	'Great Mobile Hurricane'
1860 August 11	—	Landfall West of Mobile
1860 September 15	—	Landfall West of Mobile
1870 July 30	—	Mobile
1880 August 31	—	SW Alabama & NW Florida
1882 September 9	—	SW Alabama & NW Florida
1885 September 27–28	—	Alabama & NW Florida Coasts
1889 September 23	H	SE Mississippi to NW Florida
1893 October 2	H	SE Mississippi & Alabama Extensive damage – nearly 2,000 people killed in Louisiana and South Alabama
1894 August 7	TS	Pensacola & NW Florida
1895 August 16	TS	SE Mississippi & SW Alabama
1898 August 2–3	H	NW Florida & SW Alabama
1900 September 13	TS	Weak Tropical Storm SE Mississippi
1901 June 14	TS	Mobile
1901 August 15	H	SE Mississippi
1901 September 17	TS	East of Pensacola
1902 October 10	TS	Mobile
1906 September 27	H	Pensacola & Mobile Major Hurricane – hit about 10 PM – Strongest storm to strike Pensacola since 1736 storm

1911 August 11	H	Alabama & NW Florida Coasts – major damage
1912 September 14	H	West of Mobile
1916 July 5	H	SE Mississippi to NW Florida – Extensive damage- just West of Mobile pressure at Ft. Morgan 28.38 in.
1916 October 18	H	Pensacola – eye passed over city with winds of 114 MPH
1917 September 28	H	East of Pensacola – winds 103 MPH
1919 July 4	TS	East of Pensacola
1922 October 17	TS	Between Mobile & Pensacola – weak storm
1926 September 20	H	Alabama & Florida Coasts – Major Hurricane with extensive damage – Pressure at Perdido Beach 28.20 in.
1932 August 31	H	Mobile
1934 October 5	TS	SW Alabama – weak storm
1936 July 31	H	Choctawhatchee Bay, Florida
1939 June 16	TS	Mobile Bay
1944 September 10	TS	SE Mississippi & SW Alabama
1947 September 8	TS	West of Mobile – Weak storm

1950 brought the first 'Named' storms to the Gulf Coast

1950 August 30	H	Hurricane Baker – between Mobile & Pensacola
1956 September 24	H	Hurricane Flossy – NW Florida
1959 October 8	TS	Tropical Storm Irene – NW Florida
1960 September 15	H	Hurricane Ethel – SE Mississippi
1960 September 26	TS	Tropical Storm Florence – NW Florida
1965 September 8	H	Hurricane Betsy – Florida and Louisiana – winds to 160 mph and loss of life
1969 August 17	H	Hurricane Camille – S Mississippi – Category 5 – Catastrophic damage – winds of as high as 200 mph – heavy rain and heavy tidal surge with loss of life
1975 September 23	H	Hurricane Eloise – NW Florida

1979 September 12	H	Hurricane Frederic– NW Florida – SW Alabama & SE Mississippi Severe damage to Mobile & Baldwin Counties
1985 September 2	H	Hurricane Elena – SE Mississippi – Category 3 storm – eye passed 30 miles south of Dauphin Island
1985 October 31	H	Hurricane Juan – SW Alabama & NW Florida
1992 August 16–28	H	Hurricane Andrew – Major hurricane with catastrophic damage to south Florida – came into Gulf and hit Louisiana as a Category 3
1994 July 3	TS	Tropical Storm Alberto – NW Florida & S Alabama – heavy rain
1995 August 3	H	Hurricane Erin – NW Florida
1995 October 4	H	Hurricane Opal – NW Florida – Category 3 storm as it hit Pensacola Beach with heavy storm surge – 8 foot storm surge on Alabama coast
1997 July 19	H	Hurricane Danny – SW Alabama
1998 September 28	H	Hurricane Georges – SW Alabama– NW Florida & SE Mississippi
2000 September 22	TS	Tropical Storm Helena – NW Florida
2001 June 12	TS	Tropical Storm Allison – Louisiana to North Carolina
2001 August 5	TS	Tropical Storm Barry – NW Florida – strong tropical storm with minor damage
2002 September 14	TS	Tropical Storm Hanna – NW Florida – with severe rip tides
2002 September 26	TS	Tropical Storm Isidore – Grand Isle, Louisiana – heavy rain from Louisiana to Alabama
2002 October 3	H	Hurricane Lili – Category 1 storm – central Louisiana coast – heavy surf & light rain in Alabama
2003 July 1	TS	Tropical Storm Bill – Louisiana to Florida
2004 September 6	H	Hurricane Frances – Florida then Alabama – hit Florida as a Cat 2 storm

		slow moving storm with wide spread heavy rain
2004 September 16	H	Hurricane Ivan – Alabama to Northwest Florida – came ashore at Gulf Shores as a Cat 3 storm about 3:30 am– tidal surge 8 to 14 feet – winds to 140 mph – catastrophic damage along coast – followed Highway 59 through Alabama loss of life – left State still as a hurricane with heavy rain & flooding to the NE – over 1 million people in Alabama left without power
2005 June 12	TS	Tropical Storm Arlene – near Pensacola , Florida – with 60 MPH winds
2005 July 6	TS	Tropical Storm Cindy – SE Louisiana then a major rain event over Mississippi, Alabama, and NW Florida.
2005 July 10	H	Hurricane Dennis – near Navarre, Florida with Cat 3 winds – extensive damage in NW Florida
2005 August 29	H	Hurricane Katrina – S of New Orleans and again at Pass Christian, Mississippi as a Cat 4 storm – considered the worst natural disaster in U.S. history – with loss of life and great destruction

Editors note: Other storms have passed the Alabama coast at varying times with out making land fall, but have effected currents, surf conditions, and charter fishing in the Gulf of Mexico.

Historical Hurricane Chart

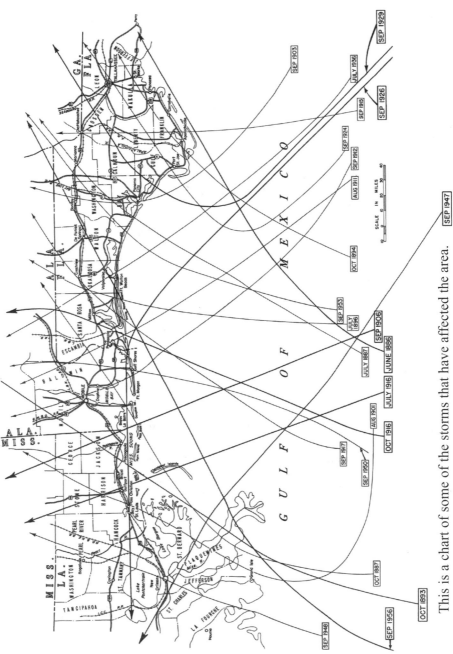

This is a chart of some of the storms that have affected the area.

Appendix

Orange Beach City Parks and Public Facilities

- Orange Beach Municipal Complex
  (City Hall–Fire Station #1–U.S. Post Office)
  4099 Orange Beach Boulevard (Highway 161)
  251–981–6979

- Orange Beach Community Development Building
  4101 Orange Beach Boulevard (Highway 161)
  251–981–1290

- Orange Beach Community Center
  27235 Canal Road (Highway 180)
  251–981–6979

- Orange Beach Public Library
  26267 Canal Road (Highway 180)
  251–981–2923

- Orange Beach Kids' Park
  26425 Canal Road (Highway 180)
  251–981–7529

- Orange Beach Waterfront Park
  26425 Canal Road (Highway 180)
  251–981–7529

- Indian and Sea Museum
  25850 John Snook Drive (near Municipal Complex)
  251–981–8584

- Marjorie Snook Park
  John Snook Drive (near Municipal Complex)

- Orange Beach Justice Center (Police–Court & Jail)
  4480 Orange Beach Boulevard (Highway 161)
  251–981–8540

- Orange Beach Fire Department
  25853 John Snook Drive (near Municipal Complex)
  251–981–6166

- Orange Beach Sportsplex
  4389 William Silvers Parkway
  251–981–7529

- Orange Beach Recreation Center
  4901 Wilson Boulevard (near Elementary school)
  251–981–6028

- Orange Beach Aquatics Center
  4853 Wilson Boulevard (near Elementary school)
  251–974–7946

- Orange Beach Tennis Center
  4851 Wilson Boulevard (near Elementary school)
  251–974–6387

- Orange Beach Senior Activities Center
  26251 Canal Road (Highway 180)
  251–981–3440

- Orange Beach Public Works
  William Silvers Parkway
  251–974–5681

- Orange Beach Elementary School
  Wilson Boulevard
  251–981–5662

Visitor contact information

- Alabama Gulf Coast Convention & Visitors Bureau
  23685 Perdido Beach Blvd.
  P.O. Box 457
  Orange Beach, AL 36561
  251– 974 –1510 or 800 –745 –7263

- City of Orange Beach Municipal Complex
  251 – 981– 6979

- The Orange Beach Fishing Association
  P.O. Box 1202
  Orange Beach, Alabama 36561
  251– 981–2300
  Email: obfishing@gulftel.com

- Information on tides: 251– 968–TIDE

- National Weather Service – Mobile
  8400 Airport Blvd.
  Mobile, Alabama 36608
  251– 633– 6443

Appendix

REDISCOVER THE THRILL OF
playing hooky

For wide-open freedom and excitement, nothing compares
to year-round sportfishing on Alabama's beautiful Gulf Coast.
We're home to the Gulf's largest, most experienced charter fleet
offering everything from back bay to blue water fishing. Choose from
half-day trips to extended excursions. And chase everything from
snapper to marlin. Outstanding accommodations and dining are
convenient to nearby marinas. So come slip away with us.
Start planning your trip today.

toll-free 1-888-644-9487

closer by the minute

GULF SHORES
ORANGE BEACH
ALABAMA

[Above is a 2004 advertisement for the Alabama Gulf Coast Convention
and Visitors Bureau.]

Bibliography

List of Trademarks:

Alemite – Alemite Automotive Products

American Red Cross

Baldwin EMC – Baldwin Electric Membership Corp.

Bruno's – Bruno's Supermarket

Cadillac – General Motors Corp.

Chevrolet – General Motors Corp.

Corvair – General Motors Corp.

Delchamps – Delchamps Supermarket

Delco – Delco Electric Co.

Edison – Edison Electric Co.

Fairbanks – Fairbanks Marine

Field and Stream magazine

Flora–Bama – Flora–Bama Package Store and Lounge

Gray Marine – Gray Marine

Greyhound – Greyhound Bus, Inc.

Gulftel – Gulf Telephone Co.

Marlboro Brand – Philip Morris USA.

Marlboro Man – Philip Morris U.S.A.

Model 'A' – Ford Motor Company

Model 'T' – Ford Motor Company

Octagon Soap – Palmolive brand of Proctor and Gamble

Texaco – Texaco Oil Co.

The Readers Digest magazine

Winn–Dixie – Winn–Dixie Supermarket

Saturday Evening Post magazine

Seatrain – Seatrain Shipping Co.

Shell Oil Co. – Royal Shell Petroleum

Sports Afield magazine

Stauter Built – Stauter Boat Works

Western Union – Western Union and Telegraph Co.

Sources:

Personal Interviews (audio taped)

Bagley, James G., Jr. Personal interviews 2002

Ballard, Lillian Walker. Personal interview November 2002

Browder, Sarah Roche. Personal interviews and notes June 2003

Caldwell, Sarah DeJarnette. Personal interviews 2004

Callaway, Amel. Personal interview 1968

Callaway, Beverly. Personal interview 2004

Callaway, Clifford. Personal interviews 2002 through 2005

Callaway, Clifford and Myrth. Long, Margaret Childress. Shipler, Michael and Pamela. Personal interviews and automobile tour of Orange Beach September 21, 2002

Callaway, Earl. Personal interviews 2002 through 2005

Callaway, Ella. Personal interviews 2003 through 2005

Callaway, Myrth. Personal interviews 2002 through 2005

Callaway, Nolan. Personal interviews and notes 2004

Childress, Dorothy Brooks. Personal interviews 1988 – 1990

Crawford, Harry and Swirn, Elizabeth Personal interview 2004

Graham, Gail Walker. Personal interviews 2002 through 2005

Gums, Bonnie L. Personal interview May 2004 and 2005

Harms, Merle Rudd. Personal interview 2004

Hough, Mary Nell Walker. Personal interviews 2002 through 2005

Huff, Charles James. Personal interviews 2003 through 2005

Johnson, Joseph L. 'Joe'. Personal interviews 2002 through 2005

Lauder, Thurston. Personal interviews and notes 2002 through 2005

Moore, Mary Lou. Personal interview 2003

Resmondo, Ronnie. Personal interview June 2004

Robinson, Bertha Walker. Personal interview 2002

Springsteen, Eva Marie Walker. Personal interviews 2002 through 2005

Smith, Herman. Personal interview August 1999

Walker, Jerry and Fell, Oscar Personal interview 2002

Walker, Roland, Jr. Personal interviews 2004 and 2005

Notes, articles, brochures, letters, programs, reports, and documents:
2001 & 2002 Charter Boat Directory. Orange Beach Fishing Association

2003 & 2004 Charter Boat Directory. Orange Beach Fishing Association

Brochures and Advertisements. Orange Beach Fishing Association
various undated

Browder, Sarah Roche. Letters on Romar Beach, Alabama 2004 – 2005

Callaway, Clifford. *Genealogy notes on Callaway Family.* 2004 and 2005

Childress, Dorothy Brooks. *Notes on moving to Orange Beach.* Undated

Clizbe, Roscoe J. *Land patent.* Bureau of Land Management Government
Land Office Records, Document Nr. 27949

Community Newsletter for the Citizens of Orange Beach. City of Orange
Beach, various dates

Orange Beach City News, City of Orange Beach, various dates

Dickey, Charles. 'Manmade Fishing Banks' Sports Afield magazine
May 1958

Hurricane History. National Weather Service – Mobile, Alabama

Hurricane History. WKRG–TV5 Weather Service – Mobile, Alabama

Johnson, Joseph 'Joe'. *Notes and records on Incorporation of Orange Beach.*
various dates

Kee, William. *Land patent*. Bureau of Land Management Government Land
Office records, Document Nr. 011505

Manchester, Harland. 'Old Cars never Die' The Reader's Digest magazine
page 107. May 1963

Orange Beach 5th Year Celebration Program. City of Orange Beach
October 14, 1989

Orange Beach Picnic Program. Orange Beach Home Demonstration Club,
August 14, 1959

Overton, Walter. *original pen & ink panels Southland Sketches*.
various dates

Patton, John J., Chief Engineer. *A Report on Perdido Pass and Vicinity*
Alabama Department of Conservation, March 14, 1962

Perdido Pass Bridge Dedication Program May 12, 1962

Smith, Mrs. Daniel B. *Millview, Florida,* a paper. Undated

Springsteen, Eva Mare Walker. *Genealogy: Callaway and Walker Families*

Suarez, Francis. *Land patent*. Bureau of Land Management Government Land
office Records, Document Nr. 09450

Suarez, Joseph. *Land patent*. Bureau of Land Management Government Land
Office Records – Document Nr. 6681

Suarez, Samuel. *Land patent*. Bureau of Land Management Government Land
Office Records, Document Nr. 011740

Survey Report on Perdido Pass Channel, AL. U. S. Army Corps of Engineers
District, Mobile – Office. December 2, 1963

'The Lure of Orange Beach Alabama' Alabama Living magazine
page 6. August 2001

'The Ocean's New Junkyard Fishing'. Field & Stream magazine
August 1959

Walker, Lemuel, Jr. *Muster Roll Company 'F', 21st Alabama Infantry*
Confederate Military Records. Alabama Department of History and
Archives, October 15, 1862

--- *Company 'F' 21st Alabama Infantry pay Records*
Confederate Military Records. Alabama Department of History and
Archives, October 1863

Books and booklets:
Alabama's Gulf Coast Vacation Guide. 2002

Official guide of the Alabama Gulf Coast Convention and Visitors Bureau
2002

An Archaeological–Historical Survey and Test Excavations at the Blakeley Site
The University of South Alabama Archaeological Research
Laboratory c1978

An Environmental Assessment of the Commercial District of Old Town Blakeley.
James H. Faulkner State Junior College c1978

Annual Report. Alabama Gulf Coast Convention and Visitors Bureau 2002

A Salute to Baldwin County–Commemorative Book
Baldwin County Centennial Commission, Faulkner, Jimmy ,Chairman,
1976

Bagge, Claude. *The Standard Guide and Handbook to the Vacation Lands of
the Deep South.* Gulf States, Elberta, AL, Copyright 1960

--- *The Standard Guide and Handbook to the Vacation Lands of the Deep
South.* Gulf States, Elberta, AL, Copyright 1964

--- *The Standard Guide and Handbook to the Vacation Lands of the Deep
South.* Gulf States, Elberta, AL, Copyright 1965

Baldwin Vignettes – Gulf Telephone Company. copyright 1983

Bowman, Dicy Villar. *The Suarez Family – 1798 – 1980.*
Copyright 1980

Brandon, William. *Indians.* American Heritage Inc.,
Copyright 1961. renewed 1989
ISBN 0–618–16732–3

Brose, David S. and White, Nancy Marie, Edited and with introduction
The Northwest Florida Expeditions of Clarence Bloomfield Moore.
University of Alabama Press, Tuscaloosa, Alabama 1999
ISBN 0–8173–0992–6

Brown, Ian W., editor. Bottle *Creek – A Pensacola Culture Site in
South Alabama.* University of Alabama Press, Tuscaloosa, Alabama
Copyright 2003 – ISBN 0–8173–1219–6

Brown, William Garrott. *A History of Alabama.*
University Publishing Company, 1903

City of Orange Beach, Alabama – Public Facilities
City of Orange Beach, Alabama c2003

Coast Living magazine. Alabama Gulf Coast Chamber of Commerce 2004

Comings, L.J. Newcomb and Albers, Martha M. *A Brief History of
Baldwin County.* Baldwin County Historical Society.
Copyright 1928

David, Sunny. *The Lost Bay–A History of Perdido Bay and Perdido Key.*
Perdido Key Chamber of Commerce, 2002. ISBN: 1–887650–38–5

Deep Sea Detective. The History Channel Video, Copyright 2003

Economic Update. The Alabama Gulf Coast Convention & Visitors Bureau
1996

General description of Perdido Bay entrance. Seafarers Pilot Book 1908

Fullbright, Day, Project Chairman and Bonkemeyer, Patricia H., Editor.
Once Upon an Island. The Gulf Shores Woman's Club. 1984

Historic Blakeley Restoration. Baldwin County Commission, Bay Minette,
Alabama c1978

Overton, Walter. *Highlights and Highways of Baldwin –
1939 Guide to Baldwin County*. The Goldenrod Studio,
Magnolia Springs, AL, Copyright 1939

--- *Tourist Guide to South Baldwin*
The Goldenrod Studio, Magnolia Springs, AL, Copyright 1938

Sheldon, Craig T., Jr., *The Southern and Central Alabama Expeditions of
Clarence Bloomfield Moore*. University of Alabama Press,
Tuscaloosa, Alabama 2001

Walthall, John A. *Prehistoric Indians of the Southeast – Archeology of
Alabama and the Middle South.*. University of Alabama Press,
Tuscaloosa, Alabama, 1980. ISBN 0–8173–0552–1

Walker, Captain Roland, Sr. *Fish Stories from Orange Beach and other
Tales of Alabama*. A paper, 2000. ISBN 0–8173–1019–3

--- *Diary of Captain Roland Walker* mid 1900s

Newspapers:
Gulf Coast Newspapers – various dates
Onlooker
The Islander
Baldwin Times
The Pelican – various dates
Birmingham Post Herald – September 20, 1982

World Wide Web:
Bureau of Land Management, United States. Federal Land Patents. 2005
<http://www.glorecords.blm.gov/patentsearch/>

Conrad, Jim. 'The Geological Time Scale'. 2004
< http://www.backyardnature.net/g/geo–time.htm>

--- "'The Loess Hills' Indians' 2004
<http://www.backyardnature.net/loess/Indians.htm>

--- "Paleo–Indians among the Loess Hills' 2004
< http://www.backyardnature.net/loess/paleoind.htm>

--- 'Ice ages'. 2004
    < http://www.backyardgeology.net/g/geology.htm>

'A Brief History of Florida'
    < http://www.dhr.dos.fl.us/facts/history/summary/>

'The Story of Madoc'.
    < http://www.celticmist.freeserve.co.uk/madocx.htm/>

'European Exploration of the Southeast and Caribbean'
    < http://www.cr.nps.gov/seac/outline/07–exploration/>

'Amerigo Vespucci' 2002
    < http://www.studyworld.com/Amerigo_Vespucci.htm>

The Avalon Project. 'Treaties'
    Yale Law School.
    <http://www.yale.edu>

'The Spanish Period'
    <http://www.pbrla.com/hxarchive_span.html>

'The Fleet Sets Sail'
    < http://scholar.coe.uwf.edu/delunaexpedition.htn>

'Bernardo De Galvez and Spain'
    < http://www.pbs.org/ktca/liberty/chronicle/galvez–spain.htm>

'Pierre LeMoune Sieur d'Iberville and the Establishment of Biloxi'
    < http://www.datasync.com/~davidg59/biloxi1.htm>

'Colonial Pensacola – Prelude to American Pensacola'
    < http://www.pbrla.com/>

'Hurricane History'
    <http://www.noaa.gov>

'Hurricane Preparedness"
    <http://www.americanredcross.org>

'Ancient – Civil War – World History'
    <http://www.ehistory.osu.edu>

Waggoner, Ben and Speer, B.G. 'Paleontology" 1994 – 1998
    <http://www.ucmp.berkley.edu>

Index
People, Places, Events, etc.

About the Authors

Margaret Childress Long:

Margaret was born in Butler County, Alabama, and moved with her family to Cotton Bayou when she was two years old, where, as the only young girl being raised on the bayou, she become known as the 'Queen of Cotton Bayou'. An eight page history Margaret wrote as a high school project is the only known history of Orange Beach. Margaret continued to gather the history of the area obtaining photographs and recording conversations with descendants of early settlers and other long time residents. She received degrees from Auburn University and the University of South Alabama and taught science in the Baldwin County school system. In 2002 Margaret was elected a member of the Baldwin County Board of Education.

Margaret and her husband Buddy live in the home on Cotton Bayou where she was raised.

Michael D. Shipler:

Michael and his wife Pam moved to Bay Minette from the Pacific Northwest in 1974 and have owned and operated Leedon Art, a gallery and custom frame shop, for the last 25 years. As a graduate from Oregon Institute of Technology, he had worked in industry as a mechanical engineer prior to opening Leedon Art.

Michael, a long time history buff, finds the hundreds of years of Southern history to be a rewarding challenge of study and research.

Over the past ten years he has written numerous articles and presented lectures and talks about the Civil War years in South Alabama.

Author's statement about the book:

The object of this book is to produce a clear history of Orange Beach, Alabama, based on the recollections of early descendants and researched facts. It is our hope that you enjoy the book and will use it as reference for many years to come.

We remain interested in further information about the area, other early photographs, or possible interviews that may arise as a result of publication of this book.

Please send any comments or information to:

Margaret C. Long, P.O. Box 2126, Orange Beach, Alabama 36561